Mariano Féliz, Aaron L. Rosenberg (Eds.)

THE POLITICAL ECONOMY OF POVERTY AND SOCIAL TRANSFORMATIONS OF THE GLOBAL SOUTH

ibidem-Verlag
Stuttgart

Bibliografische Information der Deutschen Nationalbibliothek
Die Deutsche Nationalbibliothek verzeichnet diese Publikation in der Deutschen Nationalbibliografie; detaillierte bibliografische Daten sind im Internet über http://dnb.d-nb.de abrufbar.

Bibliographic information published by the Deutsche Nationalbibliothek
Die Deutsche Nationalbibliothek lists this publication in the Deutsche Nationalbibliografie; detailed bibliographic data are available in the Internet at http://dnb.d-nb.de.

Cover photo: *Photograph taken during the April 2012 popular mobilization in Caracas, Venezuela.*

© copyright 2012 by Luciana Melina Deledicque

Gedruckt auf alterungsbeständigem, säurefreien Papier
Printed on acid-free paper

ISBN-13: 978-3-8382-0914-2

© *ibidem*-Verlag
Stuttgart 2017

Alle Rechte vorbehalten

Das Werk einschließlich aller seiner Teile ist urheberrechtlich geschützt. Jede Verwertung außerhalb der engen Grenzen des Urheberrechtsgesetzes ist ohne Zustimmung des Verlages unzulässig und strafbar. Dies gilt insbesondere für Vervielfältigungen, Übersetzungen, Mikroverfilmungen und elektronische Speicherformen sowie die Einspeicherung und Verarbeitung in elektronischen Systemen.

All rights reserved. No part of this publication may be reproduced, stored in or introduced into a retrieval system, or transmitted, in any form, or by any means (electronic, mechanical, photocopying, recording or otherwise) without the prior written permission of the publisher. Any person who does any unauthorized act in relation to this publication may be liable to criminal prosecution and civil claims for damages.

Printed in the EU

Contents

List of Abbrevations 7

Note on Contributors 15

Introduction – Mariano Féliz and Aaron Louis Rosenberg 17

Chapter 1 – *The Making and Remaking of Human Rights: Contemporary Limits and Potential Contributions of Human Rights to the Eradication of Poverty, from the Perspective of the Global South* – Camillo Perez-Bustillo 25

Chapter 2 – *"I'm Gonna Get My Share of What's Mine": Narratives of Poverty and Crime in Postcolonial Jamaica and Kenya* – Aaron Louis Rosenberg 51

Chapter 3 – *Conditional Cash Transfers: A New Paradigm for Combating Poverty in Latin America?* – Pablo E. Pérez and Brenda Brown 75

Chapter 4 – *Neodevelopmentalism in Argentina: Its Contradictions, Barriers, and Limits to Poverty Reduction and Social Change* – Mariano Féliz 101

Chapter 5 – *Alternative Paths of Social Transformation in Sub-Saharan Africa: A Case for Poverty Alleviation Programs by the Poor* – Jude Ssempebwa and Jaqueline Nakaiza 133

Chapter 6 – *Scope and Usefulness of "Right to Information" as Anti-Poverty Tool: The Bangladesh Experience* – Kazi Nurmohammad Hossainul Haque 155

Chapter 7 – *Peri-urban Dwelling and Social Transformation in Africa* – Innocent Chirisa 181

Chapter 8 – *Analysis of Women's Organizations As Drivers of Gendered Social Transformation: Experiences from Zimbabwe* – Manase Chiweshe 205

Chapter 9 – *Civil Society Movements and Rights Discourse in Post-Apartheid Socioeconomic Transformation* – Christopher G. Thomas 229

Conclusion – Mariano Féliz and Aaron Louis Rosenberg 267

LIST OF ABBREVIATIONS

AbM	Abahlali base Mjondolo
ABSA	Waters of Buenos Aires
AC	Assistant Commissioner
AIDS	Acquired Immunodeficiency Syndrome
ALBA	Alternative for the Peoples of the Americas
ALO	Assistant Land Officer
ANC	African National Congress
ANSES	National Social Security Administration (Argentina)
AsgiSA	Accelerated and Shared Growth Initiative for South Africa
AUH	Universal Child Allowance for Social Protection
BBS	Bangladesh Bureau of Statistics
BCRA	Central Bank of Argentina
BDPC	Bangladesh Disaster Preparedness Centre
BRICS	Brazil, Russia, India, China, and South Africa Emerging Economic Federation
CAFTA	Central American Free Trade Agreement
CC	Constitutional Commission
CCR	Center for Coordination of Research
CCTP	Conditional Cash Transfer Programs
CDCs	Communal Development Committees

CDF	Constituency Development Fund
CECSO	Centro de Estudios para el Cambio Social
CEDAW	Committee on the Elimination Discrimination against Women
CELAC	Conference of Latin American and Caribbean States
CEPAL	United Nations Economic Commission for Latin America and the Caribbean
CEPR	Center for Economic and Policy Research
CESCR	Committee on Economic, Social and Cultural Rights (United Nations)
CFK	Cristina Fernández de Kirchner
CIC	Chief Information Commissioner
CLACSO	Latin American Council of Social Sciences
CODESRIA	Council for the Development of Social Science Research
COSATU	Congress of South African Trade Unions
CROP	Center for Research on Poverty
CS	Civil Surgeon
DAE	Department of Agricultural Extension
DAO	District Agriculture Officer
DG	Director General
DLR	Department of Land Records
DRC	Democratic Republic of the Congo

ECLAC	United Nations Economic Commission for Latin America and the Caribbean
ECM	Electricity Commission of Malawi
ENGE	Estudio Nacional de las Grandes Industrias
FY	Financial Year
G-20	International forum of twenty major economies
G-7	Group of Seven Industrialized Nations: Canada, France, Germany, Italy, Japan, the United Kingdom, and the United States
GALZ	Gays and Lesbians Zimbabwe
GBCA	Giza Beautification and Cleaning Authority
GDP	Gross Domestic Product
GEAR	Growth, Employment and Redistribution: A Macroeconomic Strategy
GNU	Government of National Unity
GoK	Government of Kenya
GOs	Government Organizations
HIES	Household and Income Expenditure Survey
HIV	Human Immunodeficiency Virus
IC	Information Commission
ICC	International Criminal Court
ICCPR	International Covenant of Civil and Political Rights
ICESCR	International Convention on Economic, Social and Cultural Rights

ICM	Integrated Crop Management
IDB	Inter-American Development Bank
IDIHCS	Instituto de Investigaciones en Humanidades y Ciencias Sociales
IFCU	International Federation of Catholic Universities
ILO	International Labour Organization
IMF	International Monetary Fund
INDEC	National Institute of Statistics and the Census
IPM	Integrated Pest Management
IPUs	Information Providing Units
ISO	International Socialist Organization
KCC	Kampala City Council
LPM	Landless People's Movement
LWB	Lilongwe Water Board
MDG	Millennium Development Goal
MNCI	National Peasant Indigenous Movement
MOFPED	Ministry of Finance Planning and Economic Development
MOGLSD	Ministry of Gender, Labor and Social Development
MP	Minister of Parliament
MTESS	Ministries of Labor, Employment and Social Security
NAFTA	North American Free Trade Agreement

NCA	National Constitutional Assembly
NEDLAC	National Economic Development and Labour Council
NEPAD	New Partnership for Africa's Development
NGOs	Nongovernmental organizations
NK	Nijera Kori
NPT	National Popular Tradition
OECD	Organization for Economic Cooperation and Development
OHCHR	Office of the United Nations High Commissioner for Human Rights
PEL	Political Economy of Labor
PIC	Project Implementing Committee
PIE Act	Prevention of Illegal Eviction from an Unlawful Occupation of Land Act
PIO	Project Implementation Officer
PJJHD	Unemployed Heads of Households Plan
PPP	Purchasing Power Parity
PPT	Permanent People's Tribunal
PTMC	Programas de Transferencias Monetarias	Condicionadas e Inclusión Financiera
RDP	Reconstruction and Development Programme
RER	Real Exchange Rate
RSA	The Republic of South Africa

RTI	Right to Information
RTIA	Right to Information Act
SAHRC	South African Human Rights Commission
SANCO	South African National Civics Organisation
SCE	Training and Employment Insurance
SDGs	Sustainable Development Goals
SERI	Socio-Economic Rights Institute of South Africa
SKNS	Samata Nari Kalyan Samity
TAC	Treatment Action Campaign
UAC	Union of Citizen's Assemblies
UAO	Upazilla Agriculture Officer
UBOS	Uganda Bureau of Statistics
UCT	University of Cape Town
UDHR	Universal Declaration of Human Rights
UDWB	Urban Development and Works Bureau
UHO	Upazilla Health Officer
UMU	Uganda Martyrs University
UNASUR	The Union of South American States
UNCTAD	United Nations Conference on Trade and Development
UNDP	United Nations Development Program
UNHCR	United Nations High Commission for Refugees

UNO	Upazilla Nirbahi Officer
UP	Union Parishad
VGD	Vulnerability Group Development
VGF	Vulnerable Group Feeding
WAG	Women's Action Group
WB	World Bank
WC	Women's Coalition
WFA	The World Forum for Alternatives
WTO	World Trade Organization
WUAs	Water Users Associations
YPF	Yacimientos Petrolíferos Fiscale

NOTE ON CONTRIBUTORS

Brenda Brown

M.A. in Labour Social Sciences at University of Buenos Aires, Argentina. Lic. In Labor Relations at University of Buenos Aires. Reserach Fellow at Labour Studies and Research Centre (CEIL in Spanish), National Council of Scientific and Technical Research (CONICET in Spanish). Lecturer in Labor Economics at University of Buenos Aires and Lecturer in Labor Economics at National University of Moreno, Argentina.

Innocent Chirisa

Senior Lecturer, Environmental Planning and Management, Department of Rural and Urban Planning, University of Zimbabwe.

Manase Chiweshe

PhD Candidate at Rhodes University in South Africa. BSc and MSc in Sociology and Social Anthropology from the University of Zimbabwe. Lecturer in the Sociology Department at the Women's University in Africa based in Harare.

Mariano Féliz

Professor of the Department of Sociology at the Facultad de Humanidades y Ciencias de la Educación of the Universidad Nacional de La Plata. Researcher at the Centro de Investigaciones Geográficas of the Instituto de Investigaciones en Humanidades y Ciencias Sociales—IdIHCS— (Universidad Nacional de La Plata and Consejo Nacional de Investigaciones Científicas y Ténicas—CONICET).

Kazi Nurmohammad Hossainul Haque

PhD Researcher, Asia Research Centre, Murdoch University (Perth, WA). Formerly, Advisor-National Development Strategy, Action Aid Bangladesh, and Senior Research Associate/Senior Lecturer, Institute of Governance Studies (IGS), BRAC University. MA in Development Studies, International Institute of Social Studies (ISS), Erasmus University Rotterdam and MA in Public Policy, Central European University.

Jacqueline Nakaiza

Researcher and writing consultant at SNE Consultants Inc. Member of the management board of the *Journal of Development Studies*.

Pablo E. Pérez

BA in Economics. PhD in Economics (Ecole doctorale Entreprise-Travail-Emploi, Université de Paris-Est Marne-la-Vallée, France). Professor at the National University of La Plata. Researcher at CONICET on themes such as labor market, youth and employment, and social policies.

Camilo Pérez-Bustillo

Visiting Professor/Coordinator, Border Human Rights Documentation Center, New Mexico State University (NMSU), Las Cruces; Research Professor, CLACSO-Guatemala; formerly Research Professor, Graduate Program in Human Rights, Universidad Autónoma de la Ciudad de México (UACM; Autonomous University of Mexico City).

Aaron Louis Rosenberg

Associate Professor in the Centro de Estudios de Asia y África at El Colegio de México. Teaches African literature and oversees the Swahili language program. He has published on African song and literature in *Research in African Literatures*, *Wasafiri*, *The Journal of African Cultural Studies*, *The Journal of the African Literature Association* and *Estudios de Asia y África* among other journals.

Jude Ssempebwa

PhD in Management. Researcher at Uganda Martyrs University. Editor of the *Journal of Science & Sustainable Development*. PI: "The Path of Development: African Catholic Universities and the Challenges of Poverty."

Christopher G. Thomas

PhD at the University of the Witwatersrand, Johannesburg. Staff member, School of Social Sciences at the University of South Africa. Works on economic sociology, industrial restructuring, and social and economic rights.

INTRODUCTION

Aaron L. Rosenberg and Mariano Féliz

What is poverty? This seems like a logical point at which we may begin the exploration of a constellation of investigations proposed by the editors and contributors of this volume. Such an apparently simple question, however, is, as these pages will eloquently and thoroughly reveal, fraught with complications and oftentimes petrifying ambiguities. That is not to say, of course, that there has been any shortage of individuals and organizations reluctant to propose and insist upon their particular visions and definitions of poverty.

As those who work in subaltern studies would hasten to point out, however, it is precisely those individuals most intimately acquainted with the specific conditions of poverty who are most limited in their capacity to articulate and provide force to motivate the dissemination of their definitions and understandings of this phenomenon. As Gayatri Spivak explains in her fundamental essay "Can the Subaltern Speak," the mechanism of official authoritative discourse tends to exclude the voice of the powerless and disempowered precisely in the moment when their concerns are being explored and explicated.[1] Volumes such as *Voices of the Poor from Many Lands*[2] tend to play a decidedly secondary role in the formulation of policy and the scholarly and governmental understandings of poverty. This is, of course, aside from the fact of the problematic terminology employed in the text beginning with the title itself which attributes the presence of poverty to the "poor" who are implicitly associated with this quality as an intrinsic part of their being.

In part because of these limited if not blinkered perceptive capacities, scholars working on "the production of" poverty from a European or American academic post and background have tended to focus upon those aspects that coordinate most closely with their own societies' perceptions and preconceived notions as to what exactly is this elusive thing called "poverty."

---

[1] Spivak (1988, pp. 271–313).
[2] Narayan and Petesch (2002).

In large part because of the apparently functional and applied nature of existing poverty studies and the association of poverty with economic conditions and status, one of the earliest strategies adopted to describe poverty was to define the term purely in its quantitative form. One of the milestones achieved in this approach was defining absolute poverty in the 1990s as "an individual living on less than a dollar and ninety-nine cents a day." Such notions have long held sway in the minds of analysts and lay individuals throughout the globe, including in many cases the very same communities that were ostensibly under scrutiny. Such descriptive tools have contributed, of course, to the establishment and solidification of notions in development studies and policy organization and implementation which have over the course of several decades attempted unsuccessfully to at least ameliorate the conditions of individuals and groups suffering from poverty. Such conceptualizations were (or are still) founded upon the erroneous notion that any problem related to "development" faced by a society, such societies being generally considered to be nation states, can be resolved adequately, if not perfectly, by an influx of capital in the form of foreign investment provided with a plethora of strings attached by the IMF or the WB together with a horde of other international aid organizations claiming to have the resources to solve such problems. Fortunately, these purely quantitative conceptions of poverty have given way to descriptions which are founded upon the idea of poverty as the lack of rights and possibilities for social participation as in the case of publications by the UN and WB. While programs dedicated to poverty eradication were possibly the most visible of these inundations of capital, there are numerous other areas in which such apparently good intentions once again led both aid givers and recipients down the proverbial road to Hell. Efforts to alleviate corrupt practices and the institutional presence of corruption in "developing" societies throughout the Global South as well as scholarship dealing with these thorny topics were at one time founded upon the notion that corruption was rampant in these nations because of lack of resources and that those who perpetrated these nefarious acts were doing so because of insufficient compensation in their places of employment. The naïveté and superficiality of these ideas should certainly be obvious to anyone who has an even perfunctory acquaintance with any developing geography and its circumstances. As a result of the failure of such ill-founded ideas to come sufficiently to terms with the complex circumstances surrounding and giving form and force to corruption in the "developing" world, the system of thought now known as *Public Choice Theory* came into being through the work of scholars such as Duncan Black and Kenneth Arrow in the 1940s and 1950s.This theory has sought to provide a logical explanation for the enduring presence of corrupt practices in developing societies. Such explanations are designed to move beyond ideas of the ingrained nature of corruption as social practice based upon immutable cultural principles. This retrograde conceptualization feeds, of course, upon neocolonial notions of communities in the Global South at the same time as it is propagated in numerous spheres, including within the minds and mouths of members of these societies themselves. The works of scholars such as John Mukum Mbaku have gone a long way toward debunking such misconceptions and have demonstrated the extent to which corrupt practices are linked to weak state structures, misplaced intervention by foreign powers and corporations, and the impossibility of exacting punishment when corruption is carried out. Public Choice adherents, therefore, appeal for strengthening political mechanisms, treating corruption as a punishable offense— punishment severe enough to offset the benefits which any individual or group might receive from engaging in such practices.

A similar depth of understanding needs to be sought in order to adequately understand the nature of what is bandied about in scholarly and political circles when poverty is under consideration. As with many such complex issues, one of the most significant sources of confusion and misdirection comes from the terminology that is often employed to describe and comprehend the phenomenon under consideration. It is certainly true that there have been some significant changes in the manner in which these concepts are expressed by some scholars but inconsistencies abound. Seemingly, a logical place to start is from the term "the poor," which is frequently employed to refer to those who are living in poverty in a particular moment or over a given period, individually or collectively. John Iliffe's book, *The African Poor: A History*, published in 1987, eloquently describes this problem in the Global South; Iliffe is a recipient of the Melville Herskovits Prize.[3] Iliffe explains that "the hero-

---

[3] Iliffe (1987).

ism of African history is to be found not in the deeds of kings but in the struggles of ordinary people against the forces of nature and the cruelty of men" (1). Although Iliffe does use the outmoded and derogatory term "the poor" to describe those individuals living in poverty in Africa, he does simultaneously recognize that "the poor are diverse, poverty has many facets, and African peoples had their own varied and changing notions of it" (2).

At the risk of pointing out the painfully obvious, it will be helpful to consider the gravity of this terminological blunder when applied to such individuals, families, and communities. The problem inherent in such an apparently neutral world is the manner in which the term "the poor"attributes those characteristics it seeks to describe the people under consideration. Use of the term "the poor" assigns a quality to these individuals, but it also implies a series of secondary attributes which cannot be accurately assessed and therefore should be cautiously considered before they are taken for granted.

Perhaps the most egregious of these implied messages is the notion that those people who are suffering the effects of poverty are intrinsically "poor." It needs to be realized that this descriptor carries with it an entire host of signifiers. To begin with, it implies that such people are disposed if not fated to live in poverty due to some innate debility on their part. Such ideas were previously explicitly propagated as a justification for the disparate treatment of individuals living in penury as well as an explanation for the enduring presence of poverty over the millennia. The complexity of these notions is masterfully elucidated in the work of Herbert Gans, who, in a 1971 article in *Social Policy*, entitled "The Uses of Poverty: The Poor Pay All," outlines the numerous ways in which "the poor" serve strong purposes in numerous societies—purposes which he divides into "social, economic, and political" functions of great significance.[4] This is a version of humanity and its societies in which the reality of poverty is accepted as an inevitable and seemingly unalterable facet of human existence that should be accepted in this world and even embraced in order to reap the spiritual rewards that one has accumulated through such actions when he or she moves on to the next life and, it is hoped, their heavenly home. It goes without saying that in such a context

---

[4] Gans (1971, pp. 20–24).

there is no perceived necessity to ask those living with poverty what they feel about their benighted (or possibly illuminated?) condition. The excellent volume of essays ¿*El reino de Dios es de este mundo? El papel ambiguo de las religions en la lucha contra la pobreza* (2008)[5] explores the implicit and oftentimes explicit role of religions in reinforcing economic and political systems of oppression which work against those experiencing poverty. These authors demonstrate the facility with which policy and doctrine can and are often combined to ignore or even maintain conditions of poverty.

The likewise widespread idea that poverty is a purely quantifiable phenomenon draws on similar tendencies toward deliberate ignorance which mark the relative isolation that exists between scholars of poverty and the object of their studies. Defining poverty as a mere financial condition in which lack of money causes people to be "poor" is a problematic paradigm of inquiry for a variety of salient reasons. To begin with, such a limited understanding of the idea of "wealth" or capital, if you will, fails to take into account the myriad forms which resources may assume in the lives of individuals and groups throughout the globe, many of which continue to function to varying degrees and in diverse ways outside of the conventional money economy which is more often than not utilized to define success or failure, riches or penury in Western contexts, including the scholarly and the political.

The simple truth which these versions of poverty effectively obfuscate is, we would like to argue here, the real and most important aspect of this phenomenon. The chapters contained herein utilize a variety of methods, including both qualitative and quantitative strategies, in order to illuminate the various and changeable natures of poverty in the Global South. One element which they all have in common, however, is an emphasis on an understanding of poverty as what can be called a "lived experience." That is, the authors here strive to do much more than merely focusing upon purely quantifiable aspects of poverty as lack and deprivation, facts and figures which can be approached, collected, and disposed of in an apparently abstract and sterile manner. Instead, the studies undertaken in this volume seek to study poverty in an integrative manner, maintaining a comprehensive vision throughout. The lives of

---

[5] Zalpa and Offerdal (2008).

individuals living in poverty are affected by and in turn influence an immense variety of social factors, forces, and histories. These elements exist at personal, local, national, and international levels, often simultaneously. It is imperative, therefore, that any scholar grappling with issues of contemporary poverty delve into these complex and interwoven circumstances with both sensitivity and a flexibility of intellectual spirit which allow him or her to both describe and understand the phenomena of poverty as a multiplicity of feelings and encounters—which are both subjective and objective, scientific and emotional. The responses that people have to their lives can and should be a central part of our efforts to explore the geographies of poverty and to ameliorate the severity of these circumstances. Such a variegated approach to poverty as both problem and reality allows all parties involved to be heard and considered, ideally at any and all stages of the interpretive process, starting with the initial scholarly intervention and leading all the way up to the development and implementation of any relevant policy measures. Each chapter, therefore, capitalizes on these multiple potentialities:

Pérez Bustillo explores how hegemonic versions of human rights discourse and practices undermine contemporary struggles for social transformation and for the prevention, reduction, and eradication of poverty in the Global South. His study attains to recall the limits and distortions imposed upon the emancipatory potential of human rights attributable to the capitalist imperatives inherent in liberal and neoliberal appropriations of their content.

The second chapter constitutes an intriguing and groundbreaking qualitative intervention in our understanding of poverty and the manner in which it is discursively constructed and debated through popular works of creative art, specifically songs and cinema. Here, Rosenberg proposes a comparative analysis of two works of performative art and their relation to the contexts from which they emerged. From the analysis of the film *The Harder They Come* from Jamaica and the popular song "Mariana" from Kenya, the author attempts to comprehend the nature of poverty in these postcolonial settings and the tactics used by both institutionalized authorities and impoverished individuals to ameliorate such circumstances. In turn, he proposes to understand how these narratives provide valuable insights into the reasons behind violent aggression as acted out by alienated individuals.

Pérez and Brown, in their contribution, discuss the various related ways in which countries in Latin America have tackled social risks. They explain the role of conditional cash transfers in the development of a new consensus on social policies. In a provocative manner, they underline the limitations of such policies and show the extent to which these policies have been helpful in the attempt to combat income poverty in these complex and constantly evolving settings.

Féliz, in the fourth chapter, analyzes the main characteristics of the neodevelopmentalist project in Argentina, and its barriers and limitations to promote poverty reduction and social change. He provides a rich characterization of such sociopolitical projects to show that their inability to confront poverty as a widespread phenomenon comes from the articulation of structural continuities with neoliberalism and novel sociopolitical innovations in Argentina.

In their contribution, Ssempebwa and Nakaiza propose to provide a discussion on the political economy of poverty and social transformation in five sub-Saharan countries. Their analysis provides important understandings on the working of self-help and microfinance in attempts to alleviate poverty. In particular, they provide an account of how poverty alleviation programs/projects were more successful in instances where "the poor" at whom they were targeted were involved in the definition of poverty.

Kazi Haque in his study focuses upon the effectiveness and manifest limitations of the Right to Information legislation that has recently been instituted in Bangladesh. His analysis focuses upon both the users and providers of this newly legislated data and, through a variety of detailed case studies, demonstrates the capacities and pitfalls inherent in such a dispensation given the significant contextual barriers faced by individuals and groups in Bangladesh.

In his chapter, Chirisa provides a critical analysis of peri-urbanization in Africa. His insight explains how people in poverty are not just passive agents, but they take on actions to cope with their situation and build on it. He attempts to show how communities struggle to survive and resist vulnerability, tapping into their inbuilt mechanisms of resilience.

Moving farther south on the African continent, Chiweshe focuses upon the patriarchal forces in postcolonial Zimbabwe which combine with a variety of international factors linked to the nature of nongovernmental organizations (NGOs) in this moment in order to make the realization of viable women's activism an increasingly distant possibility.

Finally, Thomas presents a study on how South African post-apartheid economic policymaking followed globally hegemonic neoliberalism and worsened unemployment, inequality, and poverty, consequently increasing dependence on welfarist state support. He shows how social movements have developed in opposition to government's neoliberal policies and contemplates whether socioeconomic rights adjudication creates opportunities for reforms, bringing relief to impoverished subordinate classes.

We both wish to thank CLACSO and CROP for their support in the editing of this book as well as the people at Ibidem for their wonderful job in hewing the volume into the proper shape. Mariano wishes to thank Melina, his wife and life companion, for her unrelenting support and care, as well as for her insightful comments to my writing. The cover image for this book is one of many wonderful pictures she has produced. Aaron would like to express his heartfelt appreciation to Roxana, the mother of their wonderful baby boy Richard born during the editing of the book for enduring the long nights necessary to bring this project to fruition.

References

Gans, Herbert. "The Uses of Poverty: The Poor Pay All." *Social Policy* (July/August) 1971: pp. 20–24.

Iliffe, John. *The African Poor: A History*. Cambridge: Cambridge University Press, 1987.

Narayan, Deepa and Patti Petesch, eds. *Voices of the Poor from Many Lands*. Washington, DC: Oxford Univesrity Press and The World Bank, 2002.

Spivak, Gayatri. "Can the Subaltern Speak," In *Marxism and the Interpretation of Culture*. Eds. Cary Nelson and Lawrence Grossberg. Urbana: University of Illinois Press, 1988, pp. 271–313.

Zalpa, Genaro and Hans Egil Offerdal, eds. ¿El Reino de Dios es de este mundo? El papel ambiguo de las religiones en la lucha contra la pobreza. Bogotá: Siglo de Hombres and Clacso, 2008.

Chapter 1
THE MAKING AND REMAKING OF HUMAN RIGHTS: CONTEMPORARY LIMITS AND POTENTIAL CONTRIBUTIONS OF HUMAN RIGHTS TO THE ERADICATION OF POVERTY, FROM THE PERSPECTIVE OF THE GLOBAL SOUTH

Camilo Pérez-Bustillo

This chapter provides the reader with a thorough introduction to the complex relationship between poverty eradication and the recognition of the necessity of freedom from poverty in both economic and sociocultural terms as a determining factor in the success or failure of attempts to combat human poverty in local, national, and transnational/international contexts. The author points to the crucial flaws in the common neoliberal paradigm of economic development and social well-being insofar as its capacity to adequately encompass and rectify socioeconomic problems prevalent throughout the Global South. Ultimately the author calls into question the efficacy of institutionalized attempts to remedy these circumstances while emphasizing the necessity of strong legal responses in place of top-down strategies.

1 Introduction

This chapter explores how hegemonic versions of human rights discourse and practices undermine contemporary struggles for social transformation and for the prevention, reduction, and eradication of poverty in the Global South. My approach here is derived from long-standing critiques[1] of the limits and distortions imposed upon the emancipatory origins and potential of human rights attributable to the capitalist imperatives inherent in liberal and neoliberal appropriations of their discourse and content. It is also grounded in an understanding of the prevailing policies and practices that produce and reproduce global poverty and inequality as crimes against humanity.

---

[1] See, for example, Buchanan (1982).

Intensive efforts by the WB, the UN Development Program, the Organization for Economic Cooperation and Development (OECD), their regional and local equivalents, and key member states to incorporate "human rights-based" approaches within the overall framework of promoting "democracy," "good governance" (including enhanced dimensions of "voice" and "participation"), the "rule of law," and poverty reduction and eradication, including more "ethical" processes of development, are illustrative of the contemporary dimensions of liberal and neoliberal hegemony. Meanwhile, it is precisely these global "institutional arrangements" that continue to impose neoliberal forms of globalization, which undermine the substantive achievement of such purported objectives, and in fact produce and reproduce poverty and inequality. The Millennium Development Goals (MDGs) and their successors, the Sustainable Development Goals (SDGs), are representative examples of such initiatives and their insufficiencies (Amin, 2006; De Schutter, 2011; CROP, 2013; Pogge and Sengupta, 2014). Counter-hegemonic approaches instead seek to transform existing structures and policies in a fundamental, counter-systemic direction and to prefigure alternatives operating upon the basis of qualitatively different premises (Carroll, 2010).

My emphasis is on the need to transcend such limitations in the context of contemporary anti-poverty research and policy, and on the potential contributions counter-hegemonic movements and alternative paradigms rooted in the most excluded sectors "from below" (e.g., the poor, indigenous peoples and others victimized because of their gender, racial, ethnic, cultural and/or religious identity, as well as migrants and displaced persons) can make in this context on a global scale. This includes the need to rethink and remake contemporary approaches to the history and contemporary praxis of human rights, in the service of processes of liberation, rather than as ideological complements to contemporary structures and forms of domination (exploitation, discrimination, marginalization, exclusion, etc.). This chapter focuses initially on these conceptual aspects, and then on the BRICS (Brazil, Russia, India, China, and South Africa) grouping of key countries in the Global South and the Bolivarian Alternative for the Peoples of the Americas (ALBA, see footnote 9) in Latin America as case studies of the limits and potential of such counter-hegemonic initiatives on a global scale.

This chapter is dedicated to the memory of Berta Cáceres, a Lenca indigenous environmental rights activist from Honduras who was killed on March 3, 2016, following multiple death threats, in what has been widely reported as a targeted assassination involving government complicity, in reprisal for her long-standing leadership of grassroots movements in resistance to hydroelectric megaprojects supported by foreign investors with initial backing from the WB (Alpert/Foreign Policy in Focus, 2016; Human Rights Watch, 2016). Cáceres had been awarded the prestigious Goldman Prize for her environmental rights activism in April 2015 (Alpert/Foreign Policy in Focus, 2016; Human Rights Watch, 2016) and was widely recognized for her role in helping coordinate equivalent movements throughout the Meso-American region. Megaprojects of the kind resisted by these movements have prospered in Honduras in the wake of US support for the country's militarization following a coup in June 2009, within the context of the regional "drug war" and the promotion of "free trade" through the Central American Free Trade Agreement (CAFTA) (Alpert, 2016). Hundreds of thousands of Hondurans, primarily of indigenous origin and African descent, have been forcibly displaced within the country or have forcibly migrated toward the United States within the last decade as a result of the imposition of these policies; many of these are unaccompanied minors.

Cáceres and the movements she helped found and lead reflect the kinds of intertwined vulnerabilities and struggles highlighted in the theoretical approaches that provide inspiration for this chapter's approach. The context of Hondura is also directly related to this chapter's emphasis on a case study of BRICS, since the 2009 coup there was in part intended to prevent the country's incorporation into the emerging bloc of Latin American states known as ALBA that have sought to resist US hegemony in the region (UNHCR, 2014), as BRICS is intended to do globally, from the perspective of the Global South.

My definition of the Global South includes its geopolitical and postcolonial dimensions but goes beyond these, as Boaventura de Sousa Santos has suggested, to encompass the universal "community of victims" resulting from "all the forms of suffering produced by global capitalism. In this sense, the South is to be found throughout the world, including the North and West" (Sousa Santos, 2007). This chapter explores these issues from a critical, interdisciplinary, comparative, and intercultural perspective grounded in an intertwined approach to the relationship between the Global North and South, which lays the basis for what Sousa Santos (2009) has described as the "epistemologies of the South."

All of these issues were especially relevant as we gathered in Cairo, not far from Tahrir (Liberation) Square, amid yet another challenging moment in its ongoing process of social transformation within the overall landscape of the Arab Spring, and the contested, evolving relationship between such processes and the vindication of the rights of the poor. A key question at the time we met there (December 2012) was as to the extent to which the basic human rights recognized in Egypt's then newly adopted post-Mubarak constitution would in fact be justiciable and enforceable in practice. At the time of this writing (March 2016), these rights have been trampled amid the increasing abuses of Egypt's US-backed authoritarian, military-dominated government, whose repressive characteristics converge with the onset of a veritable "Arab Winter" throughout the region (with the partial but still uncertain exception of Tunisia) in related contexts such as Syria, Libya, Bahrain, and Yemen.

This chapter and related papers presented at CROP workshops in New Delhi, India, in October 2011, in Cape Town, South Africa, in November 2012, in Mexico City in February 2014, and in Foz do Iguacú, Brazil, in June 2015, are also intended to contribute to shaping the framework, as we approach the 50th anniversary of Rev. Dr. Martin Luther King Jr.'s call for a "Poor People's Campaign," which was launched on the eve of his assassination in April, 1968, for the convening of an international tribunal of conscience (International Poverty Tribunal) to document and assess the human costs and implications of contemporary global poverty. This tribunal would act in the spirit of the Russell Tribunal of the 1960s and 1970s and its principal successor, the Permanent People's Tribunal (PPT),[2] and would focus on a detailed exploration of the extent

---

[2] Russell Tribunal, named for its founder British philosopher and peace activist Bertrand Russell, was initially formed to judge alleged USwar crimes and crimes against humanity in the context of the Vietnam War and then extended its scope to assess equivalent crimes in the context of military dictatorships in the Southern Cone of Latin America (Chile, Uruguay, Brazil, and Argentina), with members such as Jean-Paul Sartre, Simone de Beauvoir, Isaac Deutscher, James Baldwin, and former Mexican President Lázaro Cárdenas, and later renowned Latin American writers such as Gabriel García Márquez, Eduardo Galeano, and Julio Cortázar; the PPT was established as its successor in 1979, with a secretariat based at the Lelio

to which contemporary global poverty and inequality amount to a "crime against humanity," as suggested below.

2   Central Argument and Research Questions

Contemporary visions of human rights have been reshaped by social movements in the context of the Latin American and Arab "Springs" (see Dussel, 2008; Amin, 2011, 2012b; Abdou Bakr, 2012; Hardt and Negri, 2011, 2012b; Manhire, ed. 2012; Weisbrot, 2012), as well as by similar movements elsewhere in Africa (e.g. Senegal, Mali) and of the "indignant" or "outraged" (Binebine, 2011; Hessel, 2011) in other settings as diverse as Chile, Spain, Greece, the United States, and Mexico (Byrne, ed. 2012). Is there a relationship between such processes and emerging approaches to issues of human rights, poverty, and inequality in spaces of South-South cooperation such as BRICS[3] (Brazil, Russia, India, China, and South Africa) and ALBA[4]? What is the relationship between South-

---

Basso Foundation in Rome, see http://www.internazionaleleliobasso.it/?page_id=209&lang=en. The PPT undertook a 3-year (2011–2014) process to assess systematic human rights violations in Mexico, including issues of poverty and inequality related to the imposition of neoliberal "free trade" policies through the North American Free Trade Agreement (NAFTA).

[3] South Africa joined the grouping at its summit in India in March 2012 and hosted its fifth summit in March 2013; the first summit was held in Russia in 2009, the second in Brazil in 2010, the third in China in 2011, and subsequent summits in Brazil and Russia in 2014 and 2015, respectively, and the 2016 summit in India; a preliminary framework for the group emerged from a previously held summit of Foreign Ministers from Brazil, Russia, India, and China in 2006.

[4] ALBA is the Spanish acronym for the Bolivarian Alternative for the Peoples of the Americas, an economic and political bloc of Latin American and Caribbean states which includes those most independent of US domination, such as Cuba, Venezuela, Bolivia, Ecuador, and Nicaragua, which identify with the framework of what has been described as "21st century socialism," which includes several English-speaking states in the Caribbean region such as Dominica, St.Vincent and the Grenadines, Antigua and Barbuda, and St. Lucia, as well as Suriname; Haiti is a "permanent guest member." The origins of ALBA lie in the "People's Trade Treaty" negotiated in 2006 between Cuba, Venezuela, and Bolivia. One of ALBA's most strategic contributions from a South-South perspective is its role in resisting the US efforts to consolidate its regional hegemony in Latin America through the imposition of "free trade" agreements such as NAFTA (with Canada and Mexico) and CAFTA (with Guatemala, Honduras, El Salvador, Costa Rica, and the Dominican Republic), as well as bilateral agreements with Chile, Colombia, Perú, and Panama, and the new Alliance of the Pacific which includes these plus Mexico.

based processes of poverty eradication and social transformation, and human rights, in such contexts? What implications do such initiatives have for efforts to attain or go beyond the MDGs and SDGs and other hegemonic approaches to issues relating to poverty and inequality, and as to challenges confronted by the UN system (e.g., IMF, WB, and WTO) and the G-20, in an era of economic, financial, environmental, and ultimately civilizational crisis on a global scale?

A central tension that cuts across such examples is the contested relationship between social movements of the poor "from below," based in the most marginalized sectors, which are often focused on local and regional projects of resistance and autonomy, and processes of social transformation which seek to prevent, reduce, and/or eliminate poverty, which tend to be centered around the control and exercise of state power "from above," at the national level, and on concerted action among states in regional contexts such as Latin America, Africa, and the Arab world and on a global scale. An additional cross-cutting tension is that between the marked tendency of state-centered processes to seek accommodation, to varying degrees, with the demands of global capitalist hegemony (e.g., the application of neoliberal and "free trade" policies), and the anti-systemic character of movements from below which resist such tendencies more directly.

The emergent "epistemologies of the South" (Sousa Santos) reflected in counter-hegemonic movements from below such as those which have arisen in the context of the Latin American and Arab "Springs" and within the overall framework of the "global justice movement" (Tabb, 2003) include the centrality of "indignation" as an expression of resistance against systemic injustices. The key battle cry for the Zapatista rebellion of indigenous peasants in the impoverished region of Chiapas in January, 1994, against the imposition by the United States and Mexico's ruling sectors of the North American Free Trade Agreement (NAFTA), was (in Spanish) "*Ya basta!*" (or "Enough!", in the sense of things reaching a limit which can no longer be tolerated, in both its physical and ethical dimen-

---

ALBA also plays a key role in promoting wider spaces of regional integration that exclude the United States and Canada such as the Conference of Latin American and Caribbean States (CELAC) and Union of South American states (UNASUR), and global alternatives such as the proposed Bank of the South (also promoted to some extent by BRICS). All of this is inseparable from the legacy of the leadership of Hugo Chávez.

sions), and helped inspire the emergence of the broad coalition of labor and environmentalist forces in Seattle which derailed the WTO's Ministerial Summit there in late 1999, giving birth to what has been described as the "global justice movement" (Tabb, 2003).

The concept of *"hogra,"* with its origins in the Algerian dialect of Arabic has been suggested as a key explanatory framework for the sense of indignation expressed by Mohamed Bouazizi's self-immolation in the Tunisian town of Sidi Bouzid in December 2010, which helped spark first Tunisia's "Jasmine Revolution" and then that of Egypt centered in Cairo's Tahrir Square in 2011, which together launched the Arab "Spring." *"Hogra"* has been translated into Spanish (Cembrero/El Pais, 2011) as what lies at the convergent core of related concepts for describing the subjective experiences produced by reiterated instances of "disrespect" (or "disdain" or "dishonor"), "abuse of power," and "injustice," which together generate a response grounded in claims demanding the restoration of "dignity." It was this understanding of the concept drawn from Arabic and the case of Bouazizi that led the demonstrators to mobilize against the effects of neoliberal policies in the central squares of Spain and in Greece in 2011, inspired by the images and words flowing from Cairo, to describe themselves analogously as the "indignado/as" (or the "indignant"). They in turn sparked similar movements in the United States such as Occupy Wall Street later that same year, and in Chile and Mexico among students and broader sectors of youth in 2011 and 2012. As Mahi Binebine (2011) of Morocco has explained:

> The word "hogra" is not translatable to Romance languages. It implies a sentiment which combines disdain and the arrogance of somehow who dominates with the fearful impotence of a person who is dominated. It is an ancestral sentiment inherited from feudalism and which was only reinforced during the colonial period…
> Hogra is a sentiment which also includes the thirst for justice… I am convinced that, more than a socioeconomic revolt, this is an uprising for respect and for the end of injustice, a bet in favor of dignity, respect, and freedom, against hogra.

As Hassan Abdou Bakr (Houtart et al., eds. 2012) of Egypt has emphasized, there is important common ground between ongoing revolutionary processes such as that of Egypt, which is still incomplete, and movements such as those of the "indignado/as," elsewhere in the world, and particularly those within the Global South:

> We have reached the stage when human life itself is being "commoditized" [citing sociologist Francois Houtart of the World Forum for Alternatives, WFA]. That was because of the neoliberal financial and economic policies. And the "defense of public services and 'common goods' forms a part of the resistance to those policies." This is what the revolutions of the Arab Spring are doing. People are protesting against poverty, plundering of the national wealth, by the multinationals and the local capitalistic players as well, and unemployment, as well as the disrespect of public freedoms and human dignity. In Egypt, for example, part of the protests is against selling of some public-sector companies to private investors leading to thousands of workers sent to unemployment. Revolutionary forces are calling for the recuperation of the nation-owned assets that were privatized.

3 Poverty and Human Rights

My point of departure is the compelling need to characterize contemporary global poverty and inequality as a crime against humanity. All of the acts generally recognized today as constituting crimes against humanity and/or as serious violations of international law and international human rights law—including war crimes, genocide, slavery, colonialism, torture, sexual violence and discrimination against women, racial discrimination and apartheid, and forced disappearances—have at some previous moment in history been considered legal and therefore "legitimate." Human rights norms and related conceptions of international criminal law reflect the evolving ethical consciousness of humanity, with all of its limitations, contradictions, and intermittent, nonlinear phases of advances and regressions.

The period since the events of September 11, 2011, is one of those examples of retreat from previously established standards on a global scale, which has in turn spurred responses protesting the ravages of neoliberal globalization and demanding participatory democracy and economic justice in the period prior to and following the international economic and financial crisis of 2008–2009. My approach here further assumes that contemporary human rights norms are the historical product of the struggles of social movements and their impact on evolving patterns of reflection, discourse, and policy, from the perspective of those whose suffering has been consigned to "rightlessness." This includes the legacies and contributions of movements of the poor and excluded throughout history, against feudalism, colonialism, imperialism, slavery, racism and national oppression, the exploitation of workers, and the domination of women.

The largely unwritten history of the "making" of international human rights and international law is the history of the ebbs and flows in a nonlinear trajectory as to the extent of recognition of the rights of those most exploited, oppressed, marginalized, and excluded in each historical period. Such an approach demands a distinct rupture with epistemological assumptions of a positivist, functionalist, and determinist character that are still prevalent in many circles. It also includes an insistence upon a critical understanding of legal definitions of rights in any specific historical period as minimums, not maximums ("floors and not ceilings"), and thus as points of departure, not destinations in themselves.

4 Poverty as Violence

Why is it important to differentiate between hegemonic and counter-hegemonic approaches to human rights, poverty, and global justice, and to the relationship between these concepts? My argument is that poverty must be understood as a condition resulting from the convergence of three kinds of violence which produce the deprivation of power and rights which constitute its very essence, as Rev. Dr. Martin Luther King Jr. suggested at the height of his transition from an emphasis on civil rights to human rights, and from racial discrimination to systemic injustice.

The convergent forms of violence alluded to by King and which must be explored by an International Poverty Tribunal include (1) state violence (committed by state authorities and/or their agents through their actions, omissions, and complicities); (2) structural violence (such as hunger, preventable disease, child and maternal mortality, inadequate sanitation, housing and education, the effects of multiple forms of discrimination—based on race, ethnicity, gender, nationality, immigration status, disability, age, sexual preference, etc.—environmental devastation and climate change, and other conditions that can be characterized as violations of economic, social, cultural, and environmental rights); and (3) systemic violence (such as the inequalities of property, wealth, income, and power which are attributable to the inherent characteristics of the capitalist mode of production, and to neoliberal globalization, its principal contemporary expression. Christian Marazzi (2011) has recently explored such dimensions in his exploration of the "violence of financial capital"). Serious efforts to reduce and eradicate poverty—and thus to prevent its production and reproduction—must sooner or later address all of these dimensions together and their complex interrelationship, or will necessarily fall short of accomplishing their purported objectives.

5 Poverty as Crime Against Humanity and the Right to Be Human: Ethical and Philosophical Frameworks as Necessary but Insufficient

Global poverty is the contemporary equivalent of historical crimes of a similar character that had to be wrested from the complicit silence or "norm-avoidance" (Pogge, 2002: 5) that sought to conceal or deny them, by the equivalents in each corresponding historical period of the combined pressures of counter-hegemonic social movements and critical thinking. A combination of historical and legal precedents thus leads me in turn to argue that the intertwined character of contemporary global poverty and inequality must be approached not "only" as a profound challenge to global ethics, development studies, and the philosophy of law (Sen, 1998, Pogge, 2002; Sachs, 2005), and as a "massive and systemic" (2001 CESCR Statement on Poverty, para. 4, cited by Salomon,

2011) violation of human rights that must be addressed within the framework of economic and social rights, the right to development, and "international poverty law," but also as a "serious crime" under international law.

This in turn must mean that under certain circumstances (e.g., for contemporary Mexico, the Pinochet dictatorship in Chile, and similar contexts, see Pérez-Bustillo, 2003, 2012), conduct (policies, practices, and systems or institutional orders) by state and nonstate actors that "substantially contribute to the persistence of severe poverty" (Pogge, 2002: 115) could and should lead to the application of standards, procedures, and remedies (including appropriate measures consistent with victims' rights to truth, justice, individual and collective reparations, and non-repetition of the culpable conduct) imposed by international criminal law pursuant to the Princeton Principles of Universal Jurisdiction (2001), in light of Article 7 of the Rome Statute of the International Criminal Court (ICC) (1998) (Pérez-Bustillo, 2003), and other relevant norms and standards of international law.

Article 7 defines the "crimes against humanity" which fall within the ICC's jurisdiction, and includes specific acts such as murder, extermination, enslavement, forced deportations, torture, rape, sexual slavery, persecution forced disappearances, apartheid as well as "(k) (o)ther inhumane acts of a similar character intentionally causing great suffering, or serious injury to body or to mental or physical health." The Court's definition of Elements of Crimes (2011) included in the Rome Statute stipulates that the "other inhumane acts" referred to in Article 7 section (k) must involve the infliction of "great suffering, or serious injury to body or to mental or physical health, by means of an inhumane act." Suffering of this kind culminating all too often in massive numbers of "foreseeable and avoidable" deaths and disabilities is of course inherent to living conditions characterized by severe poverty. The imperative that I seek to embrace and inject into the framework of human rights here is that of *"taking [this] suffering seriously"*; emphasis added), together with the assumption that the "spectral presence" of these victims of the contemporary global order is a "necessary condition for thinking and doing justice":

But how do we mourn for the living dead, those who are not there. These ... women, men, and children live in the present; ... exist but are denied visibility and voice; their actual physical existence/survival (bare life in terms of Agamben) is a code for their living death; ... as if they were as yet not born or had died many a time after their birth. These are the truly rightless peoples, peoples who exist only by virtue of their being expendable and disposable...

The recognition of the criminality of the conditions and conduct which produce this suffering is also then potentially the recognition of what both have described in differing but ultimately convergent contexts as the most fundamental human right of all, the "right to be human."

6 Case Studies of BRICS and ALBA

6.1 BRICS

A differentiation between hegemonic and non- or counter-hegemonic approaches must also be applied to "South-South" initiatives intended to lay the basis for fundamental social transformations such as those needed in order to seriously address contemporary global patterns of poverty and inequality. I will investigate potential case studies such as BRICS and ALBA and these are explored briefly below within this context.

My emphasis here is on the extent to which processes such as BRICS and ALBA have the potential to advance counter-hegemonic paradigms and alternatives of a systemic character (in comparison, for example, to the Non-Aligned Movement which first emerged at the Bandung Conference held in Indonesia in 1955). BRICS, for example—totaling among its members "40% of the world's population, 30% of its landmass, and a share in world GDP (in PPP terms) that increased from 16 percent in 2000 to 25 percent in 2010" (BRICS Report, 2012; UNDP HDR, 2013)— poses a distinct challenge to the current configuration of geopolitical and geoeconomic hegemony of the United States and the West, but does not imply a critique of the global capitalist system as such, nor a rejection of the hegemonic conceptualizations of modernity, development, and progress.

It certainly makes a difference, at first approximation, whether it is the United States, Western Europe, and Japan who are calling the shots within the framework of the former G-7, or whether it is the BRICS states which play the decisive role in shaping global economic and financial policies through the G-20 in spaces such as the IMF, WB, and the WTO. This has led analysts such as Walter Mignolo (2012), a leading exponent of the Modernity/(de)Coloniality project in Latin America, to emphasize the potential contributions of BRICS to the needed "dewesternization" of key spaces where the hegemony of the Global North continues to be exercised, and to the "delinking" of states within the Global South from such control.

But BRICS as currently framed implies an intriguing but currently still limited expansion and differential seasoning of the relevant decision-making table (which the 2012 Delhi Declaration of BRICS, echoed in the 2013 Declaration issued in March in Durban, South Africa, describes in paragraph 4 in terms of "strengthened representation of emerging and developing countries in the institutions of global governance" and in paragraph 8 as a "call for a more representative international financial architecture, with an increase in the voice and representation of developing countries," and in paragraph 9 in the context of the IMF's reforms of its quotas, support for enhanced protection and voice for its "poorest members"), rather than a redefinition of the game ultimately being played, unless it deploys its counter-hegemonic potential in the direction of more fundamental, systemic transformations.

It is worth noting in this context that, in the wake of the East Asian crisis of 1997–1998, it was the consulting branch ("Economic Research Group") of Goldman Sachs (a key player of course in fueling the speculative bubble which led to the Wall Street collapse in 2008), in 2001, which argued that it was in the best interests of global systemic economic and financial stability to expand the G-7 through the addition of Brazil, Russia, India, and China in order to try to make the global system less susceptible to crises it was no longer able to control (O'Neill/Goldman Sachs ERG 2001). From this perspective, BRICS highlights the incorporation into the hegemonic global framework of potential "outliers" who might pose a systemic challenge in conjunction with others if not adequately assimilated.

The ascendancy of pseudo-Communist (actually state capitalist) China and neoliberal, technocratic India thus combined together imply the fullest expression of two of the most twisted examples of capitalist globalization, the creation for the first time of a truly global market, and not a challenge to its assumptions. This picture is completed by a neutered, nonideological, Russia which is stripped of the counter-hegemonic pretensions of the failed USSR, a Brazil which represents at best a diluted version of the anti-systemic rhetoric and impulses of other more radical states in the same region such as Bolivarian Venezuela (which nonetheless has its own limitations), and a South Africa which has become specialized in "Talking Left and Walking Right" (Bond, 2006). To expect such a grouping to undo the configurations of poverty and inequality which are inherent to the systemic logic of globalized capitalism seems at minimum unlikely. Nor is it probable for such an association to prioritize human rights issues overall given their evident vulnerabilities to such issues from within. Nevertheless, BRICS is not likely to go very far if it does not find a way to differentiate and maximize its own unique identity, distinct from that of other potentially rival global and regional groupings (Chellaney and Al Jazeera, 2012; Sharma, 2012).

The declarations issued in March 2013 in Durban and in 2012 in New Delhi as the result of the 4th and 5th BRICS summits, and since,[5] are essentially slightly reworked versions of the kind of communiqué one would expect from the G-20 (or the G-7 or 8, for that matter), or from similar exercises in state rhetoric in the context of UN summits, pervaded by the same kinds of discourses and tropes which typically characterize reports issued by the WB and IMF. This includes ritualistic references in the New Delhi text (echoed in slightly different form in 2013) to (ostensibly self-evident, unexplained) premises such as the need "to restore market confidence and get global growth back on track" (para. 5); "to enable global economic recovery and secure financial stability, including through an improved international monetary and financial architecture" (para. 7); "to ensure strong, sustainable and balanced growth" (para. 7);

---

[5] See, for example, the 2015 Ufa declaration: http://www.brics.utoronto.ca/docs/150709-ufa-declaration_en.html

"and to ensure strong, sustainable and balanced growth" (para. 7, 35); and boiler-plate style references to regional experiences assumed to embody experiences along these lines, such as the New Partnership for Africa's Development (NEPAD) (para. 36). NEPAD is heavily emphasized in the 2013 Declaration, since the focus of the Durban summit was on strengthening ties between BRICs and Africa.

NEPAD has been widely criticized for its emulation of the South African strategy of accommodation to neoliberal imperatives, reflected in the way it was built initially around a core group of five states (South Africa plus Algeria, Egypt, Nigeria, and Senegal) with similar leanings, which have gradually shaped a broader equivalent consensus within the African Union (AU) as a whole reflected in NEPAD's formal incorporation into the AU structure in 2010 (para. 36). Both the Durban and Delhi Declarations suggest that NEPAD is a model for the approach which BRICS should take both as to Africa and overall (para. 36), and appears to allude to an unspoken corollary welcoming intensified Chinese investment in Africa as part of BRICS' arsenal of potential "solutions." According to Taylor and Nel (as cited by Melber 2011), the NEPAD approach is in sum intended to legitimize rather than to restructure the current global power relations in which Africa is embedded, whose inherent characteristics include increased inequality and poverty, and thus, as CODESRIA (Council for the Development of Social Science Research) has argued (para. 36) represents a "setback in the African quest for a return to a path of sustained economic growth and development" (emphasis added), instead of what the Delhi Declaration of BRICS assumes to be its culmination.

A hint of well-founded dialectically flavored irony is however evident in one section (para. 6) of the Delhi Declaration, where the BRICS states affirm "that it is critical for advanced economies to adopt responsible macroeconomic and financial policies, avoid creating excessive global liquidity and undertake structural reforms to lift growth that create jobs." This statement simultaneously applies a typical series of formulas regarding the adoption of "responsible macroeconomic and financial policies" and the need to "undertake structural reforms" traditionally directed by the IMF and WB toward emerging economies to those which are more "advanced," in a spirit of critical reciprocity, and suggests an implicit basis for questioning the use of such rhetoric at all given its hollow character. "Responsible" from whose perspective and upon the basis of what set of interests and values? What is meant by "structural" reforms? Is the term only applicable to measures which make markets more attractive and safer for investment? What about reforms which might increase the possibility of living with dignity in poor communities? Aren't poverty and inequality "structural" as well?

It would be very interesting from the standpoint of the need for a meaningful "South-South" agenda of global transformation (including issues of poverty and inequality within an expanded, reconfigured counter-hegemonic human rights framework) for BRICS to push the limits of its constraints as far as possible: to seriously seek to walk, as well as talk, "South." Some of the needed elements for this are present at least implicitly along the edges of the emerging BRICS agenda. This includes references in both the Delhi and Durban Declarations to BRICS as a potential basis for strengthening a "partnership for common development" and deepening cooperation among its members (para. 1; with the exact shape of such commonality and deepening still unspecified), and in paragraph 4 to the centrality of international law as a framework for its aspirations: "We stand ready to work with others, developed and developing countries together, on the basis of universally recognized norms of international law and multilateral decision making, to deal with the challenges and the opportunities before the world today. Strengthened representation of emerging and developing countries in the institutions of global governance will enhance their effectiveness in achieving this objective."

However, international human rights standards (hegemonic or otherwise) are not specified here or anywhere else in the Delhi Declaration as explicit components of the "universally recognized norms" referenced, and the text moreover seems to assume that "strengthened representation of emerging and developing countries in the institutions of global governance" might itself be enough to "enhance their effectiveness" in addressing contemporary global "challenges and opportunities," but "human rights" does explicitly appear as a reference for the first time in the Durban text (para. 23; as it does in para. 10 of the Ufa Declaration in 2015), including a potentially significant but still unspecified agreement to cooperate regarding human rights issues. Most social movements identified with the Arab and Latin American "Springs" and/or with the global justice movement insist that it is the existing institutions of global governance themselves that must be reformed in terms of their substantive objectives and policies, and not just procedurally in terms of which states from which regions define them. Otherwise their reorientation with enhanced representation from the "South" simply implies a shift in geographical and geopolitical direction, and not one of a systemic character. Connecting cooperation among BRICS states as to human rights and such concerns would be an interesting next step.

Additional elements of the Delhi Declaration which suggest the need for deeper transformations include its call in paragraph 10 for the IMF "to make its surveillance framework more integrated and even-handed," and its calls in paragraphs 12 and 13 for reform of the WB (in terms of its governance structure, to move it away from its current mediating role as to North-South development efforts, and to end its reliance upon an outdated donor-recipient model), and for its possible supplementation (not replacement?) by a new ("South-South"?) Development Bank, which was reaffirmed as an objective in Durban in 2013.

Paragraphs 15 and 16 of the Delhi Declaration refer to the strengthening of the WTO and of the Doha Round itself through the accession of Russia, but at the same time paragraph 17 underlines the role of UNCTAD "as focal point in the UN system for the treatment of trade and development issues." Paragraph 18 meanwhile highlights the importance of strengthening existing mechanisms to enhance intra-BRICS trade.

Paragraph 28 provides the most extended reference to issues of social development (in addition to specific reaffirmation of support for the MDGs process in paragraph 35, and additional references to issues related to the environment, climate change, and biodiversity in paragraphs 29–34, and those related to public health in paragraph 42): "[a]ccelerating growth and sustainable development, along with food, and energy security, are amongst the most important challenges facing the world today, and central to addressing economic development, eradicating poverty, combating hunger and malnutrition in many developing countries. Creating jobs needed to improve people's living standards worldwide is critical. Sustainable development is also a key element of our agenda for global recovery and investment for future growth. We owe this responsibility to our future generations." These are the principal references in the entire document to such issues and at best reflect a diluted echo of long-standing frameworks present in the international community through the MDG process and UN Summits dating back to the 1990s. Nothing is included, for example, in terms of an understanding of poverty as a violation of human rights, or as to the human rights dimensions more generally of issues related to poverty, hunger, and malnutrition.

This vacuum is particularly notable given the substantive importance of poverty and inequality as phenomena which have shaped the history and contemporary character of the economies of China, India, Russia, Brazil, and South Africa, and of the dense web of policies addressing such issues directly or indirectly (e.g., in the context of broader initiatives targeting issues of agrarian development or that of minority groups) in each of these countries. Few peoples in the world would be so well-positioned, on the other hand, to assume such a role given their accumulated experience and suffering, which makes the absence of such leadership all the more notable. The ruling sectors of the Global North which concentrate 80% of the world's wealth in the hands of 20% or less of its population pose the principal overall structural and material obstacles to the redistributive measures necessary to redress the injustices of the global economy, but the most immediate obstacles lie in their occasional rivals but ultimately de facto allies in the governing régimes in each of the BRICS states. It is difficult to imagine a substantive shift toward a counter-hegemonic, counter-systemic stance on the part of BRICS toward issues of global poverty and inequality, and more broadly toward a counter-hegemonic approach to human rights overall, without an underlying transformation in each of these régimes. It is time to begin to imagine what a counter-hegemonic approach to human rights from the perspective of the peoples of the BRICS countries might look like, and to insist that it be promoted within each of the bloc's constituent states.

Additional hints of the kinds of initiatives such an initiative might encompass include some of the recommendations formulated by the BRICS Academic Forums held in Delhi and Durban as parallel, complementary events to that of the summit itself. Some of this involves greater specificity than the more general, diplomatic language which permeates the Delhi Declaration itself, including an insistence on BRICS as a space for "progressive development trajectories" (emphasis added), including "transformations for optimal representation and participation in matters of global political, economic and financial governance" (not just economic and financial governance as is emphasized in the Delhi Declaration). The Academic Forum also recommends that the "BRICS nations must seek to create institutions that enable viable alternatives for enhancing inclusive socio-economic development agenda within and outside BRICS. Such institutions must eventually seek to set global benchmarks for best practices and standards."

Its recommendations also underline the need to address the increasing activism of nonstate actors and to assess the contributions of "indigenous knowledge and practices to deal with common challenges such as eco-friendly agricultural practices, efficient water use, disaster management and other humanitarian issues," and to emphasize issues relating to "inclusive growth and equitable development" (adjectives absent from the Delhi Declaration itself, or highly diluted). The Academic Forum's recommendations also emphasize the need within BRICS to create spaces for exchange between scholars, experts, and business leaders as well as the citizens, youths, and social, political, and cultural actors of each country. This latter component echoes the emergence on a still incipient basis within ALBA of such spaces for social movements and cultural workers. All of this in effect lays the basis in turn for imagining the gradual emergence of a much more democratic and inclusive BRICS "from below," and much more reflective of the extraordinary wealth represented by the counter-hegemonic social movements in each of its member countries, whose imaginaries range much more widely than the relatively constricted visions of its states.

6.2 ALBA Case Studies: Venezuela, Bolivia, and Ecuador

ALBA, by contrast, seems to suggest the possibility of a more proactive approach to such issues as part of a broader South-South agenda, as reflected, for example, both in its role as an emerging regional alternative to US political and economic hegemony and in Venezuela's vigorous, generally successful efforts to reduce poverty and inequality between 2002 and 2011 (with estimates ranging from 48.6% overall to 27.8% in 2010, and in terms of extreme poverty from 22.2% to 10.7%, see López Arnal 2012, based on ECLAC 2011; or of an even greater magnitude, from 54% to 27.5% overall and from 25.1 to 7.6% between 2003 and

2007, implying a 50% reduction in poverty as a whole and of 70% in extreme poverty during the period in question; many of these gains have been eroded, however, by a deep economic crisis between 2014 and 2016 spurred in part by a sharp global drop in oil prices and thus revenues. Others (McLeod and Lustig, 2011) dispute or qualify the absolute and relative character of such reductions in Venezuela and suggest that overall more moderate center-left régimes in Latin America such as those of Brazil and Chile were more effective in reducing poverty in a lasting way than the more radical, "populist" régimes of Venezuela and Argentina, in part because of the correlation in the latter two cases between reductions in poverty and their economies' greater dependency on the cyclical character of higher commodity prices. But all of those cited on both sides of this debate provide a basis to argue that regardless of whether the reductions were greater or more lasting in the more moderate or more "populist" contexts, the régimes least successful at reducing poverty and/or inequality during the same period were those most closely aligned with US-imposed "free market" policies (e.g., Colombia, Mexico; the latter once initial reductions supposedly attributable to new focalized, conditional cash transfer policies were reversed following the impact of the 2008 global crisis).

Other ALBA leaders such as Evo Morales of Bolivia and Rafael Correa of Ecuador (himself a former economist at the WB) have insisted upon poverty prevention, reduction, and eradication as key components of national social policy, including Correa's recent insistence in a speech delivered at the Santiago headquarters of the UN's Economic Council for Latin America and the Caribbean (ECLAC, better known by its Spanish language initials as CEPAL) in Chile, that poverty reduction rather than increases in economic growth should be considered the measure of a country's progress, and a "moral imperative, rather than a technical challenge". Correa also highlighted a reduction in the country's Gini coefficient measuring inequality from 0.55 in 2006 to 0.47 in 2012. Poverty meanwhile was reduced overall nationally from 37.6% in 2006 to 28.6% in 2011, and from 60.6% in the rural sector (where the country's indigenous population is most heavily concentrated) to 50.9% in 2011. Similar trends are evident in Bolivia, with reductions in overall poverty from 60.6% in 2005 to 49.6% in 2010, in rural poverty (once again, as in Ecuador, where the country's indigenous population is most highly concentrated) from 77.6% to 65.1%, and in urban poverty from 51.5% to 41.7% (Weisbrot, Ray and Johnston/CEPR, 2009; Carlson, 2012).

7 Conclusion

ALBA and the dominant political trends in its leading states (Cuba, Venezuela, Bolivia, Ecuador, and Nicaragua) pose difficult dilemmas for political analysts and activists on the left in the region because of the increasing tensions in several of these cases (Ecuador, Nicaragua, Bolivia, most notably) between their governing régimes and more radical social movements with an anti-systemic character. These dilemmas and tensions apply more broadly to similar cases in Brazil and Argentina, where the more "moderate," center-left character of their governments polarize political divisions even more emphatically, and even more so in contexts such as Colombia and Chile where powerful grassroots movements based in the countries' most marginalized sectors confront center-right governments which have little compunction in recycling the most repressive responses to their mobilizations. Common threads throughout all of these cases (from those within ALBA to those beyond in both the center-left and center-right categories) include the emergence of a form of "neo-developmentalism" or "neo-extractivism" (Zibechi, 2012) which constitutes the Latin American version of the processes of "accumulation by dispossession" (via mega-projects, mining, and overall environmental devastation, forced migration and displacement, etc.) which has been described as the essence of contemporary forms of capitalist neoliberal globalization. Zibechi and many others located within each of these countries suggest that despite their relative successes and distancing from systemic imperatives in certain respects, there is an overall continuity in the imposition of "neo-developmentalist" or "neo-extractivist" imperatives which characterizes régimes such as those of Chávez in Venezuela, Morales in Bolivia, Correa in Ecuador, Ortega in Nicaragua, Lula and Rosseff in Brazil, and the Kirchners in Argentina, in addition to their prevalence in openly neoliberal régimes such as those of Mexico, Chile, Colombia, and Honduras.

In all of these cases, the strongest responses in resistance to processes of dispossession of resources and territories come from movements of indigenous peoples and people of African descent, other marginalized sectors (e.g., the urban poor and employed and youth), and environmentalists, as in Honduras. Many of these sectors unite around the defense of the principles and rhetoric of the new constitutions of "refounded" (Sousa Santos, 2009) states such as Ecuador and Bolivia which have redefined these polities as "plurinational" and "pluricultural," arguing that the Correa and Morales régimes are violating to varying degrees the precepts of the states which they helped create (like the African National Congress in South Africa or the sectors of the opposition that have come to occupy some positions of power in Egypt, Tunisia, or Libya but have failed to act consistently with their origins or originally stated intentions).

These same frameworks of "decolonized" constitutional law have redefined the traditional conceptual boundaries of international human rights principles to include the recognition of nature or "Mother Earth" as a subject of rights, as reflected in the indigenous cultures of the Andean regions of Latin America common to countries such as Ecuador, Bolivia, Perú, and Colombia, through their shared roots in the Inca civilization, and its conception of *"Pacha Mama"* and of a "good life" understood in terms of *"Sumak Kawsay"* or *"Suma Qamaña"* (as the concept is articulated respectively in the indigenous languages of the Quechua and Aymara peoples, see Houtart et al., ed., 2012); this in turn is what is referred to as the basis for a "post-capitalist" paradigm framed in terms of the "common good of humanity" by Houtart, et.al. (id). These approaches go much further in the direction of the counter-hegemonic frameworks of human rights necessary to address issues of global systemic injustice reflected in persistent poverty and inequality, "from below," throughout the region, regardless of the ideological label attached to or embraced by the specific government at issue.

References

Abdou Bakr in Houtart, et al. (eds.) (2012) A Post-Capitalist Paradigm: The Common Good of Humanity. Brussels: Rosa Luxemburg Foundation, online at: http://rosalux-europa.info/publications/books/common-good-of-humanity/

Alpert, M. (2016) "Why was this prominent Honduran activist killed in her own home?" online at: http://foreignpolicy.com/2016/03/03/berta-caceres-murder-honduras-activist/

Amin, S. (2006) "The Millennium Development Goals: A Critique from the South," Monthly Review (March 2006), online at: http://monthlyreview.org/2006/03/01/the-millennium-development-goals-a-critique-from-the-south

Amin, S. (2011) "An Arab springtime?" 2011-06-08, issue 534, online at: http://pambazuka.org/en/category/features/73902

Amin, S. (2012a) "The Arab Revolutions: A Year After," 2012-03-14, issue 576, online at: http://pambazuka.org/en/category/features/80745

Amin, S. (2012b) "The Electoral Victory of Political Islam in Egypt," online at: http://mrzine.monthlyreview.org/2012/amin300612.html

Binebine, M. (2011) quoted in "La Revolución de la Dignidad" by Ignacio Cembrero, El País (Madrid), February 11, 2011, online at: http://elpais.com/diario/2011/02/11/internacional/1297378811_850215.html

Bond, P. (2006) Talk Left, Walk Right: South Africa's Frustrated Global Reforms, online at: http://ccs.ukzn.ac.za/files/BondTalkLeftWalkRight2ndedn.pdf

Buchanan, A. (1982) Marx and Justice: The Radical Critique of Liberalism. London: Methuen.

Byrne, J. (2012) The Occupy Handbook. New York: Back Bay Books.

Carlson, C. (2012) "What the Statistics Tell Us about Venezuela in the Chavez Era," online at: http://venezuelanalysis.com/analysis/7513

Carroll, W. (2010) "Crisis, Movements, Counter-hegemony: in Search of the New," Interface: A Journal for and About Social Movements 2 (2): 168–198, online at: http://interfacejournal.nuim.ie/wordpress/wp-content/uploads/2010/12/Interface-2-2-pp.168-198-Carroll.pdf

Chellaney, B. and Al Jazeera (2012) The BRICS Grouping: A Brick by Brick Development (Reports, April 8, 2012). Doha: Al Jazeera Centre for Studies, online at: http://studies.aljazeera.net/en/reports/2012/04/201248135926654219.htm

CROP Poverty Brief. (January 2013) "Poverty and the Millennium Development Goals (MDGs): A critical assessment and a look forward," online at: www.crop.org

De Schutter, O. (2011) "Millennium Development Goals Need More Emphasis on Human Rights: The MDGs are in Danger of Diverting Attention from the Mechanisms That Produce Underdevelopment," The Guardian (London), September 21, 2010, Poverty Matters blog, online at: http://www.guardian.co.uk/global-development/poverty-matters/2010/sep/21/millennium-development-goals-olivier-de-schutter

Dussel, E. (2008) Twenty Theses on Politics. Durham and London: Duke University Press.

Hardt and Negri (2011a) "Arabs are Democracy's New Pioneers: The Leaderless Middle East Uprisings Can Inspire Freedom Movements as Latin America did before," The Guardian (London), February 24 (Thursday), 2011, online at: http://www.guardian.co.uk/commentisfree/2011/feb/24/arabs-democracy-latin-america

Hardt and Negri (2011b) "The Fight for 'Real Democracy' at the Heart of Occupy Wall StreetThe Encampment in Lower Manhattan Speaks to a Failure of Representation," Foreign Affairs (October 2011), online at: http://www.foreignaffairs.com/articles/136399/michael-hardt-and-antonio-negri/the-fight-for-real-democracy-at-the-heart-of-occupy-wall-street

Hardt and Negri (2012) "Taking Up the Baton," http://antonionegriinenglish.files.wordpress.com/2012/05/93152857-hardt-negri-declaration-2012.pdf

Hessel, S. (2011) "Time for Outrage" (also distributed under the alternative title Cry Out!)/Indignez-vous/¡Indignaos! online at: http://therearenosunglasses.files.wordpress.com/2011/01/cry-out_.pdf

Human Rights Watch (2016) "Honduras: Investigate Environmental Activist's Killing," online at: https://www.hrw.org/news/2016/03/04/honduras-investigate-environmental-activists-killing

King, Martin Luther (1965) "The Violence of Poverty," Amsterdam News (New York City), online at: http://www.thekingcenter.org/archive/document/my-dream-violence-poverty#

Manhire, Toby (ed.) (2012) The Arab Spring: Rebellion, Revolution, and A New World Order. London: Guardian Books.

McLeod, D. and Lustig, N. (May 2011) "Inequality and Poverty under Latin America's New Left Regimes," Working Paper 1117 in Tulane

Economic Working Papers Series, online at: http://econ.tulane.edu/RePEc/pdf/tul1117.pdf

Melber, H. (2011) "South Africa and NEPAD—quo vadis?" Centre for Policy Studies, Policy Brief 31, online at: http://www.cps.org.za/cps%20pdf/polbrief31.pdf

Mignolo, W. (2012) online at: http://criticallegalthinking.com/2012/05/02/delinking-decoloniality-dewesternization-interview-with-walter-mignolo-part-ii/; http://waltermignolo.com/dheli-2012-la-desocc identalizacion-los-brics-y-la-distribucion-racial-del-capital/

O'Neill/Goldman Sachs (2001) "Building Better Global Economic BRICS," online at: http://www.goldmansachs.com/our-thinking/topics/brics/building-better.html

Pérez-Bustillo (1997, 2000, 2001, 2003, 2008, 2009, 2011, 2012) The Poverty of Rights: Human Rights and the Eradication of Poverty (ed. with Willem van Genugten). London: Zed Books.

Pogge, T. (2002) World Poverty and Human Rights: Cosmopolitan Responsibilities and Reforms. New York City: Wiley, John and Sons.

Pogge, T. and Sengupta, M. (2014) "Sustainable Development Goals: A Better Pact is Possible," online at: http://academicsstand.org/blog/2014/08/10/sustainable-development-goals-a-better-pact-is-possible/

Salomon, M. (2011) "Why should it matter that others have more? Poverty, inequality, and the potential of international human rights law" Review of International Studies 37: 2137–2155. 2011 British International Studies Association, doi:10.1017/S0260210511000362. First published online October 19, 2011: http://papers.ssrn.com/sol3/papers.cfm?abstract_id=1711657

Sen, A. (1998) Development and Freedom. Cambridge, MA: Harvard University Press.

Sharma, R. (2012) "Broken BRICs: Why the Rest Stopped Rising," Foreign Affairs (November/December 2012), http://www.foreignaffairs.com/articles/138219/ruchir-sharma/broken-brics

Sousa Santos, B. de (ed.) (2007) Another Knowledge is Possible: Beyond Northern Epistemologies. Verso: London and New York.

Sousa Santos, B. de (2009) Una epistemología del sur. México: Siglo XXI Editores.

Tabb, W. (2003) "After Neoliberalism," Monthly Review 55(02, June), online at: http://monthlyreview.org/2003/06/01/after-neoliberalism

UN CESCR (2001) Statement on Poverty and the International Covenant on Economic, Social and Cultural Rights; see text of proposed guidelines on Extreme Poverty and Human Rights, online at: http://www2.ohchr.org/english/issues/poverty/consultation/index.htm

UN Millennium Development Goals (MDG) Report 2012, online at: http://www.un.org/en/development/desa/publications/mdg-report-2012.html

UNDP Human Development Report 2013, UNDP: New York.

Weisbrot, M. (2012), "Report from the South American Spring," online at: http://www.epsusa.org/publications/newsletter/2012/mar2012/weisbrot.html

Weisbrot, Mark, Ray, Rebecca and Johnston, Jake (2011) "The Economy during the Morales administration," online at: http://www.cepr.net/index.php/publications/reports/bolivian-economy-during-morales-administration; regarding Venezuela (2010, 2008) see: //www.cepr.net/index.php/publications/reports/update-venezuela-economy, http://www.cepr.net/index.php/Publications/Reports/poverty-reduction-in-venezuela-a-reality-based-view; regarding Ecuador (2009): http://www.cepr.net/index.php/publications/reports/update-on-the-ecuadorian-economy

Zibechi (2008, 2011, 2012) Autonomía y emancipación. Mexico City: Bajo Tierra Ediciones.

Chapter 2
"I'M GONNA GET MY SHARE OF WHAT'S MINE": NARRATIVES OF POVERTY AND CRIME IN POSTCOLONIAL JAMAICA AND KENYA

Aaron Louis Rosenberg

This chapter sheds light upon the lived realities and (inter)personal experiences of those living in poverty and the manner in which such ways of perceiving and interacting with the world oftentimes result in choices that bring individuals into direct conflict with the forces of law and order. These illegal strategies of poverty alleviation are viewed through the prism of popular cultural expressions in Kenya and Jamaica by performing artists Eric Wainaina and Jimmy Cliff. While neither artist attempts to justify the use of violence and theft as tools for economic advancement, they do both construct and participate in narratives which explicate the motivations and even necessities which give impulse to these desperate and ultimately tragic endeavors to escape from the clutches of poverty.

1 Introduction

The reality of poverty in a variety of (post)colonial settings has been drawing increasing attention since the turn of the twenty-first century and the sobering realization that the first of the United Nations' Millennium Development Goals, that is, to eradicate extreme poverty and hunger, is not achieving significant rates of success in many crucial cases. Countries such as China and India with emerging industrial infrastructures have been positioned to maximize their growth and thus capitalize on the initiatives of the UN's member states. Nations in Sub-Saharan Africa and the Caribbean, however, have not necessarily been able to move forward politically or economically in the same fashion. In such contexts, criminal activity has oftentimes taken the place of gainful employment in order to compensate for the objective and felt deprivation that is experienced by members of these societies.

The reality and gravity of these situations are brought out in the studies contained in the "Strategy Paper on Urban Youth in Africa," where the authors tell us that "since the beginning of the 1990s, the population of urban youth living in poverty, and youth crime and crime by minors in cities in the developing world have increased significantly."[1] They go on to advise that it is necessary to create a "global context for concern about the plight of young people in urban settings, the extent and nature of those problems for African youth, and the urgency of the need for widespread and concerted action."[2] Of particular relevance to our study here is the intensive use of music as part of the strategy to develop youth-oriented initiatives to combat criminality and reduce poverty. As the study points out, in Kenya, Gidigidi Majimaji was involved in developing programs to encourage young people to engage in musical expression in order to "empower the youth socially."[3]

In Jamaica the contributions of scholars such as Stone[4] have been useful in determining the causes and likely trajectories of criminal activity in the Caribbean as well as in Kenya. Such feelings of deprivation have been outlined and explained by numerous authors. Ellis's study[5] of the blossoming of criminal activity in Jamaica from the 1950s to the 1980s is relevant to our project here in that it deals with precisely the period immediately following the death of the Jamaican outlaw Ivanhoe "Rhyging" Martin, who was gunned down by police in 1948, and in which Jimmy Cliff released the 1972 film *The Harder They Come*. Other explorations of the criminal world in Jamaica such as that by Headley[6] provide us with a comprehensive even if somewhat dated understanding of the manner in which the sociopolitical climate in Jamaica has facilitated the rise of organized and oftentimes violent criminal activity.

In Kenya recent studies funded by various organizations have expressed in no uncertain terms the seriousness of both rural and urban poverty. The recent rise of violent crime and criminal confrontation in Kenya with groups such as Mungiki coming to the fore as semi-organized bodies brings into focus once again the ability of disenfranchised (and even

---

[1] Kanyua and UN Habitat (2005, p. 3).
[2] Ibid., p. 4.
[3] Ibid., p. 85.
[4] Stone (1988).
[5] Ellis (1992).
[6] Headley (1994).

socially well-positioned) individuals to throw in their lot with a group of individuals involved in illegal activities.[7] This is especially true when the governing bodies in such a country are perceived to be exploitative aggressors whose rule is concerned by many to be carried out along extra-legal if not illegal lines. Such a situation is obviously compounded in a country such as Kenya where the percentage of the population living below the poverty line is approximately half of the national population.[8] This is much more than in neighbouring Tanzania with 36% of the population living below the poverty line. This level of poverty is nearly three times that of Jamaica where 17% of the population lives below the poverty line. It is likely, however, that the poverty rate in Jamaica was significantly higher at the time when the film *The Harder They Come* was being produced. This can be deduced from the fact that poverty rates in the early 1990s were at above 30% and that, according to Audley Shaw, the period from 1972 to 1980 was a "period of unprecedented economic decline."[9]

It is crucial therefore that criminal activity and criminals themselves in the Global South (and by extension much of the globe which is profoundly intertwined with these geographic, sociocultural and economic "spaces"[10]) be reassessed in light of the exigent circumstances which to a significant degree make "crime" seem like a viable and attractive option for significant numbers of people. These are numbers which are, ultimately, sufficient to make both individual and organized crime possible. The ambiguity in which the term "crime" is itself defined in both legal and social terms leaves a great deal of intellectual room for debate and disagreement. *The Oxford Online Dictionary* defines crime as "an action or omission that constitutes an offense that may be prosecuted by the state and is punishable by law." An additional definition, however, describes crime as "an action or activity that, although not illegal, is considered to

---

[7] Henninsen and Jones (2012).
[8] Australian Government Refugee Review Tribunal (2011).
[9] Shaw (2011).
[10] See, for example, Laurie Gunst's study Born Fi' Dead(1996) which does an excellent job of explaining the ways in which Jamaican criminals have responded to the need to diversify and export their criminal enterprises in order to participate in a broader sphere.

be evil, shameful, or wrong."[11] These two definitions, when taken together, go a long way toward indicating the amorphous and plastic nature of crime and those who perpetrate it in Tanzanian, Jamaican, and multiple other contexts throughout the Global South. Depending, therefore, on the perspective of those who constitute the community of reception of such actions, their strictly legal criminal nature may become significantly altered or even reversed in its implications. We might consider, for example, the legendary figure of Robin Hood, a widely disseminated character in European folklore.[12] The violent actions perpetrated by Robin Hood and his "merry men" have become the stuff of enduring, even pro-social, legend precisely because these thefts and assassinations were perceived by many to be justified if not absolutely necessary. In a similar manner, I will demonstrate below the extent to which the characters personified by Jimmy Cliff and Eric Wainaina are made sympathetic and empathetic to their audiences to the extent that they activate a sense of the ambiguity inherent in their acts of theft and violence. These sentiments are in turn, of course, given fertile soil in which to flourish due to the sociohistorical circumstances that they depict and respond to. Creative expression in African and Caribbean communities has kept pace historically and in contemporary contexts with such realities, responding to the lived experience of poverty in various ways. Escapism through the projection and celebration of wealth has long been a popular artistic foundation upon which to build both films and music produced in these regions. Of equal if not greater importance, however, are those texts which confront and describe poverty in ways which both give expression to and validate the experiences of the poor themselves.

In order to explore the representations of poverty that have been emerging from these zones, this chapter will take as its focus the life and work of the canonical performing artists Eric Wainaina and Jimmy Cliff. Each has, in quite distinct ways, carved out a productive niche for themselves in their respective countries through their musical and dramatic talents—Cliff in Jamaica and Wainaina in Kenya. While I will attempt as

---

[11] Definition of crime in English. http://www.oxforddictionaries.com/us/definition/american_english/crime. Accessed May 10, 2014.

[12] See, for example, Joseph Hunter's essay "Robin Hood" in Stephen Knight'a edited volume Robin Hood: An Anthology of Scholarship and Criticism (D.S. Brewer, 1999) for an explanation of the social significance of the Robin Hood legend.

much as possible to consider the full trajectory of each artist's work over the length of their careers, the scope of my analysis will necessarily be limited to one "work" by each artist. This category will be broadly interpreted as I will be looking at the feature film *The Harder They Come*, which stars Jimmy Cliff in its leading role as well as featuring his musical talents. This cinematic work will be considered in conjunction with the song "Mariana" from Wainaina's recent album *Love + Protest*.

As it is unlikely that many of my readers will be familiar with the work of both artists, it may be useful to provide a brief biographical sketch of each artist. This will be done in order to provide readers with a general notion of the creative background of each performing artist as well as the manner in which the works considered here fits into and can be perceived to represent general imaginative and intellectual tendencies within the oeuvre of each performing artist.

Since the beginning of his solo career in 2001, the Kenyan recording artist Eric Wainaina has repeatedly made poverty and corruption the focus of his creative works. His 2011 album *Love + Protest* continues this trajectory with the majority of the tracks confronting such issues. He has become an important public figure in Kenya who has taken an active part in the cultural life of the country, more specifically in the nation's capital, Nairobi. He has also been a featured artist in regional events such as the Sauti za Busara festival in Zanzibar in 2004 and 2008 and has collaborated with artists from throughout the African continent such as Oliver Mtukudzi from Zimbabwe and Baaba Maal from Senegal. In addition to his musical work, he has been involved in a number of theatrical productions, perhaps the most renowned of these is the musical *Lwanda Magere*[13] in which he acted as the protagonist.[14] Although Wainaina did not grow up poor and in fact was fortunate enough to study at the Berkelee School of Music in Boston, he has made his Kenyan identity an integral part of his musical expression and on each of his

---

[13] Wainaina's selection of the Luo legend of Lwanda Magere as the theme of his musical is relevant in and of itself as it represents a manifestation of his conscious effort to carry out artistic collaborations across some of the strongest discriminatory dividing lines in Kenyan society historically and in contemporary circumstances. He has worked with recording artists from the Kenyan Panjabi community and has also sung songs in Dholuo, thus effectively singing out against such forms of ethnic and racial discrimination.

[14] Wainaina (2012).

three albums has made representation and validation of the lives of Kenyans dealing with poverty a recurrent theme. One song in particular, "Mariana," adopts a novel perspective on the problem by allowing a thief to speak for himself and empathetically explain his reasons for entering into a life of crime.

The Jamaican singer Jimmy Cliff has also made activist messages an integral part of his work over the course of his lengthy career. The 1973 film *The Harder They Come*, in which he starred and for which he composed and sang much of the soundtrack, in many ways helped to establish him both as a Jamaican and as an international reggae star. The protagonist of this film and the tragic actions that unfold in the film reverberate powerfully with the tales told through Wainaina in his songs (and subsequent video productions) as we will see below. Jimmy Cliff was born James Ezekiel Chambers on July 30, 1944. As David Katz explains in his unauthorized biography of Cliff released just this year, Cliff was born into an impoverished community and for much of his younger years he was forced to struggle with the reality of poverty in both rural and urban settings.[15] As his career has now stretched out over more than four decades and includes more than twenty albums thus far released, it may be inaccurate to say that socially activist songs are the main focus of Cliff's creative output. At the same time, it would not in any way be inaccurate to state that the plot and songs which together make up the film *The Harder They Come* form part of a politically and socially engaged mindset which have been behind Cliff's oeuvre since early on. As a relevant example, his most recent album *Rebirth*, released in 2012[16] features a number of songs that deal with social justice and the problems faced by impoverished individuals and communities. The album begins with the song "World Upside Down" where Cliff states in the first verse that "Looking at world today/I am impelled to say/So much war and poverty/While few enjoy prosperity." In "The Children's Bread," Cliff attacks the capricious greed of the wealthy and their cynical waste in deliberate ignorance of the needs of the poor singing, "They took the children's bread and give it to the dogs/Making so many people's lives so hard." In "Reggae Music," he asserts that "Whenever there is injustice and tyranny

---

[15] Katz (2012, pp. 1–36).
[16] Cliff, Jimmy 2012. Rebirth. Universal Music.

Reggae music is there/Standing up for the rights and the true light." Cliff's selection of the British Punk band The Clash's "Guns of Brixton" also speaks to his preoccupation with the experiences of young and impoverished men and their seemingly inevitable one-sided confrontation with the institutionalized forces of law and order.

While I hasten to point out that it is in no way my intention to propose that Cliff and Wainaina are identical in their artistic output, sociopolitical circumstances or even message, it *is* my intention in this study to explore and illuminate the resonances (pun intended) in their work and the implications which such similarities may have in an understanding of the nature of poverty and the efforts of those battling this condition to enable themselves to rise out of impoverished circumstances. As Deepa Narayan and Patti Petesch state unequivocally in the collection of field studies, *Voices of the Poor from Many Lands*, the true experts on poverty are those who are forced to struggle with this condition every day.[17] I do not claim that the works studied here in this comparative study necessarily represent the direct interventions of impoverished individuals, which can be utilized by poverty pundits in order to realign or radically alter policy. At the same time, I do feel that a close analysis of these works, although they may have been created by artists who, by the time of their composition, were not living in poverty, can give us valuable insights into the frustrations and alleviation strategies practiced in various contexts. This is a valid enterprise in the case of both Wainaina and Cliff's creativity given the extent to which these artists, while functioning in a global market, continue to be relevant actors in the national arenas from which they emerged. These are publics composed largely of fans from disadvantaged backgrounds.

The enduring relevance which these works demonstrate for these groups is a further validation of their importance.

What can a contrastive analysis of these two works, simultaneously disparate and overlapping in generic terms, tell us about the use of creative multimedia in order to interrogate social attitudes toward wealth and poverty in postcolonial settings? Simultaneously, how are their rhetorical messages constructed and what impacts or effects are intended to be

---

[17] Narayan and Petesch (2002, p. 2).

achieved through the dissemination of these works and their persuasive ideas?

A close consideration of the works of Jimmy Cliff and Eric Wainaina permits a reassessment of definitions and conceptualizations of poverty as a constellation of phenomena both quantitative and qualitative. As Ruth Lister points out, both qualitative and quantitative studies are needed in order to provide more complete representations of the reality of poverty as lived and felt in various contexts.[18] There are certainly a multitude of quantitative studies carried out on a regular basis by both academics and poverty professionals in NGOs and government organizations. This study, while drawing upon some of the relevant data on poverty in Tanzania and Jamaica as well as other parts of the globe, is definitely of the qualitative sort.

It is my contention that the works of these two creative performing artists emerging from diverse backgrounds and geographies represent specific forms of "inherent hypertextuality" that can be linked to their experience of poverty in their respective societies. Elsewhere I have referred to "inherent hypertextuality" as "the process whereby works of verbal or other art, which emerge from similar social circumstances and respond to common societal pressures, may come to relate to each other through character development, plot, thematic content and other elements of creative composition."[19] In other contexts, I have used this concept to provide inroads into studies regarding themes as diverse as sexuality,[20] gender politics,[21] and the use and abuse of wealth and money.[22] It is my contention that this particular sort of hypertextuality can be fruitfully employed here in order to unpack narratives of those who find themselves in circumstances of abject poverty and open conflicts with their respective societies. Such an appraisal is justified by the statements of Narayan and Petesch who, having reviewed qualitative field reports from more than two dozen countries, have come to a better understanding of the "striking commonalities in the experiences of poverty across

---

[18] Lister (2005 [2004]).
[19] Rosenberg (2011, p. 41).
[20] Rosenberg (2012b, pp. 118–135).
[21] Rosenberg (2011, pp. 40–49).
[22] Rosenberg (2012a).

countries."[23] It is in no way my intention to reduce the experiences of Jamaican and Kenyan poverty to two creative works and subsequently proceed to demonstrate that these two works are identical. A careful scrutiny of the film and song can, however, reveal the power of art to articulate the lived experiences of the disenfranchised and to explain some of the reasons for such individuals' choices even when such actions may on the surface appear irrational and even self-destructive.

One recent study that I have found useful in delineating the nature and causes of the apparently regressive attacks perpetrated by the characters in these works is that of Umar Serajuddin and Paolo Verme.[24] In this paper the authors explain the importance of gainful employment in the following terms, "Participating in the labor market is important beyond the economic rewards that may derive from employment. It provides a sense of purpose and the feeling of contributing to society that has a meaning in itself. Conversely, lack of employment can provide a sense of emptiness and exclusion that can lead to anxiety and depression."[25] The writers go on to describe the importance of the conception of objective and relative deprivation which members of any community are likely to feel when they are excluded from participation as a member of the work force. Although their analysis is intended to describe the nature of these problems of exclusion in modern-day Morocco and the differentiation which the perception of deprivation undergoes according to age and gender, such ideas are also important in coming to a better understanding of the messages at work in these creative works and their capacity to represent the aspirations and frustrations of their audiences in their respective countries and beyond. Various aspects of the Moroccan situation are reflected, for example, in the report Urban Poverty and Violence in Jamaica by Caroline Moser and Jeremy Holland. Drawing on data collected in Jamaica in the 1990s they state, for example, that

> violent crimes tend to be geographically concentrated in poor urban communities, with more than half of them occurring in Kingston and St. Andrew, and almost three-quarters of murders and more than 80 percent of shootings taking place in Kingston,

---

[23] Narayan and Petesch (2002, p. 1).
[24] Serrajudin, Umar and Paolo Verme (2012).
[25] Ibid., p. 2

St. Andrew, or Spanish Town in 1994. Both victims and perpetrators of violent crime tend to be young men.[26]

In both the song by Wainaina and the film and songs as performed by Jimmy Cliff, we can perceive the declaration, discussion, and dispute of the right of impoverished male characters to aggressively take what they want from society. In an extremely limited manner these male figures attempt to create what Comaroff and Comaroff have called "parallel modes of production."[27] They explain that "criminal violence does not so much repudiate the rule of law or the licit operations of the market as appropriate their forms—and recommision their substance … they refigure the pas de deux in which norm and transgression, regulation and exception, redefine each other…."[28] Thus, confronted with the reality of their inability to escape from poverty through conventional and socially acceptable (legal) means, both men resort to violent theft and drug dealing in order to take what they need by way of the only means at their disposal. The actions of these young men which they carry out against society extend up to and include both the threat and use of extreme violence to achieve their ends. While studies such as that by Umar Serrajudin and Paolo Verme mentioned above have focused upon the conceptualization of relative deprivation as a phenomenon through which individuals compare themselves to other members of their own immediate society as bounded by the national or possibly nationally diasporic space,[29] here I would like to emphasize the capacity of individuals to, in fact, compare themselves to international communities of imagined association. It is not my intention to undermine the importance of the notion of the nation as a major paradigm of identity formation.[30] In the case of the two men whose tragic trajectories are described here, however, it is worth pointing out the extent to which their tales can be linked up to international if not global narratives of youth, poverty, and resistance. Cliff's film has been a cult classic on the international circuit for forty years and continues to prove relevant to young audiences throughout

---

[26] Moser and Holland (1997, p. 1).
[27] Comaroff and Comaroff (2006, pp. 1–56).
[28] Ibid., p. 5.
[29] Serrajudin and Verme (2012).
[30] Anderson (2006 [1983]).

the world. Wainaina's song, although marked as Kenyan by the use of Swahili lyrics and the particular realities described, was, in fact, inspired by events and situations which the singer encountered when on tour in Europe. As Wainaina himself explained to me in a recent interview, the idea for the song came from conversations that he had with his band members while on tour in Switzerland.[31] After hearing stories about Eastern European women who were travelling to Western Europe to land wealthier men and thus "epuka umaskini" or "run away from poverty," Wainaina began to draw parallels between these strategies and those of the young "beach boys" in Mombasa who spend their time trying to land wealthy foreign tourist women in order to improve their lot. Following these comparisons and before setting about the composition of the song "Mariana," he came to a profound realization, therefore, of the universal nature of this problem. Further evidence of the worldwide sweep of these issues is to be found in the references each work contains to the cinema and specifically violent action films as a widespread form of entertainment and socialization. Both men are shown to be well-versed in the popular images of outlaw rebellion which are represented in the movies. In *The Harder They Come*, Ivan spends his free time watching cowboy movies which he obviously relishes. In the film's final scene, he calls out the police and strides onto the beach like a Wild West gun slinging cowboy intent on a man to man showdown. The protagonist in "Mariana" also states:

Nilikuwa na mpango muftí	I had a foolproof plan
Kama vile kwenye muvi	just like what happens in the movies
Niliingia kwa benki	I charged into the bank
Nilisema "lala chini"	And shouted "everybody on the floor!"
Nikajaziwa tikiti	They filled up my bag with money

Thus calling on the image of another popular genre of action films with an equally lengthy history, that of bank robbery movies. In both cases this violent behavior eventually comes to engulf and destroy the protagonists themselves who end their short lives in a rain of bullets.

---

[31] Wainaina (2012).

In realization of the fact that many may not be familiar with Jimmy Cliff's film (which was released some forty years ago) and even fewer with the song recently released in Kenya by Eric Wainaina, I will here touch upon the points in both works which I feel are relevant to our study here.

Both the film and the song deal with a young male protagonist who enters into a life of crime that they turn to due to their circumstances of extreme penury and the seeming impossibility of improving their lot. In the case of *The Harder They Come*, this protagonist is Ivan Martin (based on the character of the historical figure of Ivanhoe "Rhyging" Martin, a Jamaican criminal who was shot to death by police in 1948). Here Rhyging travels from the country to the city of Kingston in order to bring his mother the painful news that his grandmother had died having sold off the family estate before her death. When he attempts to find work in Kingston he begins to suffer the physical and emotional pains of real poverty in an urban environment. His attempts to make his fortune as a Reggae singer only led to further disenfranchisement and disenchantment when he discovers that the only way to achieve fame with his masterpiece *The Harder They Come* is to sell away the rights to the song for a paltry twenty Jamaican dollars. This combination of frustration, hunger and perhaps boredom as well leads him into the arms of the church (or more accurately into the embrace of Elsa, a woman who he spies through the church windows). All of his attempts at honest employment are thwarted however, and when he has a violent falling out with the preacher, he turns to the life of a drug dealer in order to make ends meet. This racy lifestyle soon leads him into open and violent conflict with the police and he kills officer after officer before being wounded. He then holes up on a beach in order to wait for a ship which is his final chance for escape from the island. Perhaps due to his wound he is unable to grab hold of the rope ladder cast out to him as he swims toward the ship and the final moments of the film consist of Ivan coming to on the beach where he had been washed ashore. He stands up to face a dozen police officers with their automatic weapons. After a brief firefight he challenges the policemen to send out "one bad man who can draw [his pistol]" in order to engage him in a Wild West showdown. When Ivan raises his revolvers he is laid low in a hail of gunfire.

The nameless protagonist of the song "Mariana" has a similarly brief life history which converges with and diverges from that of Ivan above in significant ways. The protagonist has similarly gone through a period of particularly rough economic luck which has, as he describes it, brought him to his knees (*umenirudisha magotini*). In a manner similar to Ivan other city dwellers have robbed him of his hard-earned goods, in this case a bicycle which the narrator had bought with borrowed funds in order to start up a legitimate business as a bicycle taxi driver. He also has tried his hand at farming, the traditional solution to economic woes in East Africa as reflected in a variety of songs.[32] As a result of all of this crushing misfortune and in order to attempt to cling to his beloved "Mariana," the protagonist eventually buys himself a pistol, holds up a bank, steals a car and on the run from the police is gunned down in a thick hail of bullets.

Now, obviously there are a number of crucial similarities between these two plots as laid out in my descriptions. In the interest of time, I will not dwell on these except to emphasize the aggressive manner in which both figures lash out against society using violence as one of their few available means to achieve relief from their economic distress. In the song "Mariana," the protagonist does this ostensibly in order to vindicate himself in the eyes and affections of his Mariana. All of the money which he steals from the bank he in fact leaves at the base of a tree for her. As he states in the final verse of the song: "Kwa mizizi ya mti wetu nilikuachia zawadi ili usinitoroke" [At the roots of our favorite tree I left you a present so that you won't leave me]. There are statements of his resentment against society for his poverty and the crucial sense of debility that goes with such an impoverished state. These feelings, however, are at various points subordinated to his inability to provide for and secure his amorous relationship with Mariana.

In the case of Ivan in *The Harder They Come*, his antisocial behavior seems much more self-interested and certainly not embedded in a narrative of unrequited love. Ivan takes on women like shirts and, though he "conquers" Elsa and brings her into his orbit, he is shown in bed with another woman the night that he has his first serious showdown with the police and has to escape in his underwear after shooting various officers. The lyrics of the title track from the film, in fact, encapsulate the

---

[32] See Atomic Jazz Band's "Nitarudi Shamba," Olith Ratego's "Twende Kwa Shamba," Jamhuri Jazz Band's "Nafikiria Kurudi Shamba," Kidum's "Shamba," or Geoffrey Oryema's song "The River."

aggressively acquisitive attitude of the protagonist when Jimmy Cliff, as Ivan, sings:

> Well they tell me of a pie up in the sky
> Waiting for me when I die.
> But between the day you're born and when you die
> They never seem to hear even your cry
> So as sure as the sun will shine
> I'm gonna get my share now of what's mine.
> And then the harder they come
> The harder they'll fall, one and all.

In a likewise violent and hedonistic fashion, Ivan is shown spending the money on prostitutes, alcohol, and fancy clothes with no thought for the future. In fact, in counterpoint to the thrill-seeking Mariana in Wainaina's song above, who seeks to flee her poverty in Europe, Ivan's girlfriend Elsa is the one who tries to talk sense to him and get his flashy lifestyle under control.

In neither case are the protagonists capable of raising themselves up out of poverty into stable, productive lives. This is to say, there is no way for them to, in the terms described by Townsend and later by Nolan and Whelan, participate effectively as members of society due to a lack of resources.[33] Thus in both song and film the seemingly inescapable reality of poverty is described and agitated against even if the protagonists are not capable of realizing true realization through their violent and illegal actions. As Lister points out, "One of the most striking developments in the contemporary politics of poverty is the growing demands for poverty to be understood as powerlessness and a denial of fundamental rights and for the voices of those in poverty to be heard in public debates."[34] We can therefore see how these works of creative, even popular art, enter into debates about the nature of poverty. More specifically they speak about the manner in which young men in postcolonial settings, doubly isolated from the centers of political and financial power due to their status as both disenfranchised and young, seize for themselves the symbols of power and wealth. Though their moments of au-

---

[33] Nolan and Whelan (1996).
[34] Lister (2005 [2004], pp. 10).

thority are fleeting and sorely limited, focused as they are upon the strength of fear which the loaded pistol confers before its bullets are spent, the song and film do represent at the least a sensitive understanding of the dynamics of poverty socially and psychologically in the lives of those who suffer under its pressure. It is in fact specifically through the failure of each of these individuals to find a feasible way to escape from poverty that makes their messages much more realistic and therefore potent. The myth of the so-called free market is that it is a self-correcting system that naturally adjusts itself as an economic structure in order to provide the ideal distribution of opportunities ideally to all. What the protagonists are stating in these two works is that the arrangement of the world's resources in this way is in fact far from free and certainly is not equal. Their defeat and death at the hands of the police, seen as the protectors of the wealthy and their interests at the direct expense if not destruction of the poor, on a certain level affirms the old adage that crime does not pay. At the same time, however, it can also be seen as a powerful representation of the manner in which the impoverished individual who no longer serves the interests of those who have wealth and power risks elimination. This is, of course, an eradication that is almost assured should such individuals demonstrate their willingness to violently work against this construct. Such sentiments were emphatically expressed by the urban residents interviewed by Moser and Holland in and around Kingston.

Summarizing the attitudes of these individuals from various townships, they state:

> Police are a central part of the everyday life of the urban poor, yet are perceived as reinforcing fear and divisiveness. Focus groups in all communities felt that the relationship between the police and the urban poor served only to exacerbate existing conflict [...] Young people in particular argued that through their wholesale harassment of youth on street corners, the actions of the police "mek the youth dem behave wickeder." Their actions instill fear and hatred amongst the youth.[35]

---

[35] Moser and Holland (1997, p. 31).

More recent accounts which point to the lack of trust and cooperation between police and young people in Jamaican urban contexts include the study by Gayle and Levy in which the authors describe an atmosphere of police exploitation and intimidation including extortion and sexual solicitation.[36]

When I lived in Nairobi in the early 1990s, I had the opportunity to witness a similar atmosphere of intimidation at work. The rule of thumb was, in fact, that if one saw the police coming toward you on the street it was always best to cross to the other side of the road in order to avoid coming face to face with them and risking a confrontation which would almost certainly result in the extortion of a bribe and possibly in outright physical abuse or worse. Such realities are candidly explored in youth music known as genge in Kenya. Some of the most articulate examples of this can be found on the self-titled debut album of the group Necessary Noize in which an account of fatal police brutality is laid out for the listener's consideration.[37] The crushing frustration which accompanies such a tense and brutally oppressive situation is eloquently and intimately expressed when Wainaina sings "Nimechoka kusota", or "I am tired of suffering," and whispers to his Mariana with his dying breath "Ukiuliza kwa nini kwa makumbusho yangu/Waeleze nilikataa kuishi/Na matumaini pekee [When they ask you why in remembrance of me/tell them that I refused to live/On hope alone]." Through these parting words we can clearly detect the reverberations of such feelings with the brazen proclamation of Jimmy Cliff as Ivan when he sings to us that "I keep on fighting for the things I want/Though I know that when you're dead you can't/But I'd rather be a free man in my grave/Than living as a puppet or a slave." From the mouths of both men we hear the equation of wealth not only with power but indeed with the sensation of freedom and free will itself. Thus Marx's description of money as the "universal social power,"[38] recognizing as it does both the instrumental and socially integrated nature of wealth as function, goes a great distance in explaining the actions of our primary actors here in their attempts to assume and therefore exploit the transcendent, even if transient and literally

---

[36] Gayle and Levy (2009).
[37] Necessary Noize (2000).
[38] Marx and Engels (2005[1888], p. 14).

expendable, power of wealth. The power of narrative art, as sound and vision, to make such realities more potent and salient for us is only reinforced through the comparison of these stories of poverty and rebellion against it.

2 Conclusion

A comparative analysis of the film *The Harder They Come* and the song "Mariana" is justified and highly productive despite the multiple ways in which these texts can be seen to be radically different. Geographically they are on opposite sides of the globe although both from the Global South. They are separated by nearly half a century in their chronology and are performed in Jamaican Patois and colloquial Kenyan Swahili respectively. An inherently hypertextual examination of these works, however, lays bare the powerful reverberations of film and song as narratives of poverty and disempowerment in postcolonial settings. By placing their protagonists' actions side by side we can come to a more profound understanding of the potential of art to "speak truth" to those in power at the same time as it activates the sensibilities of those whose lives and experiences are generally isolated from the centers of influence even in the case of those who are authorized to dictate policy regarding poverty itself as concept and reality.

A salient correlation can be carried out between these creative works and a cross section of the scholarship related to poverty and youth empowerment in situations of extreme impoverishment in the nations where these creative works were given their impulse and to which they most directly speak. This in turn allows us to come to a more profound understanding of the ways in which young men, manifestly isolated from the centers of economic power and authority in their respective societies, understand their deprivation and attempt to strategies, whether feasible or not, to break out of the cycles of deficiency and desperation into which they have been thrust by a combination of factors largely beyond their control. The dismissal of acts of aggression and violent crime which are often linked to the conditions of such disenfranchised men can thus be understood, through a more nuanced exploration of these sociological and psychological dynamics to be the logical if not inevitable outgrowth of the lack of alternative prospects to which such men can turn in their attempts to solve their physical, social, and emotional needs.

3 Appendix

The Harder They Come   Jimmy Cliff

Well they tell me of a pie up in the sky
Waiting for me when I die
But between the day you're born and when you die
They never seem to hear even your cry

CHORUS
So as sure as the sun will shine
I'm gonna get my share now of what's mine
And then the harder they come the harder they'll fall,

One and all
The harder they come the harder they'll fall

One and all

Well the oppressors are trying to keep me down
Trying to drive me underground
And they think that they have got the battle won
I say forgive them Lord
They know not what they've done

CHORUS

And I keep on fighting for the things I want
Though I know that when you're dead you can't
But I'd rather be a free man in my grave
Than living as a puppet or a slave

CHORUS

The harder they come, the harder they'll fall

One and all
What I say now, what I say now
What I say now, what I say one time
The harder they come the harder they'll fall

One and all

Cliff, Jimmy. "The Harder They Come." The Harder They Come. Island Records, 1972.

Mariana	Eric Wainaina
Mariana Mariana	Mariana Mariana
Nimechoka kusota	I'm fed up with suffering
Nimeamua leo ni leo	I've made a drastic move
Nitaibadili picha	I want to change my life once and for all
Mariana Mariana	Mariana Mariana
Niliomba unipe mwaka	I asked you to give me a year
Usiutupe upendo wetu	To not throw away our love
Na usiamke kutoka ndoto yetu	To not wake up from our dream together
Nilinunua baiskeli	I bought a bicycle
Kupitia mkopo wa benki	With a bank loan
Kusafirisha abiria	In order to make money ferrying passengers
Lakini iliibiwa	But somebody stole it
Mariana Mariana	Mariana Mariana
Ulitafuta visa	You started to look for a visa
Ya nchi ya Yuropa	To run off to Europe
Utaniacha juu ya pesa	You want to dump me because I've got no money
Hakuna atakayeweza	There is noone capable
Kukupenda vile nakupenda	of loving you the way that I do

Najua upendo hauliwi	I know that love won't fill your stomach
Lakini moyo haudanganywi	But the heart cannot be so easily fooled
Nilinunua shamba	I bought a piece of land
Na nilipanda mimea	And I got to planting crops
Ya kuuza marikiti	I was going to make a killing at the market
Lakini ukame	But the drought drove me back
ukanirudisha magotini	onto my knees
Mariana Mariana	Mariana Mariana
Nilikuwa nimechoka	I was so tired
Kwa vile umaskini	Seeing that this poverty
Utafanya unitoroke	Would make you leave me
Mariana Mariana	Mariana Mariana
Nilikomboa bunduki	I bought a gun
Niliamua leo ni leo	Not thinking about tomorrow
Nilikuwa na mpango muftí	I had a foolproof plan
Kama vile kwenye muvi	Just like what happens in the movies
Niliingia kwa benki	I charged into the bank
Nilisema "lala chini"	And shouted "everybody on the floor!"
Nikajaziwa tikiti	They filled up my bag with money
Basi mimi ni huyu	And I was king of the world
Nikajivuta upesi	I tore out of there
Nikauficha mzigo	And ran off to hide the bag
Na nimeiba gari	I had to steal a car
Naenda mwendo kasi	And now I'm driving like a bat out of hell
Lakini kasi haishindi risasi	But still not as fast as the bullets
Zinaninyesha kama mvua	That are falling on me like rain
Naomba Mungu atanipokea	I hope that God will take me into heaven
Ukiulizwa kwa nini	When they ask you why I did it
Kwa makumbusho yangu	At the funeral
Waeleze nilikataa kuishi	Tell them that I refused to live
Na matumaini pekee	surviving on hope alone
Mariana Mariana	Mariana Mariana
Jambo la mwisho	One last thing

Kwa mizizi ya mti wetu	Buried amongst the roots of our lovers' tree
Nimekuachia zawadi	I left you a gift
Ili usinitoroke	So that you will never leave me

Wainaina, Eric and the Best Band in Africa. "Mariana." *Love + Protest.* Eric Wainaina, 2011.

Transcription and translation by Aaron Louis Rosenberg

Bibliography

Anderson, Benedict. 2006 [1983]. Imagined Communities: Reflections on the Origin and Spread of Nationalism. London: Verso.

Australian Government Refugee Review Tribunal. 2011. "Country Advice Kenya: Kenya—KEN38528-Mungiki-Police Protection." 14 April.

Cliff, Jimmy. 1972. "The Harder They Come." Island Records.

Comaroff, John and Jean Comaroff. 2006. "Law and Disorder in the Postcolony: An Introduction," in John Comaroff and Jean Comaroff (eds.), Law and Disorder in the Postcolony. Chicago: University of Chicago Press, pp. 1–56.

Ellis, Hyacinthe. 1992. Identifying Crime Correlates in a Developing Society: A Study of Socio-economic and Socio-demographic Contributions to Crime in Jamaica, 1950–84. New York: Peter Lang.

Gayle, Herbert and Horace Levy. 2009. "'Forced Ripe!': How Youth of Three Selected Working Class Communities Assess their Identity, Support, and Authority Systems, including their Relationship with the Jamaican Police." Mona, Jamaica: University of the West Indies.

Gunst, Laurie. 1996. Born Fi' Dead: A Journey through the Jamaican Posse Underworld. New York: Henry Holt.

Headley, Bernard 1994. The Jamaican Crime Scene: A Perspective. Mandeville, Jamaica: Eureka Press.

Henninsen, Erik and Peris Jones. 2012. "Crisis and the Regeneration of the Self: The Mungiki Movement's Power of Mobilisation." Norwegian Institute for Urban and Regional Research. Accessed at http://aegis-eu.org/archive/ecas4/ecas-4/panels/41-60/panel-60/Erik-Henningsen-Full-paper.pdf (10 October).

Hunter, Joseph. 1999. "Robin Hood," in Robin Hood: An Anthology of Scholarship and Criticism. Cambridge: D.S. Brewer, pp. 187–196.

Jamhuri Jazz Band. 1971. "Nafikiria Kurudi Shamba." Wanyama Wakali. Philips.

Kanyua and UN Habitat. 2005(?). "Strategy Paper on Urban Youth in Africa." Accessed at: http://www.unhabitat.org/downloads/docs/5647_23903_2472_altedit.pdf (accessed October 20, 2012).

Katz, David. 2012. Jimmy Cliff: An Unauthorized Biography. Northampton, MA: Interlink Books.

Kidum. 2003. "Shamba." Shamba. Ug Records.

Lister, Ruth. 2005 [2004]. Poverty. Cambridge, UK and Malden, MA: Polity Press.

Marx, Karl and Friedrich Engels. 2005(1888). Communist Manifesto. Project Gutenberg, pp. 14.

Moser, Caroline and Jeremy Holland. 1997. Urban Poverty and Violence in Jamaica. Washington, DC: World Bank.

Narayan, Deepa and Patti Petesch. 2002. Introduction. Voices of the Poor from Many Lands. New York: Oxford University Press, pp. 1–16.

Necessary Noize. 2000. Necessary Noize. Audio Vault.

Nolan, Brian and Christopher T. Whelan. 1996. Resources, Deprivation and Poverty. London: Oxford.

Oryema, Geoffrey. 1993. "The River." Beat the Border. Realworld.

Ratego, Olith. 2005. "Twendeni kwa Shamba." Osuga: Ketebul.

Rosenberg, Aaron. 2011. "Form and Theme as Unifying Principles in Tanzanian Verbal Art: Elieshi Lema and Orchestra DDC Mlimani Park." Wasafiri 26(1), pp. 40–49.

Rosenberg, Aaron. 2012a. "Naikumbuka kesho: The Nostalgic Present in Tanzanian Verbal Arts." Unpublished. Presented at Florida International University. September 28, 2012.

Rosenberg, Aaron. 2012b. "Remembered Intimacies: Tradition and Gendered Power in Tanzanian Creative Expression." Research in African Literatures 43 (1, Spring), pp. 118–135.

Serrajudin, Umar and Paolo Verme. 2012. "Who Is Deprived? Who Feels Deprived? Labor Deprivation, Youth and Gender in Morocco." Policy Research Working Paper 6090. The World Bank.

Shaw, Audley 2011. "The Other Side of the Truth: Figures don't lie, the PNP can't grow the economy." The Observer, Jamaica. 28 December. http://www.jamaicaobserver.com/columns/The-other-side-of-the-truth_10460378 (accessed October 10, 2012).

Stone, Carl. 1988. "Crime and Violence: Socio-Political Implications," in P. Phillips and J. Wedderburn (eds.), Crime and Violence in Jamaica: Causes and Solutions. Kingston, Jamaica: Department of Government, University of the West Indies.

The Harder They Come. 1972. Dir. Perry Henzell. Perf. Jimmy Cliff. International Films.

Townsend, Peter. 1979. Poverty in the United Kingdom: A Survey of Household Resources and Standards of Living. Berkeley: University of California Press.

Wainaina, Eric. 2012. Personal interview with the author via Skype. 6th of June.Wainaina, Eric and the Best Band in Africa 2011. "Mariana." Love + Protest. Eric Wainaina.

Chapter 3
CONDITIONAL CASH TRANSFERS: A NEW PARADIGM FOR COMBATING POVERTY IN LATIN AMERICA?

Pablo E. Pérez and Brenda Brown

Pérez and Brown analyze the strategies behind the implementation of Conditional Monetary Transfer Programs (CMTP) in Latin America since the 1990s. Those policies were a new attempt at engaging the pervasiveness of unemployment. In fact, the authors explain that these policies come as an oddity since they have multiplied even after the so-called progressive governments.

They attempt to study the different CMTP in the region and its main characteristics, providing a critical reflection on the diagnosis they rely on and on the policies themselves.

1   Introduction

The beginning of this century was characterized in Latin America by the development of a variety of government proposals that fundamentally questioned the neoliberal ideas of the 1990s. These were and are proposals in which the state plays a key role in national development strategies and their implementation. Such policies have come to be referred to as "new developmentalism" or "neodevelopmentalism."[1] This new role assumed by the state generates changes in public policy in general and social policies in particular. Although the priority assigned to output growth and employment has led most countries to an improvement in economic and social indicators, socioeconomic problems affecting a large part of the population persist in a variety of contexts: unemployment, informality, poverty, and indigence remaining persistent issues to date among a plethora of other unresolved problems.

In order to solve this problem, political authorities have expanded a set of social policies in Latin America, mostly driven by international finan-

---

[1]   See Bresser Pereira (2007), Santos et al. (2013), and Féliz (2015).

cial institutions and their objectives. These policies—called Conditional Cash Transfers Programs (CCTP)—supply monetary benefits as long as beneficiaries can demonstrate that they have met certain conditions (popularly such transactions are referred to as funding "with strings attached"). Such policies supposedly aim to reduce poverty levels, not only in the short-term—by way of stimulating monetary profits—but also via medium-term strategies which are designed to break intergenerational cycles of poverty via "human capital accumulation."

In 1997, only three countries in Latin America had such programs underway; ten years later, almost all of the countries in the region have at least one program of this type in effect (Lavinas, 2013). It is estimated that such programs reach 70 million people (Valencia Lomelí, 2008). Several of these policies aim to reduce poverty by promoting work placement for social policy beneficiaries and providing social benefits to workers who are not currently in the formal sector of the economy.

The implementation of CCTP on a massive scale is part of a reconfiguration of the social protection system worldwide which can be traced back to the period of the mid-seventies when such programs were characterized by their promotion of a new way to manage social risks. This strategy aims to promote self-sufficiency, individualism, and self-responsibility in risk coverage of the target population. In its analysis of the theory and practice of such strategies, this chapter works toward the realization of two main objectives: (1) investigate the characteristics that have been adopted in Latin America in order to facilitate this new configuration of the social protection system and (2) analyze the relation between this new configuration and the dynamics of capital accumulation in the region, understanding that the new development mode—which recovers some of the Latin American structuralism' and its basic precepts but also incorporates patterns of prevailing liberal model—has its counterpart in the transformation of the current model of social protection in the region.

This chapter consists of four sections: the first one points out different ways that countries recognize the right to protection against social risks, introduces some theoretical elements about the functions of social policy, and suggests a new configuration of social risks in Latin America. The second section analyzes the diagnosis behind the CCTP and discusses why there has been a relatively universal consensus in Latin America as to the efficacy of these programs. The third section discusses some of the CCTP peculiarities. Finally, we reflect on the results achieved by the CCTP programs in the region.

2 From Social Rights to Social Protection

2.1 Risks, Rights, and Conditions for Social Protection

All of the advanced capitalist countries recognize some form of a general social right to protection against basic social risks such as unemployment, disability, illness, and old age rights. Access to such assistance, however, is almost never unconditional, since to receive a benefit, claimants must meet those conditions as stipulated in the relevant government policies. They must be able to demonstrate their being sick, being disabled, or unemployed. Conditionality usually is related to the type of agreement that the society sets with social security.

Esping-Andersen (1993) distinguishes three classical types of agreements in modern societies. The first is the essentialist model, dominant in Anglo-Saxon countries, where rights to such services are based on an urgent and demonstrable need to ensure the "deserving" character of beneficiaries. The practice of social assistance, with its origin in the tradition of the Poor Law of 1834, is characterized by the unquestioned right of government agencies to check the livelihood and income of those who are applying for assistance. A second type of agreement infrastructure recognizes the essential role of rights in relation to formal work. This kind of protection system, which predominates in Latin America, has its origins in the tradition of insurance as developed first in Germany and then throughout Europe. Here rights are conditioned upon and perpetually linked to a system of interaction between the labor market and financial contributions. Finally, the third type of agreement guarantees universal rights to citizens, regardless of their individual relationship with the labor market. The capacity to request assistance as a beneficiary depends upon one's status as a citizen or resident in the country for a certain time. These systems operate as ideal types; in reality today all countries have a mixed program which selectively draws upon the characteristics inherent in all of these three systems.

In Latin America, social protection systems are inclined to include a preponderance of elements associated with the second type of agreement. These programs extend rights in relation to formal work. The trend since the nineties, however, as one result of the deepening of the neoliberal offensive, is to connect the social protection system toward the essentialist Anglo-Saxon model. In that sense, Filgueira (1998) argues that the shift from a development model founded on the domestic market to one which is export-oriented is related to the transformation of our model of social protection. These policies, centralized, sectorialized, and managed from the state social policies, will lead to models of decentralized social policies, "targeted" and, in some cases, delegated to the private sector, such as those that have multiplied over the past two decades.

In order to link the realities of social policy to the development model requirements which we are considering here, it is necessary to analyze the nature and breadth of state intervention in the process of the labor force reproduction, mainly through its regulatory role in labor markets. We are particularly interested in examining the institutionalization of nonparticipation in wage labor, selecting those involved in the process of social production who regularly participate in the labor market, and analyzing the presence of those who are relegated to the category of intermittent workers or inactive members of society. All of these analyses are to be carried out under the umbrella of social policies and their regulatory potential.

2.2 The State and the Reproduction of Labor Force. The Functions of Social Policy

At this point we return to the perspectives of Offe (1990) and Jessop (2002), for whom social policy is primarily a national strategy intended to regulate the incorporation of labor force into a given labor market according to the necessities of capital accumulation.

If the state wants to ensure—and quantitatively control—the transformation of the labor force into wage-labor, it organizes and sanctions different forms of participation in the labor market. We can readily identify two mechanisms of state policy which act to that effect: (1) social control via the criminalization and prosecution of modes of subsistence that are potential alternatives to the wage-labor relation (e.g., the prohibition of begging) and (2) the state-organized procurement of norms and values, the adherence to which results in the transition of individuals into the wage-labor market. The long-term and intensive application of these two mechanisms of state policy produce a situation in which the working class "by education, tradition, and habit looks upon the requirements of that mode of production as self-evident natural laws" (Offe, 1990).

It is simultaneously necessary that authorities handle changes in labor demand; Offe (1990: 98) points out the need for the state and its various divisions to establish "catchment areas" which lie outside of the conventional labor market. These are zones where the labor force can be accommodated either permanently (old-age pensions, payments for disabled workers) or temporarily (institutions of health care and further education); but on condition that access to them must be controlled by the state through admission requirements. Otherwise the "compulsion to sell" which gives a strong impulse to individuals to enter and remain within a normal labor force market would relax. Regulating the labor participation of certain groups of workers such as young workers, women, older workers, and migrants is a way in which fluctuating labor demand is reconciled with a comparatively inelastic labor supply (Offe and Hindrics, 1985).

In turn, in order to access social assistance, beneficiaries must prove not only their manifest needs but also demonstrate that they are legally deserving of such benefits, that is, subordinated to the guidelines and economic, political, and cultural standards dominant in society and institutionally enforced. Offe considers such conditions an exchange transaction in which material benefits for the needy are traded for their submissive recognition of the "moral order" of the society which generates such needs.

Added to that, Jessop (2002: 46) explains that in capitalist social formations, social reproduction is organized mainly through and/or around the (changing) wage relation, which often causes problems because (1) employees are free to spend their wages without regard to the needs of capital. Thus workers may not reproduce their labor-power (including specific skills, abilities, knowledge, work—capacity); (2) When capital trends to prioritize its self-valuation rather than the reproduction and welfare of labor-power, such labor-power could be destroyed or weakened through over-exploitation (excessive hours or work intensity) or through "collateral" damage (such as accidents or occupational diseases)[2]; (3) workers find it hard to defend their collective interests in reproducing their labor-power—especially where there is a large pool of unemployed but employable workers. Therefore, the state must ensure a continuous and adequate skilled labor supply, as well as compensating for the effects caused by the commodification of both social reproduction and social cohesion (Jessop, 2002).

However, the state should not be regarded as a simple instrument or functional mechanism for the reproduction of capitalist relations of production. What the state does, how it does it, and with what tools are all realities which are specified in a complex process. This system of interactions expresses the contradictions of the struggle, usually mediated and charged with multiple meanings, among conflicting interests: capitalists attempting to achieve higher quotas of surplus value, and workers striving to defend their working and living conditions (Thwaites Rey and Castillo, 1999).

2.3 A New Configuration of Social Protection in Latin America

The proliferation of CCTP in Latin America has been carried out in the context of a change in the nature of the social protection system worldwide. Over the past three decades, many welfare states have moved to downsize or dismantle such social safety nets, shifting from comprehensive coverage toward more individualized models—"targeted" or "means-tested"—and from decommodified provision of goods and services to a greater emphasis on cash benefits (Lavinas, 2013). While the postwar welfare state recognized the needs of its citizens on both an individual and collective level and based upon these granted "rights" that guaranteed equal access to public services, the new model which is presently emerging offers "rewards" in return for fulfilment of obligations. This new social protection scheme is known under the neologism of "workfare" which merges the word "work" to "welfare" in order to encapsulate a new economic and philosophical social contract.

---

[2] The private capital interests are not required to invest in human capital or compensate for its depreciation unless they be profitable, for this reason there is a general tendency of capital to invest insufficiently in education and training.

The workfare model arises as a reconfiguration of the social protection system in the central countries, whose foundation is based upon the need to explain the nature of the changes which have been realized in the labor market during the last quarter of the twentieth century and in the second decade of the twenty-first century. The central argument is that the unemployment rate experienced by central countries since the 1980s began to alert states as to their need to allocate increased budget toward the development of passive policies (such as unemployment insurance) therefore jeopardizing the sustainability of the protection system that had prevailed since the World War II up until that time (Bonoli, 2010).

This social protection system is based on a new strategy intended to manage social risks where the objectives of equality and social justice are no longer concerned with material outcomes, but instead with the creation of opportunity structures (Dean, 2007). The primary role of social policy is, in such a scenario, not the distribution of resources to provide for people's needs but to mitigate risk and to enable people individually to manage risk (World Bank, 2000). The welfare state is effectively replaced by an active state that grants individuals certain capital (as human or social capital), so that they are then prepared to responsibly handle a "patrimony" that will allow them a swift and complete reinsertion into labor markets. It is believed that such a well-orchestrated reintegration of workers and labor imperatives will serve to reduce the dependence on state resources in the long term.

As a result of these radical reinterpretations of the nature of social assistance and security, the social protection of vulnerable sectors begins to be conditioned upon the potential beneficiary's disposition to seek a job, stay trained, participate in the health system, and send their children to school. This is so mainly because neoliberal economists tend to associate poverty with individual irresponsibility, or with the failure to effectively manage risk (Dean, 2007). Because of the nature of these radical alterations to the institutionalized perspective toward risk management there are many who feel that the world as a whole is moving toward a period of risk explosion and increased commoditization of benefits (Castel, 2004).

We understand that the proliferation of PTMC in Latin America responds to this reconfiguration of social protection system worldwide. However, the region has some peculiarities: (1) the welfare state has never developed in the same magnitude as in Western countries; (2) the high levels of informality and the limited and uneven development of insurance against unemployment have an effect on poor and insipient risk coverage[3] via the contributory system. In this sense, the CCTP as an umbrella network of systems allows for governing bodies to reach (in a focused and residually way) those groups that historically were not covered by the social protection system. Thus, in Latin America the concept and structures of workfare are not being implemented in order to dismantle the welfare state (as it never existed as such in the region), but are expected to bring about circumstances in which beneficiaries have a short period of participation in the programs, after which they will be able to avail themselves of certain assets that enable them to overcome their vulnerability and to be placed in the labor market as quickly as possible.

Organizations such as the UN or the ILO originally presented these programs as a mechanism for strengthening social protection and its extension as a first step toward a "social protection floor". This proposal assumed as its objective the capacity to generate horizontal successive extensions (increasing the number of people covered by social protection) as well as vertical ones (improving the quantity and quality of services and social security guarantees). This strategy is presented as a "ladder of social security" which consists of three steps with three different performance levels, corresponding to different levels of guarantees. In the center of the model are those commonly contributory social insurance schemes. Among members of compulsory contributory schemes, those who desire and can financially do so are able to seek coverage at a qualitatively higher level—third step—through additional voluntary schemes regulated by the state. The first step would include a large number of workers who are not yet covered by formal social security schemes.

While we consider it marked progress that there are authorities ready and willing to oversee the application of a social protection floor (espe-

---

[3] The contributory character of these safe and the high rates of informality that the region presents have a negative effect on the coverage. According to the ILO in 2012/2013, only 4.6% of the unemployed people had received unemployment insurance. ILO data, obtained from: http://www.social-protection.org/gimi/gess/RessourceDownload.action?ressource.ressourceId=37042 visited the 23/03/16

cially in terms of its impact on poverty rates), we understand this proposal to be grossly insufficient due to the fact that it does not foster a significant change in the tax logic that prevails in the region. The novelty of this initiative lies in the fact that it is designed to promote "good coordination" between the contributory and noncontributory system in order to achieve inclusion of the entire population in any of these systems (ILO, 2014). However, there remain distinct benefits for each of the systems which now exist, as well as different resources distributed upon each of the "steps" of the "ladder of social security."

3 Conditional Cash Transfer Programs, Human Capital and Employability. The end of poverty in Latin America?

3.1 Diagnosis

Some institutions (especially the Inter-American Development Bank – IDB-) argue that the CCTP is an "endogenous innovation" of Latin America; however, other authors show that the intellectual antecedents of this socioeconomic strategy are to be found further north due to the fact that these institutional reforms are conceptually based on the confluence of two sets of ideas: the idea of human capital (Schultz, 1961; Becker, 1983) that aims to eradicate poverty in the long term; and the idea of fighting poverty in the short term targeting social spending. The strategy to break intergenerational cycles of poverty is based on the idea that any significant increase in human capital will result in an increase of employability that will allow beneficiaries to leave their conditions of poverty by being integrated, in the future, into the labor market, or in jobs with higher incomes. The low education levels and poor health of vulnerable sectors are seen as an obstacle to prosperity because they prevent these individuals and communities from participating fully in the market, both as workers or as consumers.

Employability[4] is defined as the probability of a person to find a job. In the case of the array of programs under analysis in this chapter, we should understand such initiatives as forces promoting a type of em-

---

[4] For a discussion of this issues, see Barbier (2000) and Gazier (1990).

ployability that Gazier (1990) has called initiative. This is a strategy that combines attitudes, skills, and qualifications that are deemed necessary to deal with rapid changes in a globalized economy. It also points to individual responsibility and the ability to build and mobilize social networks in order to bring about the necessary changes. Each worker appears in this vision of the market in society as the supreme manager of his or her own career path, emphasizing the individual character that determines access or not to the work world, and therefore, the fate of being or not being poor. Training and activation pursue the same objective: increase the individual's autonomy and empowerment effectively providing them with the means to carry out their projects rather than simply assist superficially in their realization. Nowadays, the role of the state is primarily perceived to be the provision of assistance to individuals in order to enable citizens to acquire a reasonable portion of these assets—what Gautié (2004) called the actions of the Social Patrimonial State—so that such initially disadvantaged people can have access to a patrimony that strategically positions them to assume a role as the "entrepreneur" in charge of their own life.

From this point of view, however, it is easy to see why there are many who do not recognize the poverty and unemployment problems which are arising as a result of structural issues related to the accumulation mode adopted, the structural characteristics of the Latin American labor markets, macroeconomic policies developed, and so forth. This vision tends to blame the victim who suffers the problems which are supposedly being addressed, redirecting the focus of institutional networks of support away from the structural problems that developing countries have to confront on a daily and even momentary basis and instead emphasizing poverty and its associated problems as deriving from a shortage of human capital.

3.2 The Consensus

Because they understand that attempting to alleviate social problems with conventional systems in Latin America compromises the public resources, international organizations recommend targeting on the poorest, giving them tools and assets to improve risks management through the establishment of networks of "co-responsibilities"—and also encouraging their complete economic and social integration. It is in this sense that CCTP are considered to be the programs which use the public funds in the best way directing them toward those with greater needs.

In this context, and trying to make more effective investment in social spending, international financial institutions suggest targeting the most vulnerable groups (IDB, 1998) seeking to boost their economic integration. In addition to these techniques, the requirement of actors recognizing the "co-responsibilities" impinging upon their lives will allow beneficiaries in the short or long term to become self-sufficient and therefore move away from state assistance. The central argument of targeting, based on the model of social policy introduced after World War II in the region, did not have the capacity to serve the poorest and was exploited primarily by workers sectors which were well-unionized and the urban middle classes. To achieve greater and effective social equity and reach the most vulnerable sectors (out of the contributory system) it has been necessary to remodel the building of social policy and target public spending specifically in these sectors (Isuani, 2012).

Targeting spending in CCTP allows for wide coverage at a very low cost. The Economic Commission for Latin America and the Caribbean— ECLAC—(2011) notes the significant growth of such types of programs in Latin America during the last decade: while coverage (% of total population) increased from 5.7% in 2000 to 19.3% in 2010 (see table in annex to this chapter). During the same period the executed budget doubled, growing from 0.2% to 0.4% of GDP. This is one of the main attractions of these programs for governments as they can expand their social policy without making any important fiscal sacrifices.

One of the reasons why the coverage is wide and the budget relatively limited is the fact that CCTP provide low economic benefits. This is due to the fact that they do not aim to discourage the participation of beneficiaries in the labor market. Based on an orthodox conception of market function, policy makers (and the organizations that promote them) argue that distributing large amounts of money (close to the minimum wage of each country) to the needy would simply cause the beneficiaries to fall further into the poverty trap. The notion behind this vision is the perception that, without working, if individuals are able to gain assistance benefits that guarantee similar incomes comparable to those which could be obtained from a job, such resources would only serve to discourage such individuals seeking access to the labor market and the revenues to be gained by participating actively as a member of the work force. Nevertheless, the limited amount of benefits required impacts the program's potential to reduce poverty. This is to say that the impact is moderate when one considers both the household consumption and poverty lines (Valencia Lomelí, 2008). It thus appears that, based on quantitative data, these programs can be successful in reducing the gap or the severity of poverty, but often have a low impact on the poverty rate itself (Skoufias, 2000).

4 A New Social Protection for a New Developmentalism? CCTP in the New Developmental Model

We have noted that the CCTP have extended considerably in the region during the 2000s. Lavinas (2013) identifies three reasons for this rapid expansion. First, the choices made by a wave of progressive governments that pushed social concerns to the forefront of the political agenda in Latin America. Secondly, the author points out that the continent, from the 2000s on, has undergone a renewed, albeit unequal period of economic growth, where strong international commodity prices boosted export revenues (the 2008 crisis also generated a massive arrival of money seeking higher returns in emerging markets). These factors in turn have given governments a margin of fiscal maneuver which they had previously lacked. The third factor was institutional, because after initial skepticism, the WB and other international credit agencies promoted the CCTP, putting it forward as an essential part of its new strategy of social risk management to which we have referred above.

Our perspective, while not entirely inconsistent with this view, focuses intensively upon the dynamics of capital accumulation as evolving in Latin America. This infrastructural system, popularly referred to as neodevelopmentalism, has its counterpart in the transformation of the model of social protection in the region.

What do we mean by neodevelopmentalism? Bresser Pereira (2007) places it somewhere between the zone of development discourse and conventional orthodoxy. Unlike the developmentalism paradigms of the fifties, this contemporary vision is not protectionist, but emphasizes the need for a competitive exchange rate—that must be fluctuating but managed—to avoid the problem of Dutch disease, a valid concern to date in Latin American economies. At the same time, the economy tends to be oriented toward exports and the state plays a central role in the organization and implementation of any development strategy. Other Latin American scholars, depending on the perspective with which each of us identifies neodevelopmentalism, tend to describe it as a growth scheme linked to the rent of land through agricultural products, hydrocarbons, and minerals. This is a situation in which the state plays an active role in establishing a new mode of regulation that creates optimal institutional conditions for the arrival and permanence of transnational investment while displaying compensatory social policies of income redistribution (Santos, Narbondo and Oyhantçabai, 2013). To Féliz (2015), developmentalism provides a set of practical guidelines for the construction of a new project of capitalist development in the periphery. These are practices that include a new form of state intervention together with a new set of public, social, and labor policies which are designed to contain social conflict and canalize it productively to maximize the benefits of capital (Féliz, 2015).

Additionally, the search for new economic and social bases for capital accumulation during this period of expansion has also necessitated a search for new forms of state intervention designed to ensure increased valorization of capital and the reproduction of the labor force and its actors under such new conditions (Jessop, 2002). As a result the new role assumed by the state generates changes in public policy in general and social policies in particular.

While the policies implemented have resulted in growth and increased output and employment which has led in most countries to an improvement in crucial economic and social indicators, high rates of poverty, unemployment, and labor informality persist and exclude a large number of people from the benefits of social security which developmentalism promises. Additionally, these people are limited in their consumption potential and largely excluded from the variables needed for forms of capital valorization established according to this new model of accumulation. This is where the so-called CCTP are brought into play in the multiple level attempt to (1) regulate the entry of labor according to the requirements of capital accumulation, (2) compensate for the inequality which produces market conditions in the distribution of resources, and (3) to contain and canalize the socio-labor conflict within certain acceptable limits.

The basic structure of the CCTP involves the provision of monetary and nonmonetary resources to families or individuals in vulnerable situations, with the condition that recipients must carry out certain behaviors associated with attempts to improve human capital, so that they can later be hired in order to work at a lucrative job. We can separate CCTP into two broad categories according to the characteristics of the populations which these types of programs target. The first type includes those programs seeking to promote the employment of people of a conventional working age. The route out of poverty is thus the beneficiary's participation in the labor market. A second type of program aims to break the intergenerational transfer of poverty in vulnerable families, transferring money to beneficiaries in exchange for the accomplishment of specific goals related to health and education of children and adolescents present in the home (which would give them the necessary tools to enter the labor market in the future).

5 The CCPT, the Intergenerational Transfer of Poverty and the Activation of Social Protection

Most CCTP transfer incomes on a monthly basis to families living in poverty or indigence subject to compliance with certain duties, generally related to health and nutritional controls and children's school attendance in such homes. The goal is to modify the family strategies used to address social risks. The underlying diagnosis is that poor households often face declining real incomes with the incorporation of children and young people into the labor market through various forms of precarious rather than stable employment. This premature insertion has negative effects in the long term, especially with regard to the accumulation of human capital, since in many cases it replaces essential schooling with work (Barba Solano and Valencia Lomelí, 2011).

For this reason, the characteristic population of the CCTP are children of families in vulnerable situations This is the case of the Abrazo program, developed in Paraguay since 2005 and aims to eradicate child labor by giving monthly income to low-income families if they meet three compensations: (1) that children attend health services and achieve good nutrition indicators; (2) that they comply with 85% school attendance per month and promotion of curricular year; (3) children to stay away from economic activities. Also the Juancito Pinto bonus, which runs in Bolivia from 2006, aims to eliminate child labor and increase school enrollment by delivering an annual bonus to those children and adolescents who compute a school attendance of 80% in public schools.

Another set of CCTP tries to respond to the problems of poverty by encouraging the labor participation of beneficiaries, making work pay, that is attempting to link more closely cash benefits with active training measures and incentives for rapid job placement. In this case the aim is to increase human capital and improve the employability of the unemployed (through education, training and vocational training), while looking for a quick insertion of beneficiaries into the labor market, encouraging the abandonment of social assistance policies through a system of declining benefits.

Most of the required compensations are associated with training programs, qualifying practices, training in jobs, or completion of their basic education. However, they may also imply compensations involving the application of individuals to certain jobs or to accept the proposed job offer from employment offices. This is one of the ways these PTMC attempt to ensure that the unemployed maintain habits related to the labor market since, based upon various academic and political spaces, scholars hypothesize that provision of an income without compensation discourages the work culture as such, so those who receive this benefit will lose interest in finding a job. In addition, this focus ensures that greater consensus would be achieved in the implementation of benefits programs targeted toward capturing public opinion since such programs would not be giving money for nothing, and fears about the effects of dependency that could generate social policy without compensation would dissipate (Eransus Pérez, 2006).

Indirectly it is uncertain whether or not the permanence over time of the status of "unemployed," precludes or gives greater force to the possibility that some people choose to remain in this situation (getting a social plan) or alternately lose the incentive to sell their labor force. Here we find relevant Offe's perspective about the state's need to punish forms of existence different from participation in the labor market if it wants to ensure the transformation of the labor force in wage labor. Only the state—through the social policies inherent in a national space—politically regulates who is allowed to live outside the wage relation and those who do not need to do so.

Within this type of program, we should mention My First Job Worth (Bolivia), a program for skill development for youth 18–24 years of age, or the "Uruguay Works" program targeted at adults between 18 and 65 years, aimed at improving the employability of people living in socioeconomic vulnerability through training and community value tasks.

However, perhaps the clearest example of this type of program can be found in Argentina around 2004, when the Unemployed Heads of Household Plan (PJJHD) was disbanded. This program—which surpassed two million beneficiaries during 2003—was essential to increase aggregate consumption levels that made possible the recovery of economic activity after the 2001–2002 crisis and to contain social tensions in a context of a strong redistribution of income against lower-income sectors. However, with economic growth and improving social indicators, the government decided that it was necessary to order the beneficiaries to allow the design of more specific policies. To this end, the government required that the Ministries of Labor, Employment and Social Security (MTESS) and Social Development develop a classification of PJJHD beneficiaries according to their employability. According to this decree two groups are differentiated: (1) those with a greater chance of reentering the labor market, who are encouraged to move to the Training and Employment Insurance (SCE), where it provides them with tools to help them reintegrate in the labor market, and (2) those "whose characteristics or conditions are difficult or impossible to relocate occupationally" (MTESS, 2004) who become dependent on welfare (Families for social Inclusion Plan), with the attendant obligation to ensure the health and school attendance of their children.

We note here four core issues which we have advanced in the theoretical section. First, we confirm that in a context of increased economic activity and employment the government seeks to "activate" social policies designed to incorporate inactive labor force into the market on a relatively permanent basis. In other words, we see how social policy regulates the incorporation of labor force into the market according to the needs of capital accumulation, and also plays an important role in its qualitative administration, ensuring the provision of skills, habits, behaviors, and abilities necessary for its incorporation in the manner which the labor market demands (Gough, 1982). Second, it is highlighted in the PJJHD example how the state regulates and selects those involved in the labor market as well as those who will remain as inactive workers in the area of social policies. Third, we recognize in the obligation of beneficiaries to ensure the health and school attendance of their children, the exchange transaction which Offe speaks of, through which, in order to access social assistance, beneficiaries must prove not only their needs but also their worth. That is to say that they must subordinate themselves to the economic, political, and cultural guidelines and norms dominant in society (e.g., to keep children away from economic activities, although this is actually a practice with a long history in Latin America). Fourth, since virtually all workers who are transferred to the Families Plan (and therefore are in charge of the care of children and fall outside the labor market) are women. We also notice that social policy can be generative and modulate the specific characteristics of inequality itself (in this case between men and women), naturalizing and institutionalizing inequalities between certain groups while ostensibly reducing them in other arenas (Adelantado et al., 1998).

After several years of economic growth in the region, nearly half of workers remain trapped in conditions of labor informality, a sign that this would not be a system failure that can be absorbed when the economy grows but it's functional to the dynamics of accumulation of peripheral capitalism. Thus, some CCTP recognize these high levels of informality and labor precariousness that characterize Latin American labor markets. This is the case of the Universal Child Allowance for Social Protection (hereinafter AUH), implemented in Argentina in 2009 as a noncontributory subsystem within the family allowance scheme and intended to alleviate the precariousness of informal and unemployed workers, who because of their condition do not receive family allowances.

With the implementation of the AUH public spending scheme in social and employment programs, the impact of such programs is that the number of beneficiaries has been doubled, reaching 5 million beneficiaries in 2009, a period made all the more complex by (1) economic deceleration and the decline in job creation (as a product of the crisis) and (2) the political weakening of the government, because of the confrontation with the agricultural sector revolving around Resolution 125[5] and the election results of June 2009.

Paradoxically, although this type of CCTP tries to recognize the labor rights of workers in vulnerable employment situations, such individuals are not usually recognized as rights holders, but instead as beneficiaries of social programs. Furthermore, although it is difficult for any government to confront the political cost involved with the discontinuation of such programs, in accordance with a broad consensus in Latin America, freezing the income transferred to beneficiaries in an inflationary period is sufficient to dismantle them, since there is no law that supports indexing benefits.

Since one of the objectives of these programs is to reduce inequalities between registered and unregistered workers, it draws attention to the requirement for compensations required to program beneficiaries but not those who belong to the contributive system. Again, we find here the repressive component of social policy at work, the allocation of a monetary assistance in exchange for beneficiaries meeting certain social behavior patterns that other sectors can neglect. Moreover, we note that in a context of recession and declining employment, social policy significantly increases coverage and extends itself as a "catchment area" of the labor force, giving priority to programs aimed at maintaining income and consumption levels and compensations relating to education and health.

This type of CCTP reinforces the idea of linking subsidies to the promotion of a beneficiary-world employment relationship, which would find greater acceptance from the different sectors of society (Bonvecchi and Smulovitz, 2008). Policies that are disengaged from the labor market for the provision of income suggest the inherent complexity of breaking a paradigm that has hundreds of years of existence, in which the insertion into the labor world is seen as essential to ensure an income, and thus,

---

[5] Through this resolution, the Argentine government tries to set a new sliding tax scheme for exports in the agricultural sector.

access to the satisfaction of human needs at a basic as well as advanced level (Isuani, 2008).

However, one must think primarily in terms of social inclusion only in the case of those receiving benefits as employment poses a risk of reductionism on issues affecting persons who apply for such financial benefits, where the lack of a job is not the only problematic factor. Often there are also deficiencies in housing, health, education, and so on. In turn, the emphasis on the paradigm of activation which is placed on labor insertion creates certain questions: Is any form of employment positive for social integration? In turn, what are the negative effects that job insecurity has on people living in poverty? In a context of deepening problems linked to employment, it is necessary to rethink activation strategies with regard to the most vulnerable people, since the conditions of exploitation of some, far from favoring the objective of integration would be worsening the situation of exclusion of some households (Pérez Eransus, 2006).

Overall, it can reinforce positive impacts in terms of a reduction in extreme poverty rates as a result of the implementation of these programs; however, despite its broad coverage it seems to be insufficient to effectively combat poverty levels experienced by those living in the region (CEPAL, 2007). In addition, it is clear that this impact is significant when measuring income poverty but loses relevance when it is used to observe their impact on structural poverty, usually associated with the satisfaction of basic needs related to housing access and conditions, health services, educational level of households, issues whose resolution would imply another level of commitment from public policies.

6 Final Considerations

In this article we have discussed some of the features adopted in Latin America related to the reconfiguration of social protection systems. We focus upon the fact that the CCTP are part of this reformulation of social policy at the regional level which adheres to the new social protection scheme known as workfare. From a study of the various CCTP implemented in Latin America, we have determined what is the general diagnosis that supports the implementation of these programs and what have the causes of their widespread organization.

In turn, recovering the perspective proposed by Offe (1990) and Jessop (2002), we have recognized that during the period analyzed, social policy can be seen regulating the incorporation of labor force into the market according to the requirements of capital accumulation. These policies activate social policies in times of economic growth in order to incorporate labor force to the market and expand the coverage of income maintenance programs, with considerations related to improving human capital (education and health) in periods of economic recession.

The CCTP allow people previously excluded from consumption possibilities to access basic necessities, but do not guarantee their escape from poverty nor definitively greater opportunities for upward mobility. At the same time, these programs do not generate ownership rights and serve to promote control and management mechanisms of poverty by the state. Meanwhile, although they promote the access by the poor to health and education services, they have not expanded the supply and quality of these services nor generated greater homogeneity of services within the rest of society.

We have noted that these programs are characterized by the provision of wide coverage at a relatively low cost, hence much of their enduring popularity and evident consensus. Nevertheless, difficulties are evident when one considers the sustainability of long-term financing, especially for lower-income countries which depend on credits from international agencies for funding. In fact, in most cases, the financing of CCTP is not based on tax reforms and mechanisms of more equitable redistribution of wealth, but instead predicated upon the use of existing public resources, sometimes the contributive system, or the demand of international credits. A regressive taxation like those predominant in Latin America becomes difficult to manage while increasing social transfers at the level of what is at stake in such cases (Salama, 2011).

While several of these CCTP extend noncontributory social coverage to new groups such as informal workers, we do not believe that these programs crystallize a profound change in the system of social protection. Instead their implementation reproduces a dual system of protection consistent with the persistence of a segmented labor market characterized by high informality. We note here that social policy not only attempts to compensate for the inequality originally produced in the labor market (between formal workers and those who are not) but also modulates institutionalized inequality itself (by requiring compensation to some workers and not others).

This reorientation of social policy toward greater coverage allows for the stimulation of consumption in the domestic market, reactivation of the economy and contribution to the reproduction of the labor force without any significant increase in wages (beyond productivity increases) maintaining thus the competitiveness of the economy in larger contexts.

We can then ask what might be the possible alternatives to the current problems of exclusion and unemployment. Progress has been made in the debate among academics and social organizations on the possibility of considering other forms of inclusion beyond the working world. In recent decades, the phenomenon of the working poor began to interpolate labor insertion as the only mechanism for social inclusion and escape from poverty.

A step forward in this area would be the recognition of citizenship as a guarantee of rights, a moving away from the current system in which the labor market is the almost exclusive mechanism for access to social protection. Full formal employment has not proven to be the "normal" situation in capitalist economies, even in developed ones, so a profound rethinking of the social protection system linked to formal employment seems to be a pending if not urgent matter. The immediate challenge is to expand coverage for those who fall outside of the social protection of the state, trying to include the greatest percentage possible of the population within the circles of consumption necessary to maintain a worthy life.

Poverty, unemployment, and precarious employment are events fully functional to capitalist systems of accumulation, and while we do not dispute the basic pillars on which such persistent social realities rest, we can hardly propose that the benefit schemes analyzed here present a structural change in which a real solution to the problems that afflict our societies is promoted.

7 Annex

Coverage (% of total population) and executed budget (% of GDP) for Latin America and the Caribbean, 2010.

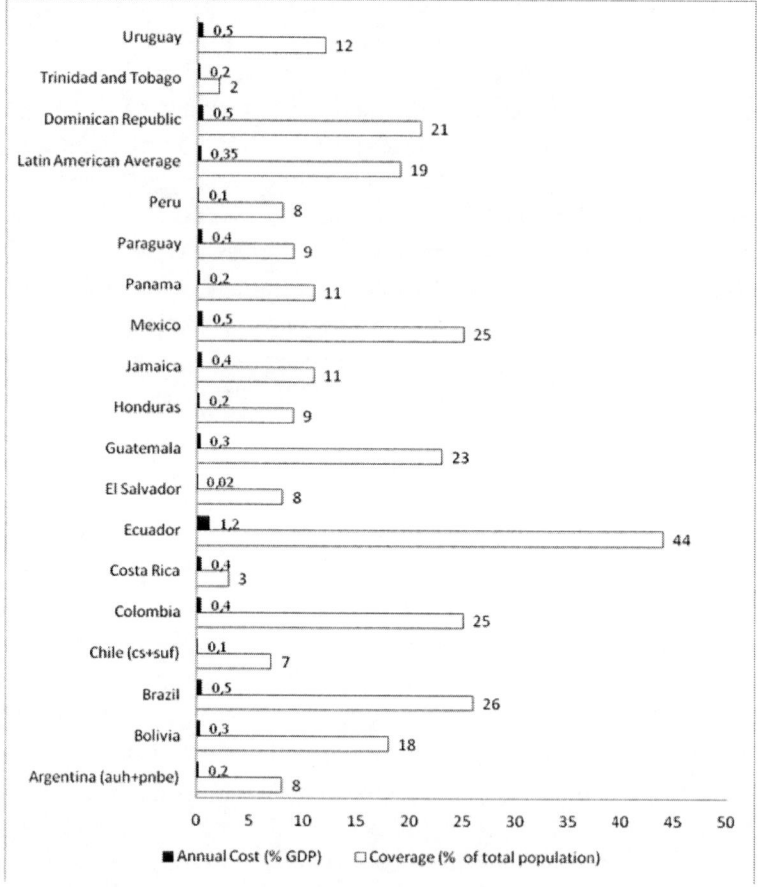

Source: Prepared on Data Base (ECLAC, 2011).

References

Adelantado, J., Noguera, J., Rambla, X., & Sáez, L. (1998). Las relaciones entre estructura y políticas sociales: una propuesta teórica. Revista Mexicana de Sociología, 3/98(3), 122–156.

Banco Mundial (BM). (2000). Social risk Management: a new conceptual framework for social protection and beyond. Social Protection Discussion paper N° 0006, World Bank.

Barba Solano, C., & Valencia Lomelí, E. (2011). Hipótesis no comprobadas y espejismos de las transferencias monetarias condicionales. In Barba Solano y Cohen (Coords.), Perspectivas críticas sobre la cohesión social. desigualdad y tentativas fallidas de integración social en américa latina. Buenos Aires: CLACSO.

Barbier, J.-C. (2000). A propos des difficultés de traduction des catégories d'analyse des marchés du travail et des politiques de l'emploi en contexte comparatif européen. Documento de trabajo N° 3. Centre d'étude de l'emploi (CEE), Universidad de París.

Becker, G. (1983). El Capital Humano. Madrid: Alianza.

BID. (1998). Para salir de la pobreza. El Enfoque del Banco Interamericano de Desarrollo para reducir la pobreza. BID.

Bonoli, G. (2010). The political economy of active labour market policy. REC-WP 01/2010. Working Papers on the Reconciliation of Work and We lfare in Europe RECWOWE Publication, Dissemination and Dialogue Cen tre, Edinburgh.

Bonvecchi, A., & Smulovitz, C. (2008). Atender necesidades, crear oportunidades o garantizar derechos. Visiones sobre la política social. In G. Cruces (Comp), Los Programas Sociales en Argentina hacia el Bicentenario: visiones y perspectivas. Buenos Aires: Banco Mundial.

Bresser Pereira, L. C. (2007). Estado y mercado en el nuevo desarrollismo. Nueva Sociedad, 210, 110–125.

Castel, R. (2004). La inseguridad social, ¿Qué es estar protegido? Buenos Aires: Manantial.

CEPAL. (2007). Las transferencias condicionadas en América Latina: Luces y sombras. Presented at the Seminario Internacional: "Programas de transferencias condicionadas: La experiencia de diversos países." Brasilia: CEPAL.

Dean, H. (2007). The ethics of welfare-to-work. Policy and Politics 4(35), 573–590.

Esping-Andersen, G. (1993). Los tres mundos del Estado del bienestar. Valencia: Edicions Alfons el Magnànim-IVEI.

Féliz, M. (2015). Argentina neodesarrollista: Debates sobre el modelo [en línea]. La Plata: EDULP. En Memoria Académica. Disponible en: http://www.memoria.fahce.unlp.edu.ar/libros/pm.383/pm.383.pdf

Filgueira, F. (1998). El nuevo modelo de prestaciones sociales en América Latina: residualismo, eficiencia y ciudadanía estratificada. In B. R. Roberts (Ed.), Ciudadanía y Política Sociales (pp. 32–73). San José de Costa Rica: FLACSO/SSRC.

Gautié, J. (2004). Repensar la articulación entre mercado de trabajo y protección social en el posfordismo. Cuadernos de Relaciones Laborales 22(1), 147–184.

Gazier, B. (1990). Assurance et chômage, employabilité et marches transitionnels du travail. Université Paris 1/ MATISSE, CNRS UMR 8595, 1–18.

Gough, I. (1982). Economía Política del Estado de Bienestar. Madrid: Blume Editores.

Isuani, A. (2008). La política social argentina en perspectiva. In G. Cruces, J. M. Moreno, D. Ringold, & Rofman (Eds.), en Los programas sociales en Argentina hacia el Bicentenario. Visiones y Perspectivas (pp. 169–197). Buenos Aires: Banco Mundial.

Isuani, A. (2012). Política social y transferencias monetarias en América Latina. Revista de Análisis Público Universidad de Valparaís, 1(1), 14–41.

Jessop, B. (2002). The future of the capitalist state. Cambridge: Policy Press.

Lavinas, L. (2013). 21st century welfare. New Left Review 84, 5–40.

Offe, C. (1990). Contradicciones en el Estado de Bienestar. Madrid: Alianza.

Offe, C., & Hindrics, K. (1985). The Political Economy of the Labor Market. In C. Offe (Ed.), Disorganized Capitalism: Contemporary Transformations of Work and Politics (pp. 10–51). Cambridge: Policy Press.

Pérez Eransus, B. (2006). Rentas mínimas y políticas de activación. Documentación Social, 143, 77–92.

Salama, P. (2011). Luchas contra la pobreza en América Latina. El caso de la pobreza rural en Brasil. Revista Problemas Del Desarrollo, 165(42), 7–34.

Santos, C., Narbondo, I., & Oyhantçabai, G. (2013). Seis tesis sobre el neodesarrollismo en Uruguay. Revista Contrapunto, 2, 13–32.

Schultz, T. W. (1961). Investment in Human Capital. The American Economic Review, 51(1), 1–17.

Skoufias, E. (2000). ¿Está dando buenos resultados Progresa? Deocumento de trabajo de IFPRI—SEDESOL, México.

Thwaites Rey, M., & Castillo, J. (1999). Poder estatal y capital global: los límites de la lucha política. In A. Borón, J. Gambina, & N. Minsburg, Tiempos violentos; Neoliberalismo, globalizacion y desigualdad en America Latina (pp. 124–137). Buenos Aires: Colección CLACSO—EUDEBA.

Valencia Lomelí, E. (2008). Las transferencias monetarias condicionadas como política social en América Latina. Un balance: aportes, límites y debates. Annual Review of Sociology, (34), 499–524.

Chapter 4
NEODEVELOPMENTALISM IN ARGENTINA: ITS CONTRADICTIONS, BARRIERS, AND LIMITS TO POVERTY REDUCTION AND SOCIAL CHANGE

Mariano Féliz

Neodevelopmentalism is the keyword that describes Argentina's new mode of development since 2003. Born from the ashes of neoliberalism, it has signified a wide range of policy changes that have effectively modified living conditions in the country. However, this new mode of development has been unable to transform the structural factors behind widespread inequality and poverty and unable to promote radical progressive social change.

Mariano Féliz's main argument is that while showing significant changes in policies (macroeconomic, social, and labor) since 2003, neodevelopmentalism has not broken with the neoliberal social, political, and economic structure: transnationalization of the economy, natural resource-based growth, and extended precariousness of labor.

The chapter shows why the political ideology of the groups in power has blocked significant social change in the country, even if there are social and political movements inclined to promote and favor such changes.

1 Introduction

In the last twenty years Latin America has gone from hardcore neoliberal rule to a process of sociopolitical transformations that can be presented as generally post-neoliberal and in most cases neodevelopmentalist (Féliz, 2012; Thwaites Rey, 2010; Svampa, 2011). Through this process dominant classes in Argentina have exorcised neoliberal ideological predominance and advanced in the constitution of a new hegemonic rule based on the original combination of developmentalist economic discourse with an increasingly radical national-popular political ideology and rhetoric (if not practice) (Féliz, 2013; Svampa, 2011b). This new symbiosis has been politically productive for the capitalist fractions that emerged as dominating after three decades of neoliberalism, those of transnationalized capital, since it provided them with the means to build a renewed hegemony over society. However, the consolidation of this new hegemonic project has limited the potential for radical change that seemed to have had emerged from the sociopolitical turmoil that led to the violent crisis and exit from neoliberalism in Argentina in late 2001 (Dinerstein, 2002). In fact, over ten years after that crisis, the main tendencies outlined through neoliberal reforms have strengthened, resulting in the persistence of wide and deep social inequalities and pervasive poverty and precarization of life.

This article seeks to analyze the main characteristics of the neodevelopmentalist project in Argentina, its barriers and limitations to promote poverty reduction and social change. We will show that these restrictions come from the articulation of structural continuities with neoliberalism and novel sociopolitical innovations. We will also discuss briefly some of the potential alternatives to overcome the limits of this project.

2 Why Neodevelopmentalism is the Supersession of Neoliberalism?

Neoliberalism cannot be understood just as a "mode of development" (Neffa, 1998) in capitalism. Furthermore, it was a project of the capitalist classes worldwide to regain full political control on the production and reproduction of society in its capitalist form (Duménil and Lévy, 2009; Harvey, 2009). Neoliberal rule in Latin America advanced fiercely since the early seventies through several tactics that included, in variable combinations, social and political repression as well as socioeconomic restructuration. In Argentina, political repression reached its peak during the dictatorship of 1976–1983. Since then and in next 20 years, capitalist restructuration was pushed forward through formally democratic governments with variations of orthodox (1989–2001) and so-called heterodox (1983–1989) structural adjustment programs, only possible as repression, economic stagnation, and instability, and the ideological triumph of individualism weakened an ever-present popular resistance and reduced its effectiveness (Féliz and López, 2012: 25–34). The result was the advancement of concentration, centralization, and transnationalization of capital through state reform, the total or partial privatization of public enterprises and services (social security, education, health, etc.), the deregulation of the economy, the flexibilization of the labor market and the opening up of the economy to capital movements in its different forms, among other changes (Féliz and Pérez, 2004; Basualdo, 2006). The neoliberal project allowed for a substantial political recomposition of capital since it helped to rearticulate power within its dominant fractions. In Argentina, by the late nineties the new hegemonic fractions were the transnational corporations that had gained control of the main enterprises in most economic branches: within the biggest 500 local firms, those with more than 50% of foreign capital ownership rose from 46.8% of them in 1997 to 65% in 2009 (Féliz and López, 2012: 53). A few local conglomerates were able to transform themselves into transnationalized capitals and/or local associates of foreign capitals.

The neoliberal project in Argentina created numerous sociopolitical and economic contradictions that led to a deep crisis in the late nineties. In that decade, economic inconsistencies grew out of a chronic process of public and private indebtedness, increasing current account deficit and growing unemployment. These tensions transformed a recession that begun in 1998 into a prolonged crisis that created the perfect framework for the tendency of the profit rate to fall to manifest as stagnation, as growing deflationary pressures and eventually as massive capital flight and currency devaluation in late 2001 (Féliz, 2009, 2011).

Meanwhile, economic contradictions coupled with growing social unrest. During the second half of the nineties, laboring classes regained their ability to successfully confront the neoliberal momentum. The movements of unemployed workers (mostly young and female) gained a place as the new dynamic factor in the political recomposition of the working class. Together with fractions of the traditional working class (particularly, state employees in the provinces and teachers), impoverished peasants, small entrepreneurs, and others, these new social subjects were able to confront the attempts by the government to find a way out of the crisis by trying to radicalize the neoliberal project.[1] In December

---

[1] Attempts for the radicalization of the neoliberal project in Argentina included proposals such as the full dollarization of the economy (i.e., complete substitution of national currency by the US dollar). The first attempts were made during the

2001 the organic crisis of neoliberalism led to a violent exit (Bonnet, 2006; Dinerstein, 2002). A popular uprising during the 19th and 20th of December terminated with De la Rua's government, replaced two weeks later, through a turbulent transition, by a new peronist coalition.

Dominant classes were forced to find a way to regain social control. The new president Duhalde (elected by the Parliament, not by popular election) took steps to create conditions for successful capitalist accumulation and at the same time put a cap on popular unrest. In order to attain the first objective, the government took several measures (Basualdo, 2006): (a) partial default on public debt, (b) currency devaluation, (c) partial nationalization of dollar-denominated private debt, (d) freeze on privatized utilities' tariffs, and (e) tax on selected primary exports. As a whole, they allowed for (a) the recovery on the profitability of private capital, (b) a trade balance surplus and (c) a surplus in public finances (Féliz and López, 2012). This came at a huge social cost: between 2001 and 2002, real wages fell by 19% on average, the income poverty rate jumped to 53% of the population in May 2002, real consumption dropped 12.6% during the first trimester of 2002, and the price index for food stuffs went up by 48.6% within the first six months of 2002 (Féliz, 2012: 5). To contain social unrest and create the political conditions for the constitution of a new hegemonic bloc, the government put into place a new massive program of income support, the program *Jefes y Jefas de Hogar Desocupados* (Unemployed Heads of Households program, JJHD). In a few months, this program multiplied ten times the number of recipients of income support, reaching almost 5% of the population (Féliz and Pérez, 2007).

These policies were accompanied by selective repression of popular protests, in particular those led by the most radical factions of the movements of the unemployed. The assassination by police forces of two members of these movements on June 26, 2002 led to an unexpected call for national elections, which occurred in early 2003. N. Kirchner won the Presidency with only 22% on the popular vote. On May 25, 2003, the newly elected president was appointed. While its "economic" bases were

---

peronist president Menem in its second administration (1995–1999). He was followed by De la Rúa (1999–2001), which represented a newly formed coalition called Alianza dominated by the traditional social-democratic Radical Party.

seeded earlier, this date can be said to mark the political birth of the neodevelopmentalist project.

3 Structural Continuities with Reformist Policies: Neodevelopmentalism as the New Political Ideology of Capital

As the neoliberal project fell apart, dominant fractions of capital in Argentina pressed for the constitution of a new strategic project. In 2002 such a project began to be organized as the new strategy to guarantee the continuity of capitalist development in Argentina under the conditions created though neoliberalism but at the same time as its dialectical supersession. This means that while the new project was born out of (the crisis of) neoliberalism and it appropriates of its heritage, neodevelopmentalism redefines state intervention, political composition of classes, and macroeconomic dynamics.

In structural terms neoliberalism was the process that historically preconstituted the bases for a new strategy of capital accumulation (Féliz, 2012; Féliz and López, 2012). Capital restructuration in Argentina led to the consolidation of a new pattern of valorization articulated around a neoextractivist strategy. Mining and agricultural production (mainly based on the soya complex) became the new dynamic fractions of capital regarding Argentina's participation in the world economy. The cycle of capital organized around exporting primary commodities and manufactured by-products of agricultural production and minerals, under the control of transnational corporations (Féliz and López, 2012: 53–55). In this framework, the production and appropriation of land rent became one of the two main sources of surplus profitability of the period (Féliz, 2012b). The other source of excess profitability was the widespread precariousness of employment that led to increased systemic superexploitation of labor.

The exit out of neoliberalism required recreating the conditions for successful valorization and accumulation of productive capital. In order to do so, Kirchner's government took three main actions regarding macroeconomic policy. Firstly, after the process of partial default on public debt, currency devaluation, and partial nationalization of private dollarized debt in early 2002, the new government had to take steps toward making public debt payable not only for the state but also for the economy as a whole.[2] In 2002, public debt amounted to 166.4% of GDP. Interest payments implied transfers of surplus value from productive capital to financial capital equal to about half of total surplus value (Féliz, 2012: 11–12). Such conditions made capitalism unfeasible in economic and political terms. Thus, debt restructuration became a priority. The government paid the full debt in cash before it was due to the IMF (in 2006) and restructured most of the defaulted debt with private holders in two stages (2005 and 2010). At the same time, the government attempted to soften the fiscal restriction by complementing the reduced interest payments on public debt with a lid on state employee's wages and increasing the marginal rates of the new tax on rent producing exports (mainly soya, wheat and oil). This combination allowed the state to regain control over its finances: primary fiscal surplus reached 2.8% of GDP on average between 2002 and 2006 (Féliz and López, 2012: 72). The third element of the new macroeconomic strategy was a new real exchange rate (RER) policy (Féliz, 2012: 6). The new objective was to maintain the RER at a high and stable level to favor exports and keep imports down with the goal of sustaining a positive result on foreign trade and increasing foreign exchange reserves. During the first five years after exiting neoliberal rule (2002–2006), the current account surplus remained at 4.7% of GDP on average, while international reserves grew to 47 billion dollars in 2007.

The recovery of macroeconomic conditions for accumulation and growth favored employment creation and reduction in unemployment: 2.7 million jobs were created between 2002 and 2007 as unemployment fell to 7.5% in late 2007. However, creating conditions of political stability required that the government take additional steps toward insuring its legitimacy. With this aim, Kirchner's government favored what might be called reformist policy measures that allowed for a partial recovery of living conditions and, especially, expectations of its future improvement (Féliz and López, 2010; Pérez and Féliz, 2010). After the crisis of 2001, a

---

[2] This implies that the government accepted that the public debt (particularly, its foreign part) was to be payed (even if restructured) and not repudiated for economic, political, social, and even ethical reasons, as many political forces were demanding.

generation of young activists born in the heat of struggles against neoliberalism led a new wave of struggles outside and within traditional unions, putting pressure on its leadership and on the state (Féliz, 2012). Between 2003 and 2005, the government was forced to decree unilateral wage increases, to hike in several occasions the minimum wage, and to give way to demands for collective bargaining. While in the nineties formal labor-capital negotiations stalled as unions preferred to give in to pressure from capitalists through informal agreements, after 2002 worker's organizations successfully demanded for negotiations to be instituted in formal collective agreements, under state tutelage.[3]

Besides the reactivation of traditional labor policies, the government took steps to contain social unrest outside more formalized employment. In an attempt (successful in the end) to keep mobilization under control, the massive program JJHD was progressively transformed and replaced by other forms of social intervention (Féliz, 2012). The new programs tended to focalize benefits and perfect controls on recipients while maintaining its wide scope (Pérez and Féliz, 2010). The latest program created in 2009, the *Asignación Universal por Hijo* (Universal Child Benefit, AUH), included almost 3.5 million families with children who receive a cash benefit for each child if families proved that they were sending them to school and to sanitary controls. The program expenditures amount to 0.58% of GDP.

Arguably the new orientation of state policy can be characterized as neodevelopmentalist (Féliz, 2012: 15). Even though new policies have not implied significant structural changes in the economy, the state now takes active steps toward ensuring both the process of capitalist accumulation and its legitimacy after neoliberalism. During neoliberalism, the capitalist class insisted that the state be a means for restructuration and liberalization. The so-called "roll back of the State" was in fact a call for the actual state to dismantle itself; in sociopolitical terms the state was meant to become a residual-police state. In neodevelopmentalism, in contrast, dominant classes demanded that the state became a proac-

---

[3] State tutelage implied not only supervision but—in many occasions—direct intervention of the Ministry of Labour in an attempt to keep capital-labor accords within "rational parameters" according to macroeconomic policy (Féliz, 2012: 14). Demand for "moderation" of labor's demands is part of the neodevelopmentalist platform (Féliz, 2013).

tive means for capitalist reproduction and social control through political hegemony. The active pursuit of "development" became a way to create a renewed consensus around capitalism.

For this reason, we sustain that after neoliberalism, neodevelopmentalism turns into the new political economy (and ideology) of capital. During neoliberalism, neoclassical economics was the theoretical justification for structural adjustment within the Washington Consensus promoted by the WB. After the bankruptcy of neoliberalism in most of Latin America, neoclassical economics was displaced as the "toolkit" for policy making by a new version of the structuralist economics promoted mainly by the UN's Economic Commission for Latin America and the Caribbean (ECLAC), also followed in its own way by the IDB as well as by the WB (Féliz, 2013). This new consensus (post Washington Consensus; Fine, Lapavitsas, and Pincus, 2003) proposes a set of policy interventions that in Argentina is oriented toward building "serious capitalism," as the President Cristina Fernández de Kirchner (CFK) anticipated in a recent speech (Página/12, 2011).[4] These new reforms no longer imply radical, pro-capital structural reforms but mainly a sort of fine-tuning in line with the reforms of second and third generation of WB type.[5]

New public policies change significantly but inherit the pervasive commoditization and privatization of social relations. Neodevelopmentalist policies retain a confidence on capitalism as a means for socioeconomic development. At the same time, the state recovers a legitimate place in the orientation of capitalist reproduction. For that reason, new policies included renationalization of some formerly privatized enterprises and social services. Between 2002 and 2010 the national airline *Aerolíneas Argentinas* (Argentinean Airlines), the mail service *Correo Argentino* (Argentinean Mail), the water service *Aguas de Buenos Aires* (Waters of Buenos Aires, ABSA), the main oil and gas corporation (YPF) as well as the pension system, among others, were renationalized.

However, these nationalizations remained within neoliberal heritage. Several examples come to mind. First, all nationalized companies remained organized as private corporations (of state ownership), as stock

---

[4] CKF was first elected in 2007.
[5] In fact, both the WB and the IDB still promote their new political economy through the financing of dozens of social, infrastructure and state-reform projects in Argentina.

enterprises, many with stocks in national and foreign capital markets, regulated by private enterprises commercial legislation, with employees bound by (mostly neoliberal) private employment regulation, and so on; thus, production for profit remains their top objective. Second, the renationalization of social security implied the transformation of the private pension funds created in 1993 into a single state fund. No attempt was made to create a new system based on sustainable funding (Féliz, 2008). The nationalized system remains unsound and based on the logic of capital: accumulated funds of the privatized system are now invested by a government agency, *Administración Nacional de la Seguridad Social* (National Administration of the Social Security, ANSES) in much the same orientation as in the private system since a considerable part of the resources are used to buy new emissions of public debt. Third, the recently nationalized YPF has only been partially nationalized: 25% of its shares are still in the hand of private investors. Furthermore, the government's strategy is to find new private foreign investors to pursue the goal of turning Argentina into an oil-exporting nation by promoting the exploitation of so-called "shale-oil&gas" reserves.

As we have referred before, the political orientation of the neodevelopmentalist project was in the hands of an alliance led by a fraction of the Peronist party steered by the Kirchner family: Néstor, who died in 2010, was president between 2003 and 2007, and Cristina Fernández de Kirchner (his wife) was elected in 2007 and again in 2011 (until 2015).

One of Argentina's paradoxes is the Peronist party, which was born in the 1940s within the national-popular tradition (NPT). In a nutshell, the NPT attempts to channel popular demands within the limits of capitalist rule by aiming for a class compromise, under state tutelage (Svampa, 2011b), between national capitalist class and the core of the working class. In such alliance, labor was included as a subordinate partner to an imagined dynamic nationalistic capitalist class that should create, under the promotion and orientation of the state, the conditions for development, which was basically understood as industrialization based economic growth plus employment creation and progressive redistribution of income.[6]

---

[6] While the NPT in Argentina had also a more revolutionary tradition, the reformist alternative has been dominant throughout Argentina's history (Svampa, 2011).

Until the 1970s, the Peronist party sustained a developmentalist project where the state had a fundamental place in promoting capital accumulation. During the first stage (1943–1951) it induced light industrialization based on national capital (Féliz and Pérez, 2004). Later on, in line with ECLAC's structuralist proposals and its developmentalist counterparts in core economies, Peronism begun to promote foreign capital participation in the economy (Féliz, and Pérez, 2004; Féliz, 2013). In the 1990s, however, under Menem's governments (1989–1995, 1995–1999), the Peronist party became the main promoter of the neoliberal project. After a short transition of De la Rua's government (1999–2001), Peronism regained political hegemony but abandoning neoliberal ideology and bringing back developmentalism. However, after neoliberalism and in the context of transnational capitalism, neodevelopmentalist ideology and policy are tightly bound by the imperative of competitiveness (Féliz, 2013). In a peripheral economy such as Argentina this implies the impossibility of the development of the national-popular project as was traditionally construed within peronist ideology. In particular, the place of a dynamic national capitalist class is diffused, as local (transnational) capital and its worldwide interests becomes the fundamental actor in accumulation. In a sense, neodevelopmentalism is a version of the old developmental, national-popular project without its (national) class subject.

4 Barriers and Limits of Neodevelopmentalism as a Development Project

Neodevelopmentalism reproduces traditional contradictions in Argentina's capitalism in new ways. The confrontation between different forms of capital (especially, rentier versus nonrentier capitals, national versus local/transnational capitals and financial versus productive capital) and between capital and labor, interact in a particular historical period bringing about specific barriers and limits to the hegemonic project of development.

See more on the peronist NPT in Svampa (2011), Mazzeo (2011), and Rougier and Schorr (2012).

Barriers within a development project represent disequilibria whose resolution can be contained and displaced in time and space through policy or through the unplanned or concerted action of different social actors involved. Limits, on the contrary, imply blockages in the capacity to fulfil the main objectives of a development project. As such, overcoming limits requires the supersession and replacement of the hegemonic project.[7]

4.1 High Inflation, Low Competitiveness and Poor Fiscal Performance: Three Barriers to Neodevelopmentalism

In neodevelopmentalism we can identify three important barriers that come about from the movement of its own contradictions.

Inflation has historically been one of the main barriers in Argentina's capitalist development. While in the nineties it appeared as a problem of the past (Féliz and Pérez, 2004), inflation has resurfaced, becoming the main and foremost important barrier within neodevelopmentalism. The currency devaluation at the exit of neoliberalism created an important inflationary momentum. As the local currency price of the dollar jumped by 248% between December 2001 and December 2002, domestic peso consumer prices increased by 40.9%. This was exacerbated by growing world prices for exported primary products, and the subsequent acceleration of class struggle for income appropriation.

Up until 2007 growing aggregate demand (particularly in export and consumption) was accommodated mostly by the use of existing productive capacity, since investment grew slowly and tilted toward luxury housing construction (Féliz and López, 2012). However, from 2008 lack of adequate investment begun to create structural productive bottlenecks in several branches (Katz, 2012). Coupled with the market power of price setting capitals in most sectors due to high concentration, this has led to sustained inflation of over 20% annual rate.[8] Such high infla-

---

[7] As proposed by Lebowitz (2003), we derive our distinction between barriers and limits from Marx's discussion on barriers and limits that capital poses itself in its own development.
[8] In 2007, the government attempted to "hide" inflation through a political intervention of the state's statistical office Instituto Nacional de Estadísticas y Censos (National Institute of Statistics and the Census, INDEC). Through this intervention it kept "official" inflation rate usually below the 10% annual rate. However, there is significant social, academic, and political consensus and

tion rate became a significant barrier to the ability of the neodevelopmentalist project to fabricate consensus based on redistribution of income and inclusion through employment. Inflation at high rates tend to stagnate wages even for the most organized fractions of the working class.

High inflationary tendencies push developmentalism in Argentina against a second important barrier: growing lack of international competitiveness of capital. One of the main changes in macroeconomic policies after 2001 was the attempt to sustain a high and stable real exchange rate (RER). The "expensive" dollar was the key element in the competitiveness policy (Frenkel and Rapetti, 2004). With a highly devalued currency, local capitals were to be able to compete internationally (even if their structural competitiveness was thin) since devaluation meant a huge immediate reduction in relative unit labor costs: participation of labor costs in total costs for big corporations fell 53.5% in 2002–2003 in comparison with the average for 1993–2001.[9] This policy was coupled with generalized and growing subsidies for electricity and transport. Total direct subsidies to corporations reached 4% of GDP in 2011 (Bona, 2012: 107). While these subsidies also benefited the working class (through lower tariffs for some public services), they worked also as an indirect benefit to local capital competing with imports or trying to export since they helped to keep at bay wage demands.

The attempt to maintain competitiveness through exchange rate policy and subsidies was successful for a while but as a tendency it is doomed. Inflationary pressures tended to appreciate the real exchange rate (i.e., increase the price of local commodities expressed in foreign currency) (Féliz, 2007). The decentralized action of different capitals that tried to use inflation for their own benefit resulted in a falling RER after 2003 as general prices increased more than nominal devaluation. Furthermore, a lack of investment expenditure and low productivity growth put pressure on relative real labor unit costs (Féliz, 2009), which are the structural source of competitiveness within capitalism (Shaikh, 1991).

---

    practice indicating that actual inflation rate has been well over 20% annually. See ATE-INDEC (2008).

[9]   Our estimates are based on data from the Encuesta Nacional a Grandes Empresas (National Survey to Big Enterprises, ENGE) of the INDEC.

The systematic use of devaluation as a means to recover lost competitiveness was initially limited since the government attempted to use nominal exchange rate policy to curb inflation. Only after 2007 when falling international competitiveness was becoming increasingly problematic did the government take steps to attack the issue. A combination of normative wage caps and slow but progressive nominal devaluation became the main policy tools (Féliz, 2012). However, these proved basically unsuccessful as a growing fraction of manufacturing branches showed increasing foreign trade deficits (Azpiazu and Schorr, 2010). By 2011, most of the trade surplus was the result of positive net exports in primary production, food manufacturing, and mining. That is, only those capitals linked to the production and appropriation of rent from natural resources had actual (structural) international competitiveness.[10] For the rest of them, superexploitation of labor and public subsidies were the main source of competitive ability, albeit an insufficient one.[11]

This leads to the third significant barrier: the fiscal barrier. In the first few years of this period, the state was able to generate a significant fiscal primary surplus that allowed it to fulfil interest payments on restructured public debt without resorting to increasing indebtedness. However, the need to subsidize nonrentier capital that couldn't keep up with international competition while at the same time maintaining debt compromises and managing growing demands (and needs) for social policies was putting a significant pressure on the fiscal accounts.

The inability of the peronist social coalition to transform the tax base of the state creates increasing difficulties for financing the neodevelopmentalist (posneoliberal) form of the welfare state. The only major change had been the creation of export taxes in 2002 but the latest attempt at a hike in its rates led to an important uprising of farmers and exporters of foods stuffs in 2008 (Sartelli et al., 2008; Grigera, 2009). The budgetary restriction of the state had been progressively loosened after the renationalization of social security since surplus resources are "loaned" to the state's Central Administration. Later on, the creation of the *Fondo de*

---

[10] Besides, this sectors are dominated by the biggest transnational corporations (e.g., in agrobusiness, Monsanto and Danone; in mining, Barrick Gold).
[11] Of course, since the labor market is unified (even if fragmented) structurally competitive rentier capitals also take advantage of systemic superexploitation of labour as a source of extra profits.

Desendeudamiento (Fund for Debt Reduction) and a change in the Organic Charter of the *Banco Central de la República Argentina* (Argentina's Central Bank, BCRA) facilitated central government's borrowing from the BCRA. However, primary fiscal deficit kept rising.

The most ardent social contradictions were manifest within the state. Financial creditors have a reduced weight but the state still prioritizes debt payments.[12] The fait of productive capital becomes tantamount to development as such; thus, promoting its competitiveness through fiscal aid, exchange rate policy, and other means is a key policy goal. As the social and political promises of neodevelopmentalism became sources of political stability and consensus, social and labor policies become of greater importance.

In its essential determinants, barriers within the neodevelopmentalist project boil down to the structural consequences of neoliberalism and the failure of national-popular ideological project to confront them. The neoextractivist strategy reproduces the historical contradiction between rentier and nonrentier productive capitals. While the former obtain extraordinary profits, the later live of the appropriation of such rents directly or through public policies, complementing land rent appropriation with extensive use of superexploitation of labor. However, in the context of transnationalization of the economy, higher profits do not result in an investment shock. This occurs for two main reasons. First, income from rents are not reinvested for they are not needed to reproduce high profits that derive from the property of low-cost natural resources; thus, corporations can transfer their extra profits outside the local cycle of capital without jeopardizing their ability to maintain their extraordinary profitability. Second, since 2007 the crisis in capitalism created a drain of local profits toward the center in the case of global corporations that need every hour of value they can get to confront the crisis and restructure their international operations. Both reasons result in an investment rate of big capital corporations that stayed at 19.3% of their value added in 2009 (in contrast with a 24.7% on average between 1993 and 2001), keeping the economy's investment rate at just 22.4% of GDP (Manzanelli, 2011: 26). In the context of expanded aggregate demand, the lack of

---

[12] "As the world plummets, Argentina pays its debts" (our own translation), stated president CFK in a recent discourse (Infonews.com, 2012).

adequate investment has led to the aforementioned inflationary barrier. At the same time, significant employment growth with low investment has led to poor productivity growth and thus to falling competitiveness. Besides, as growth in productivity remains low, the limited possibilities (within capitalism) for using relative surplus-value strategies restricts the ability for increasing fiscal pressure on productive capital.

Barriers and structural restrictions were building up for neodevelopmentalism in Argentina. The ideological construction of the forces in government (Kirchnerism's version of Peronism) proposed a demand-led growth strategy (Amico, 2008), which was in line with the demands of the social forces that emerged and headed the neoliberal project to its political crisis. However, Kirchnerism's inability, and unwillingness, to displace structural restrictions inherited from neoliberalism turned barriers into ever-growing limits. Some of the main political promises of the peronist national-popular version of capitalist development became impossible to attain.

4.2 From Barriers to Limits within Neodevelopmentalism

The sociopolitical hegemony of the neodevelopmentalist discourse in Argentina has been based on the notion that a demand-led growth regime through reindustrialization will guarantee the progressive redistribution of incomes and employment-based social inclusion (Rougier and Schorr, 2012: 68; Féliz, 2013). According to this, economic growth based on industrialization will allow a process of "development from within" (export led), which contrasts with the developmentalist motto "development towards the inside" characteristic of the so-called import substitution stage (Sunkel, 1991).

However, the barriers that the neodevelopmentalist project posses on itself grow into limits to the possibilities of development within its own national-popular framework. Furthermore, those limits bring forth the discussion about the alternatives to capitalist development strategies within the periphery.

Limits of Industrialization in the Periphery

Argentina's hegemonic development project proposes that industrialization has to be the base of growth and socioeconomic development. The argument is based first of all in the idea that the country suffered from deindustrialization throughout neoliberalism and that this (deindustrialization) was directly responsible for growing poverty, worsening income distribution and increasing precariousness of labor (Rougier and Schorr, 2012). Thus, growth via reindustrialization should turn around social indicators, allowing for the so-called "growth with social inclusion." The actual experience of neodevelopmentalism in Argentina calls into question the reality of the argument.

The neoextractivist insertion in world markets together with the significant transnationalization of production (particularly, manufacturing) creates a very real limitation to the possibilities of industrialization in Argentina. Since transnational corporations control most investment and accumulation decisions, the local leverage over the development of a process of industrial growth is constrained by those corporations' global strategies. This situation puts Argentina as producer/exporter of primary commodities and, at the most, of these commodity's basic manufactures. In that respect, through massive subsidies neodevelopmentalist policies have been able to promote foreign investment for the assembly of consumption equipment with a majority of foreign parts, technology, and design. The result has been the reproduction of dependent industrialization (Rougier and Schorr, 2012). In general terms, it can be said that industrial growth has not resulted in "reindustrialization" but has been simply part of the general expansion process: even if manufacturing industry's real GDP grew more than total GDP between 2002 and 2011 (107.2% and 95.4%, respectively) in contrast with 1998, the previous peak, industry's growth is not so significant (51.4% to 59.5%, respectively).

Limits to Employment and Wage Growth

In this context, economic growth has promoted employment growth. However, contrary to the official account, job creation has not been able of guaranteeing social inclusion, at least not in any sensible way. As we stated, the years of recovery of economic growth (97.4% growth in GDP between the 4th quarter of 2002 and the 4th quarter of 2011) were marked by the partial improvement in living conditions for most of the working people. This, however, has been a slow process: in 2005, four years after the 2001 crisis, formal salaried workers had just recovered their pre-crisis (2001) real wages; informal workers had to wait until

2010 to reach that level and state employees' wages were still 32.6% below its 2001 level in 2013.[13]

Employment growth and the recovery in wages led for quite a few years to an increasing participation of wage in aggregate income (Fernández and González, 2012). In 2008, workers reached, according to the official statistics, a 43.8% participation in value added, similar to the 1993 estimation (44.7%). After 2008 there is no official data, in part due to the mentioned problem with the estimation of inflation. Several estimates show that in the five years to 2013 the participation of wages in income had receded significantly mainly to increasing inflation and also due to the reduction in the rate of employment creation: urban employment growth fell from a 3.2% annual rate between 2004 and 2007 to only 1.7% annual rate between 2008 and 2011.

The national-popular peronist tradition recalls the 50% participation of wages on income that was recorded in the late 1940s and early 1950s.[14] Although not backed by the data, the CFK's speeches talk of the indicator having reached that historical "fifty-fifty" goal. Even if that figure were true (actual data suggests it is not), the significance of the objective has to be put into perspective. First, a 50% participation of wage on income means that about 90% of the population (working people) controls half of total income while 10% has control over the other half (in particular, investment expenditure that guides the cycle of capital as a whole). The "democratic" 50–50 is in fact not so democratic. Second, in the 1940s when the mythical 50% had been achieved, most working families had one member working on a fulltime job (8–9 hour a day, maybe 45–50 hours a week); the rest of the family worked unwaged at home or didn't work. In any case, now working families need two or three members to be active part of the labor market, providing a total of 100 or more hours a week of waged labor, to arrive at just over 40% participation in total income. This is a sign of one major limit of Argentina's economy: the extended precariousness of employment.

---

[13] Our own estimations based on data from the INDEC.
[14] According to Rougier and Schorr (2012: 97), in 1954 workers accrued 49.6% of total income. In 1974, the statistical reading reached its historical peak: 49.7%.

Precariousness as Limit to Development

In the course of neoliberalism, the conditions of employment deteriorated greatly (Féliz, 2011). Several forms of precarious labor developed and extended across the economy. The incidence of unregistered employment in the private sector of the economy remained at almost 38.3% in 2009 (Féliz, López and Fernández, 2012); in the public sector, labor unions' accounts mark different forms of precarious employment at close to 2/3 of total posts. Neodevelopmentalism has been unable to undergo any significant transformation in this respect mainly, as we commented before, because superexploitation of labor came to be a structural condition for the successful reproduction of capital within Argentina's value-space. Even if statistically nonregistered employment is "a problem" of small enterprises, most big firms make extensive use of indirect forms of precarious employment through externalization of activities and processes through formally independent small and medium size firms.

One of the main effects of extended precarization of employment is the permanence of low wages and ample income poverty even as the economy presents record growth rates and unemployment statistics are close to its lowest levels in 30 years. Wages have remained all the way through the first ten years of neodevelopmentalism well below the so-called *Canasta Familiar* (Family Basket) for a very significant fraction of the labor class. In 2011 more than 55% of workers had incomes below this standard (Katz et al., 2012). Besides, even if legal minimum wages have multiplied by more than 7 times since 2002, the number of workers with wages below that level remained at 42.3% in 2009 (Féliz, López and Fernández, 2012). Argentina clearly suffers from the problem analyzed by Marini (2007) and that he called superexploitation of labor: a significant proportion of the working class lives with incomes far below what is needed to maintain and reproduce its labor-force. Such is still the "cost" of dependent capitalism in its new pattern of reproduction in the age of transnational capital.

Thus, contrary to official expectations, economic growth does not trickle down in better incomes and jobs. Even if industrialization goes further, without significant changes in the role of Argentina's value-space within the world market, it is not likely that living conditions will improve significantly. The country that in the seventies had reached a significant position in terms of capitalist economic development (Azpiazu and

Schorr, 2010) now seems stuck as a peripherical value-space that has been pigeonholed by transnational corporations as supplier of cheap agricultural manufactures and primary products, in contrast with those that have been placed as suppliers of cheap industrial manufactures (e.g., China, India, Brazil). In such a place, labor's appropriation of income will tend to be pulled down (Fernández and González, 2012).

Besides, persistent precarization in its different forms is the main means for capitalist corporations to control production and distribution of value. More than deindustrialization, that is an ambiguous idea (Grigera, 2011), capitalist restructuration during neoliberal rule allowed capital to structurally shift power in the shop floor in its favor, taking advantage of new technological developments to dismantle the so-called fordist social and technical association of labor. The capitalist use of technology has favored the flexibility and movement of constant capital, thus making it easier for capitals to regionally fragment the labor-force (Ceceña, 2000). The immediate consequence of such process has been the political decomposition of labor (Cleaver, 1985).

The resulting income dynamic creates a situation where between 15% and 30% of the urban population in Argentina lives in conditions of statistical income poverty, while close to 10% borders statistical hunger.[15,16] The severity of the problem of production of poverty in Argentina can be put into perspective with a brief historical comparison. In the early 1970s income poverty reached about 9% of urban population in Greater Buenos Aires (Montoya and Mitnik, 1995). Such was the result of relatively high wages and employment levels. At that time, there were almost no social income transfer programs but a significant extension of the welfare state in a peripheral setting. Today, as neodevelopmentalism consolidates as hegemonic project, income poverty remains at more than twice the rate of the 1970s but with a huge array of social policies that transfer income directly to families. While these programs (with all its deficits) are an absolute necessity, they also illustrate that magnitude

---

[15] Since official estimates have been seriuosly questioned, here we refer to alternative estimations (ATE-INDEC, 2012).

[16] We talk of statistical hunger since estimations refer to people whose incomes are below the money value of a mininum food consumption basket. This basket represents the minimum consumption of calories required to avoid hunger. However, since people's consumption includes other expenditures, even if their income is over that level, many of them are probably suffering from malnutrition.

of the problem. Argentina's capitalist strategy of development produces poverty and deprivation at a staggering rate; public policies only keep at a leash the potential political problem that the situation presents.

Besides income poverty, poverty as deprivation of well-being or lack of functionings (Sen, 1997) is much more extended: the lack of adequate housing remains a problem for almost 3 million families, and it has not been reduced at all in a decade due to failed public programs and insufficient family incomes; public transportation is in crisis, even after millions of dollars in subsidies have been poured into a public (but mostly privatized) system; public education and health are in poor shape, and greater numbers of poor middle-class families spend ever-growing shares of their incomes in expensive and insufficient private sector schemes. Privatization and precarization of everyday life has become rampant fact in today's Argentina.

5 Beyond Neodevelopmentalism? The Political Economy of Radical Social Change

As neodevelopmentalism builds barriers and limits to its own political and economic reproduction, so social movements, popular organizations, and radical political forces begin to find ways to propose an alternative orientation for capitalist development in the periphery, if not a way to opt out from capitalist rule altogether (Féliz, 2009b).

Those alternatives do not represent a definite and coherent plan, but attempt to signal to the need for new foundations for policy—economic, social or otherwise. In a sense, we propose that if neodevelopmentalism has become the new political economy of capital, those alternatives from below pave the way for a "political economy of labour" (Lebowitz, 2003) for new policies for radical social change.

The political economy of capital was clearly analyzed by Marx (Lebowitz, 2003) and it is based on a social relationship (capital) that imposes as a natural force the logic of capitalization, valorization, and mercantilization on society. The expression M – C [MoP, LF] – ... P ... – C' – M' characterizes simply but precisely the content of such relationship.[17]

5.1 Toward a Political Economy of Labor

An alternative political economy has to confront the capitalist rationality that tends to be imposed by the force of dominant social relations. In fact, working people confront that hegemonic tendency through their daily struggles to improve their living conditions within society (i.e., the actual post-neoliberal society).[18] Through other values and from the need to reproduce their own material conditions of existence they pose the elements of what they want for a better (good) living.

These practices delineate a political economy of labor (PEL) that begins by placing people and their immediate relationships at the center (Lebowitz, 2003). In a way, it proposes to invert the capitalist ratio and build a circuit whose point of departure could be represented as the inversion of the cycle of capital: HB – D (C) – ... P' ... – HB'. This inverted relationship implies a process of production of the world (P') whose axis is the reproduction of human beings (HB) in new conditions (HB') not just as means but also as ends themselves, and where commodities (C) and money (M) are only means toward those objectives.

A popular alternative to capital's program (today, in Argentina, an alternative to neodevelopmentalism) should begin from these practices and experiences of struggle. In a sense, this alternative should radicalize national-popular propositions by going over its politico-ideological limits. This new program must promote popular participation and construction of popular power as the basis for a new policy that will allow the beginning of a path to transcend the neoliberal heritage: transnationalization, peripherical extractivist industrialization, and precarization of life and labor.

---

[17] Let's remind that M stands for money, C for a series of commodities (LF, labour force, and MoP, means of production), P is a productive process that allows to create new commodities (C') but to valorize the original value (M'>M).

[18] This rejection to the practices of capital is not always (nor mostly) conscientious. However, as Dussel (1998) explains labour has an immanent—constitutive—exteriority regarding capital that allows it to confront its tendency to include everything (life, work, free time, nature) as part of itself. Labour is never completely subsumed in capital (Cleaver, 1992).

Those propositions and alternatives from below are the building blocks of a new political economy. Such political economy should confront capital's basic assumptions and present the basis for policies to promote the general interests of the working people.

Essentially, the political economy of labor confronts capital's political economy on the basics of four main elements.[19]

First, it opposes competition with cooperation (Lebowitz, 2003). Capitalist competition leads to the degradation of working conditions, intensifying labor exploitation and destroying the environment. This occurs because of the pressure imposed by dominant relations on individual capitals to subsist. This tendency is the original source of precarization of labor (Féliz and Chena, 2005). Working people confront such tendencies by organizing collectively in trade unions, by building base collectives and neighborhood assemblies, thus showing that cooperation and solidarity are the best strategy for improving and defending their conditions of living. To the decentralized (even individual) bargaining proposed by firms, workers have historically proposed association. In such a way they have tried to overcome the mediation of capital in the labor market, trying to impose through the state legislation that will provide better and more stable conditions for work.

In the second place, the hierarchical organization of capitalist production is questioned by modalities of workers' cooperation. In this way, workers look to displace the separation imposed by capital on them and the means of production. The PEL shows how capital is inefficient since it privileges profitability and not cost reduction. Capital results to be completely unnecessary since workers on their own can have the ability to manage enterprises with lower costs of supervision (Bowles, 1985). In Argentina, a movement of workers' coops account for the potential of autonomous worker's organization.

Third, against production for production sake (for private profit), the PEL recovers the need to produce for the satisfaction of needs and privileges the protection of the environment. Argentina's neodevelopmentalist project is based on a process of indiscriminate appropriation, use, and destruction of the riches from the soil and the underground. Agricultural production with limitless use of agrochemicals and open-pit mega-

---

[19] For further discussion on alternatives, see Féliz (2009b, 2009c, 2011b).

mining are both samples of forms of appropriation of common goods to the only goal of the valorization of capital. As forms of the PEL, in Argentina the *Unión de Asambleas Ciudadanas* (Union of Citizens' Assemblies, UAC) and the *Movimiento Nacional Campesino Indígena* (National Peasant Indigenous Movement, MNCI) are examples of the possibility of thinking and creating a world that has respect for nature, while taking the human being as part of herself, and promoting a way of development that makes use of natural riches without plundering or destroying them (Roux, 2008).

In the fourth place, the limitless expansion of capitalist markets and private property is replaced in the PEL by a willingness to widen the common space and the distribution of goods and services without the mediation of money. With privatization of the common, capital pretends to become the only mediation for the production and reproduction of life (De Angelis, 2007). The PEL proposes increasing public spaces, common (and in common) production of vital needs and the extension of rights to public services to confront its mercantilization. In such a line, we find the struggles for open source software and the public production of medicines for free distribution, the recuperation of community spaces, public education and health free and universal.

As a synthesis, the PEL confronts the values of capital with the dreams, desires, and wishes of the working people. It privileges solidarity over selfishness, the unity of the people over the regional concentration and centralization of capital, vital time over abstract labor time, the movement of people, cultures, and experiences over the exchange of money and commodities. Those values can orient another development project that can be constituted from today's experiences (Féliz, 2009b).

5.2 From the Political Economy of Labor to Radical Policies for Social Change

From those basic foundations, social movements and popular political organizations in Argentina have been proposing alternatives to the neodevelopmentalist project. These alternative policies involve several elements, which we'll present briefly (Féliz, 2012c).

Macroeconomics of wage

Macroeconomic policy should give priority to the expansion of conditions for production and reproduction of workers' daily needs. This implies radically improving working conditions by increasing wages and reducing precarization. The increase in the mass of wages will provide the adequate incentives for enterprises (capitalist and not) to increase production of popular goods and services. To warrant such policy, economic policy should, to begin with, (a) reduce the weight of soya production that takes up a sizable amount of arable land, (b) attack sumptuary consumption (manifestation of the cultural dependency of dominant classes; Furtado, 1974) that has become a drain on foreign currency and deviates to unproductive use of available resources and surplus value, and (c) reduction of the economy's transnationalization to give domestic social actors (not necessarily capitalist, but mainly social and public endeavours) greater weight in decisions regarding investment. Taking steps in this direction will allow for a radical change in the direction of aggregate demand (from surplus-value to popular consumption) to be satisfied in the short run with adequate local (or regional) supply thus avoiding (or softening) the current neodevelopmentalist inflationary and competitive barrier.

Social security beyond salaried work

Promoting actual economic democracy should be one of the main objectives of a new social security scheme. To complement and accentuate income redistribution in the labor market, the social security system should be universalized, isolating the right to basic goods and services from work. Through a radical tax reform that taps resources from existing sources (i.e., financial capital, rents from natural resources, extraordinary profits, which are now exempt or lightly taxed), the state could warrant the funds for a substantial generalization of the right to basic income (Féliz, 2011c) as well as a general improvement and universalization of public education, health and other policies that provide basic services. This policy combination will allow a radical development process to surpass the fiscal barrier.

Social self-management as a project

One of the most pressing limitations of public policies is the lack of popular participation in their definition, control, and management. A popular program should create the means to transform the state (and society) from a bureaucratic, hierarchical machine into an instrument of popular self-management of common tasks. In such direction, state policies should promote and finance the autonomous self-organization of the population in productive and social endeavors and undertakings. This might include the management of natural riches, the financial system, housing policies, public enterprises, and so on, and even the political economy in a general sense.

These and other policy orientations would allow popular organization to begin to transcend the limits of peripherical capitalist development in its current neodevelopmentalist form.

6   Preliminary Conclusions

The consolidation of the neodevelopmentalist project in Argentina has also meant the fortification of its barriers and limits. While superseding neoliberalism, due to its ideological and political constitution, neodevelopmentalism has not been able to overcome most structural restrictions to an inclusive development path in the periphery. Transnational control over the whole cycle of capital, a peripherical extractivist insertion within the world's distribution of labor and in consequence the extended precarization and poverty remain the unanswered questions of the hegemonic project. This inability creates a significant contradiction between the promises of developmentalism's national-popular tradition and the reality of neodevelopmentalism in a peripheral economy in the era of transnational capital.

These contradictions have not yet materialized in an outright crisis of the neodevelopmentalist project (that would signify its limit as development project) since political forces in the state (peronist Kirchnerism) have been able to displace barriers and contain its potential for crisis. However, as barriers and limits become ever more pressing, the elaboration of alternative policies (and alternative political alliances to put them in place) becomes a growing necessity. Popular movements have long proposed such alternatives, which build on what's been dubbed the political economy of labor. However, such alternatives will not materialize in actual policies unless social forces within labor are able to politically reconfigure the sociopolitical playing field, dialectically overcoming (radicalizing) the national-popular discourse and practice.

References

Amico, F. (2008) "Argentina: diferencias entre el actual modelo de dólar alto y la convertibilidad," Investigación Económica, LXVII(264), pp. 63–93.

ATE-INDEC (2008) "Índice de precios al consumidor IPC-GBA del año 2007: ejercicio alternativo ante la imposibilidad del cálculo del IPC-GBA debido a la intervención del INDEC," working document, 4, January, Junta Interna/Comisión Técnica ATE-INDEC, Buenos Aires.

ATE-INDEC (2012) "La manipulación de datos en el INDEC. Impacto en la medición de la pobreza e indigencia," working document, 7, September, Comisión Técnica ATE-INDEC, Buenos Aires.

Azpiazu D. & M. Schorr (2010) Hecho en Argentina, industria y economía. 1976–2007, Siglo Veintiuno Editores, Buenos Aires.

Basualdo, E. (2006) Estudios de historia económica argentina. Desde mediados del siglo XX a la actualidad, FLACSO/Siglo veintiuno editores, Buenos Aires.

Bona, L. (2012) "Subsidios a sectores económicos en la Argentina de la post Convertibilidad: interpretación desde una perspectiva de clase," in Féliz, M. et al. (editors) Más allá del individuo. Clases sociales, transformaciones económicas y políticas estatales en la argentina contemporánea, pp. 103–124, Editorial El Colectivo, Buenos Aires.

Bonnet, A. (2006) "¡Qué se vayan todos!: Discussing the Argentine crisis and insurrection," Historical Materialism, 14 (1), pp. 157–184, Koninklikje Brill NV, Leiden.

Bowles, S. (1985) "The production process in a competitive economy: Walrasian, Neo-Hobbesian and Marxian models," American Economic Review, 75 (1), pp.16–36.

Ceceña, A. E. (2000) Tecnología y organización capitalista al final del siglo XX, in Marini, R. M. & M. Millán (editors) La teoría social latinoamericana. Cuestiones contemporáneas, Tomo IV, 1996, pp. 95–104, Universidad Nacional Autónoma de México, Ediciones El Caballito, México.

Cleaver, H. (1985) Una lectura política de "El Capital," Fondo de Cultura Económica, México.

Cleaver, H. (1992) "Theses on secular crisis in capitalism: the insurpassability of class antagonism," Rethinking Marxism Conference, Amherst.

De Angelis, M. (2007) The beginning of history. Value struggles and global capital, Pluto Press, London.

Dinerstein, A. C. (2002) "The Battle of Buenos Aires. Crisis, Insurrection and the Reinvention of Politics in Argentina," Historical Materialism, 10 (4), pp. 5–38, Koninklikje Brill NV, Leiden.

Duménil, G. & D. Lévy (2009) Crisis y salida de crisis. Orden y desorden neoliberals, Fondo de Cultura Económica, México.

Féliz, M. (2007) "¿Hacia el neodesarrollismo en Argentina? De la reestructuración capitalista a su estabilización," ¿Coyuntura favorable o nuevo modelo?: Economía argentina, Anuario EDI 3, pp. 68–81, Ediciones Luxemburg, Buenos Aires.

Féliz, M. (2008) "Jubilaciones: ¿volver al '93 o crear un verdadero sistema de previsión social?," Prensa de Frente, 29 October, <http://www.prensadefrente.org/pdfb2/index.php/a/2008/10/29/p4084> accessed October 29, 2008.

Féliz, M. (2009a) "Crisis cambiaria en Argentina," Problemas del Desarrollo. Revista Latinoamericana de Economía, 40 (158), pp. 185–213 julio-septiembre, México.

Féliz, M. (2009b) "¿No hay alternativa frente al ajuste? Crisis, competitividad y opciones populares en Argentina," Herramienta. Revista de debate y crítica marxista, 42, pp. 147–160, Buenos Aires.

Féliz, M. (2009c) "Frente a la economía política del capital, la economía política de la clase trabajadora: Alternativas populares ante la crisis capitalista en Argentina," Herramienta Web, 2, September, Buenos Aires. <http://www.herramienta.com.ar/herramienta-web-2/frente-la-economia-politica-del-capital-la-economia-politica-de-la-clase-trabajado> accessed October 19, 2012.

Féliz, M. (2011a) Un estudio sobre la crisis en un país periférico. La economía argentina del crecimiento a la crisis, 1991–2002, Editorial El Colectivo, Buenos Aires.

Féliz, M. (2011b) "Neoliberalismos, neodesarrollismos y proyectos contrahegemónicos en Suramérica," Revista Astrolabio. Nueva época, 7, pp. 238–265, Córdoba.

Féliz, M. (2011c) "The macroeconomic limits of income's policy in a dependent country. The need and possibilities for radical reforms in social policies in Argentina after the crisis (2001–2008)," in Puyana Mutis, A. & S. Ong'wen Okuro (editors) Strategies Against Poverty. Designs from the North and alternatives from the South, CLACSO-CROP, Buenos Aires.

Féliz, M. (2012a) "Neo-Developmentalism Beyond Neoliberalism? Capitalist Crisis and Argentina's Development Since the 1990s," Historical Materialism, 20(2), pp. 105–123, London.

Féliz, M. (2012b) "Neoextractivismo, neodesarrollismo y acumulación de capital en Argentina. Perspectivas para los movimientos sociales," Jornadas Internacionales "Rosa Luxemburgo en el Sur" (Montevideo), 27 y 28 de Julio de 2012, Facultad de Humanidades y Ciencias de la Educación (UDELAR), Montevideo.

Féliz, M. (2012c) "El desarrollo más allá del capital. Economía política del trabajo y luchas populares por el cambio social en Argentina," Centro de Estudios del Desarrollo Económico y Social, Facultad de Economía, Benemérita Universidad Autónoma de Puebla, Puebla (México). In press.

Féliz, M. (2013) "Sin clase. Neodesarrollismo y neoestructuralismo en Argentina (2002–2011)," Século XXI: Revista de Ciências Sociais, January–June, Santa María, Brazil. In press.

Féliz, M. & P. Chena (2005) "Tendencias del mercado de trabajo en la economía periférica. Algunas tesis para el caso de Argentina," in Neffa, J. C. (coord.), Desequilibrios en el mercado de trabajo argentino. Los desafíos en la postconvertibilidad, CEIL-PIETTE/CONICET, Asociación Trabajo y Sociedad, Buenos Aires.

Féliz, M. & E. López (2010) "Políticas sociales y labourales en la Argentina: del Estado 'ausente' al Estado posneoliberal," in Féliz, M., Deledicque, L. M., López, E. & F. Barrera (editors), Pensamiento crítico, organización y cambio social, Centro de Estudios para el Cambio Social, Editorial El Colectivo, CONICET, Buenos Aires.

Féliz, M. & E. López (2012) Proyecto neodesarrollista en Argentina ¿Modelo nacional-popular o nueva etapa en el desarrollo capitalista? Editorial El Colectivo, Buenos Aires.

Féliz, M. & P. E. Pérez (2004) "Conflicto de clase, salarios y productividad. Una mirada de largo plazo para la Argentina," in Boyer, R. & J. C. Neffa (coords.), La economía Argentina y su crisis (1976–2001): visiones institucionalistas y regulacionistas, Miño y Dávila/CEIL-PIETTE del CONICET / Trabajo y Sociedad / Caisse des Depôts et Consignations de Francia, Buenos Aires.

Féliz, M. & P. E. Pérez (2007) "¿Tiempos de cambio? Contradicciones y conflictos en la política económica de la posconvertibilidad," in Boyer, R. &J. C. Neffa (comp.), Salidas de crisis y estrategias alternativas de desarrollo. La experiencia argentina, Institut CDC pour la Recherche/CEIL-PIETTE/CONICET, Editorial Miño y Dávila, Buenos Aires.

Féliz, M., López, E. & L. Fernández (2012) "Estructura de clase, distribución del ingreso y políticas públicas. Una aproximación al caso argentino en la etapa post-neoliberal," in Féliz, M. et al. (editors), Más allá del individuo. Clases sociales, transformaciones económicas y políticas estatales en la argentina contemporánea, Editorial El Colectivo, Buenos Aires.

Fernández, A. L. & M. L. González (2012) "La desigualdad en los ingresos laborales. Su evolución en la posconvertibilidad," Apuntes para el Cambio, 3, Buenos Aires.

Fine, B., Lapavitsas, C. & J. Pincus (editors) (2003) Development Policy in the Twenty-First Century: Beyond the Post-Washington Consensus, Routledge, London.

Frenkel, R. & M. Rapetti (2004) "Políticas macroeconómicas para el crecimiento crecimiento y el empleo," OIT—Oficina Regional para América Latina y el Caribe, Conferencia de empleo MERCOSUR, Buenos Aires.

Furtado, C. (1974) El desarrollo económico: un mito, Siglo Veintiuno Editores, Buenos Aires.

Grigera, Juan (2009) "Right-wing Social Movements? The Argentinean 'Development Model' in Question," Historical Materialism Sixth Annual Conference, London.

Grigera, Juan (2011) "La desindustrialización en Argentina. ¿Agresión a la manufactura o reestructuración capitalista?," in Bonnet, Alberto (editor), El país invisible, Peña y Lilo/Continente, Buenos Aires.

Harvey, David (2009) "¿Estamos realmente ante el fin del neoliberalismo?," Herramienta. Revista de debate y crítica marxista, 41, Buenos Aires.

Katz, Claudio (2012) "Contrasentidos del neodesarrollismo," Rebelion.org <http://www.rebelion.org/noticia.php?id=154325> accessed October 19, 2012.

Katz, Claudio, Lucita, Eduardo, et al. (2012) "Afloran los límites del modelo," Working Paper, Economistas de Izquierda, Buenos Aires <http://www.rebelion.org/noticia.php?id=147522> accessed October 19, 2012.

Lebowitz, Michael (2003) Beyond Capital. Marx's political economy of the working class, Palgrave Macmillan, London.

Manzanelli, Pablo (2011) "Peculiaridades en el comportamiento de la formación de capital en las grandes empresas durante la posconvertibilidad," Apuntes para el Cambio, 1, pp. 23–37, November/December, Buenos Aires.

Marini, Ruy Mauro (2007), "Dialéctica de la dependencia," in Marini, Ruy Mauro, América Latina, dependencia y globalización, 1973, CLACSO-Prometeo, Buenos Aires.

Mazzeo, Miguel (2011), Poder popular y nación. Notas sobre el Bicentenario de la Revolución de Mayo, Editorial El Colectivo y Ediciones Herramienta, Buenos Aires.

Montoya, Silvia &Oscar Mitnik (1995) "Dinámica de la pobreza y la distribución del ingreso. Gran Buenos Aires, 1974–1994," XXX Reunión Anual Asociación Argentina de Economía Política, Universidad Nacional de Río Cuarto, Córdoba.

Neffa, Julio C. (1998) Modos de regulación, regímenes de acumulación y sus crisis en Argentina (1880–1996). Un enfoque desde la teoría de la regulación, Trabajo y Sociedad—PIETTE/CONICET—Eudeba, Buenos Aires.

Página/12 (2011) "CFK: 'Propongo volver al capitalismo en serio'," Diario Página/12, 3 November, Buenos Aires <http://www.pagina12.com.ar/diario/ultimas/20-180432-2011-11-03.html> accessed October 19, 2012.

Pérez, Pablo E. & Mariano Féliz (2010) "La crisis económica y sus implicancias sobre la política de empleo e ingresos en Argentina," Revista Ser Social, 12(26), pp. 31–58, Brasilia.

Rougier, Marcelo & Martín Schorr (2012) La industria en los cuatro peronismos: estrategias, políticas y resultados, Capital Intelectual, Buenos Aires.

Roux, Rhina (2008) "Marx y la cuestión del despojo. Claves teóricas para iluminar un cambio de época," Revista Herramienta, 38, pp. 61–74, Buenos Aires.

Sartelli, Eduardo, Harari, Fabián, Kabat, Marina, Kornblihtt, Juan, Baudino, Verónica, Dachevsky, Fernando, & Gonzalo Sanz Cerbino (2008) Patrones en la ruta. El conflicto agrario y los enfrentamientos en el seno de la burguesía, Ediciones ryr, Buenos Aires.

Sen, Amartya K. (1997) Inequality reexamined, Harvard University Press, Cambridge.

Shaikh, Anwar (1991) "Competition and Exchange Rates: Theory and Empirical Evidence," Working Paper, Department of Economics, New School for Social Research, New York.

Sunkel, Osvaldo (1991) El desarrollo desde dentro. Un enfoque neoestructuralista para la América Latina, Fondo de Cultura Económica, México.

Svampa, Maristella (2011a) "Argentina, una década después. Del 'que se vayan todos' a la exacerbación de lo nacional-popular," Revista Nueva Sociedad, 235, pp. 17–34.

Svampa, Maristella (2011b) "Extractivismo neodesarrollista, Gobiernos y Movimientos Sociales en América Latina," Revista Problèmes de l'Amérique Latine, 81, pp. 103–128.

Thwaites Rey, Mabel (2010) "Después de la globalización neoliberal: ¿Qué Estado en América Latina?," OSAL, Año XI, 27, april, Buenos Aires.

Chapter 5
ALTERNATIVE PATHS OF SOCIAL TRANSFORMATION IN SUB-SAHARIAN AFRICA: A CASE FOR POVERTY ALLEVIATION PROGRAMS BY THE POOR

Jude Ssempebwa and Jacqueline Nakaiza

Jude Ssempebwa and Jacqueline Nakaiza's study of the elaboration and execution of "social transformation" programs in Uganda and Kenya together with data from the Democratic Republic of the Congo, Mozambique, and Rwanda provides a much needed stock taking of the projected lofty aims and oftentimes stunted potential gains of these politico-economic agendas. The researchers investigate a series of difficult and complex questions relating to the means by which the efficiency and rentability of such programs can and should be measured at the same time as they delve into the reasons behind the successes and failures of these institutionalized responses to the thorny issue of poverty. After a careful consideration and correlation of their findings, the authors make a convincing case for the elaboration and enactment of user-friendly strategies which solicit and usefully incorporate input and participation by individuals and communities living with poverty rather than those plans which utilize trained individuals and a top-down approach to problem identification and resolution.

1 Introduction

In many Sub-Saharan African countries social transformation is at the nucleus of the political economy of poverty. Defined as the process by which households improve their ascribed status, social transformation has also received notable attention from scholars, activists, and NGOs in and outside the region. Subsequently, there is an enormous and diverse body of literature on the subject. Flagship among the foci of this literature is the interplay between economics and politics; the policy options for social transformation that this interplay presents; and the implementation and outcomes of these policy options. Among others, this literature affirms two things that point to need for new research on the political economy of poverty and social transformation in the region. First, it indicates that governmental, diplomatic, civil society, and charitable organizations have invested heavily in poverty alleviation programs in the region (see, e.g., Moyo, 2009). Second, it indicates that many households are stagnating in extreme poverty, notwithstanding the fact that successive household welfare surveys have reported notable improvements in household welfare. Why? What explains the persistence of extreme poverty despite years of enormous investment in poverty alleviation programs? Why have some poverty alleviation programs/projects been more successful in alleviating poverty than others? What lessons may be drawn from both the successful and less successful programs/projects for policy reform?

Review of the literature (e.g., Crook, 2000; Daxbacher, 2004; Dorr, 1992; Mehrotra and Delamonica, 2007) leads to the conclusion that, hitherto, these questions had not attracted satisfactory scholarly attention. Rather, the literature occurs in three major categories: (1) poverty status reports, discussing the causes, nature, incidence, and consequences of poverty (e.g., Abuka et al., 2007; Ayako and Katumanga, 1997; Bird et al., 2003; Deininger and Okidi, 2003a); (2) poverty alleviation program/project reports, mainly narrative explanations of the performance of these programs (e.g., Ministry of Finance Planning and Economic Development [MoFPED], 2001; Ministry of Gender, Labour and Social Development [MoGLSD], 2003); and (3) commentary on poverty and poverty alleviation programs, discussing aspects of the literature in the first two categories (e.g., Bansikiza, 2007; Due et al., 1990; Ellis and Bahiigwa, 2001; Johnson, 2004; Kisekka, 2011; Lawson, McKay and Okidi, 2003; Muhumuza, 2007; Mukui, 2005; Nduhukhire-Owa-Mataze, 1999; Stevenson and St-Onge, 2005). Thus, a gap in knowledge on the political economy of poverty and social transformation in the region pertains to the fact that even though some of the authors in each of the categories of related literature make an indication of the reasons underlying the performance of individual poverty alleviation programs, they do not synthesize multiple experiences to propound generic propositions that may be applicable across varied settings.

To plug this gap, this chapter synthesizes the findings of five studies of aspects of the political economy of poverty and social transformation conducted in the region between 2009 and 2012. Conducted by teams of researchers based at the Catholic University of Eastern Africa, Uganda Martyrs University (UMU), Université Catholique de Graben, Universidade Catholica do Mocambique, and Universite Catholique de Kabgayi—under the auspices and technical guidance of the Centre for Coordination of Research of the International Federation of Catholic Universities—the studies respectively delved into: (1) Caritas' self-help and government's revolving loan programs in Kenya; (2) growth of a savings and internal lending community and the correlates of stagnation in and mobility from poverty in central Uganda; and (3) perceptions of poverty and poverty alleviation programs in DRC, Mozambique, and Rwanda. The chapter discusses the studies with the conclusion that, despite their diversity, two findings that are common to all of them are that: (1) poverty alleviation programs/projects were more successful in instances where the poor at whom they were targeted were involved in the definition of poverty; and (2) many poverty alleviation programs/projects were implemented among/for people who did not perceive themselves as being poor and these tended to be ineffective. Thus, the chapter propounds a case for a paradigmatic shift in the political economy of poverty and social transformation in the region—from relegating the poor as passive consumers of poverty alleviation programs/projects to appreciating them as partners in the design and implementation of these programs/projects.

2 Lessons from Selected Successful and Unsuccessful Poverty Alleviation Programs

The studies conducted in Kenya and Uganda examined four similar poverty alleviation programs (i.e. Caritas Kenya's Self-Help Program and Government of Kenya [GoK]'s Revolving Loan Fund; and Nkozi Agribusiness Training Association [a Savings and Internal Lending Community], and Uganda Government's Revolving Loan Fund Programs) but which succeeded to differing levels.

2.1 Caritas Kenya's Self-Help Program and GoK's Revolving Loan Fund

Kenya's vision 2030 underscores government's commitment to poverty alleviation through implementation of macro and microeconomic interventions that address the factors that exclude the country's poor from gainful economic activities (GoK, 2007). Pursuant to this vision, the government is implementing a devolved fund—including a constituency development fund, poverty eradication revolving loan fund, water services trust fund, constituency bursary fund, free primary education fund, local authority transfer fund, disabled fund, HIV/AIDS community initiative account, community development trust fund, road maintenance levy fund, and rural electrification levy fund (Centre for Governance and Development, 2007). According to the Office of the Deputy Prime Minister and Ministry of Finance (2011), for example, the poverty eradication revolving loan fund is aimed at providing the poor with access to the capital that they need to break their vicious cycle of poverty and exclusion. However, as in many parts of the Global South where similar programs have been implemented, the fund has not been as effective as hoped. Fears have been expressed that, in some provinces, it is not reaching the most deserving poor. For instance, a Centre for Governance and Development report faults the constituency development fund thus:

> The [constituency development fund] CDF is one of the popular initiatives in Kenya's development history and which has elicited greater debate on the potential of devolving resources to local development level. The implementation of the fund has however witnessed challenges relating particularly to issues of governance. In many ways, this has also affected monitoring and evaluation thus compromising the Fund's effectiveness and efficiency. According to the Fund's quarterly bulletin, the main challenges ... revolve around operational issues of ... formation of [constituency development committees] CDCs, types of fundable projects and procurement procedures ... the major challenges facing the Fund are inequalities in constituency attributes ... the Fund experiences gross data inadequacy ... projects are also poorly chosen with those having widespread spill over benefits to some constituencies often being ignored. There seems to exist [sic] a "fiscal illu-

sion" that [the] CDF is free. This tends to de-motivate beneficiaries, especially in monitoring the Fund's efficient utilisation. In a number of instances, clear documentation has been noted in which politics plays a significant role in decision making in the Fund's management. Quite often, individuals and regions within the constituency that are supportive of the incumbent [Member of Parliament] MP often receive preferential treatment (Centre for Governance and Development, 2007: pp. 15–16).

Conversely, there are reports that Caritas Kenya (a charitable socioeconomic development arm of the Kenya Catholic Bishops' Conference) is implementing a household self-help development program that is comparable to the revolving loan fund component of the GoK's devolved fund albeit the former is transforming the lives of the very poor in a cost-effective and sustainable way (see, e.g,, Murori, 2010).

A team of researchers based at the Catholic University of Eastern Africa delved into the design and implementation of the household self-help development program—to gain insight into the factors responsible for its effectiveness. This was done following an ex-post facto design, through which the design and implementation of the program were contrasted with those of the GoK's revolving loan fund, to highlight best practices in the design and implementation of poverty alleviation programs (Lukwata et al., 2012). Data were collected from managers and beneficiaries of the two programs and from relevant documentary sources.

The findings were that Caritas' program has been successful because: (1) it identifies the very poor through a participatory approach and limits its interventions to them; (2) involves participatory needs assessment and beneficiary capacity building; and (3) its interventions are tailored to individual beneficiaries' felt needs and resources (Table 1).

Table 1: Attributes of Caritas' Self-Help Program and GoK's Revolving Loan Fund

Attribute	Caritas Self-Help Program	GoK Revolving Loan Fund
Focus	• Poorest people as identified by local community and verified by Caritas field staff	• All interested persons
Gender	• Women	• Men and women
Scope of activities	• Participants' priority needs	• Enterprise development
Funding	• Participants' savings	• GoK
Organization	• Informal, with rotational leadership	• Formal, with more permanent leadership
Management	• Participants, guided by their chosen management structure and Caritas field staff	• Relevant local government and commercial intermediary
Rules and Regulations	• Guidelines agreed upon by participating persons and registered with relevant statutory authorities	• Central and local government laws governing loan program
Savings and repayment schedule	• Tailored to participants' needs and capacity	Standardized
Assessment	• Participatory assessment of resources and strengths at participants' disposal	• Feasibility evaluation of enterprise proposal
Capacity building	• Training in management of meetings, writing of bylaws, bookkeeping, conflict resolutions, savings mobilization, borrowing and loaning	• None

Source: Adapted from Lukwata et al. (2012).

Table 1 shows that Caritas' Self-Help program and GoK's revolving loan fund contrast in a way that the former is beneficiary-led. Caritas facilitates the poor participating in its development program to identify and prioritize their needs and to indentify and harness the resources (including social capital) at their disposal to meet these needs—a precursor to evolution of an effective loan mobilization, utilization, and recovery incentive system.

2.2 Nkozi Agribusiness and Training Association and Government of Uganda's Revolving Loan Fund

It is noteworthy that the conclusion from the study of Caritas' program corroborates evidence from a host of studies suggesting that interventions against poverty in whose design and implementation the poor play a prominent role tend to require significantly less financial investment and to be more effective than those that don't. For instance, CRS (2010) reports that Savings and Internal Lending Communities in East Africa have not only succeeded in banking traditionally unbanked poor people but also mobilized phenomenal savings that have been loaned out to these poor with impressive recovery rates. Incidentally, in a number of instances, these communities have prospered while more heavily capitalized government and commercial credit schemes are failing in the same communities. Table 2 presents an example from Uganda.

Table 2: Growth of Nkozi Agribusiness Training Association (2010–2012)

Year	Groups	Men	Women	Total Number of Members	Total Savings (UGX)	Value of Loans
2010	53	226	605	831	3,923,900	0
2011	92	524	1,300	1,824	117,043,950	90,414,700
2012	286	1,987	4,365	6,352	567,153,310	444,282,850

Source: Nkozi Agribusiness and Training Association.

Table 2 shows that from 53 groups, 831 members and UGX 3,923,900/= in 2010, Nkozi Agribusiness and Training Association, a member-based savings and internal lending community in a rural county of central Uganda, reached 6,352 people who generated a turnover of UGX 444,282,850/= albeit government of Uganda sponsored revolving loan schemes implemented in the area failed (see, e.g., Microfinance Support Centre, 2007; Mubiru, 2006; Ogwang, 2007).

3 Case for Poverty Alleviation Programs by the Poor

The main lesson from the study of the critical success factors in Caritas Kenya's Self-Help Program and Nkozi Agribusiness and Training Association is that involving the poor in the definition of poverty and in the designing and implementation of poverty alleviation programs could enhance the effectiveness, efficiency, and sustainability of the programs. The inference here is that efforts to alleviate poverty should prioritize poor-people-led poverty alleviation programs. This proposition and the findings of researches into stagnation in and mobility from poverty in Uganda and into poor people's perceptions of poverty and poverty alleviation programs in DRC, Mozambique, and Rwanda underscore a need for poverty alleviation programs by the poor.

3.1 Correlates of Stagnation in and Mobility from Poverty in Central Uganda

Study of the correlates of stagnation in and mobility from poverty in central Uganda addressed one main question: how come the poverty alleviation programs that are enabling some households in the region to transit from poverty are not working for the households stagnating in poverty? (Ssempebwa et al., 2012). The rationale underlying the question derives from the persistence of poverty in many households in the region despite decades of implementing a multiplicity of poverty reduction programs. Review of related literature indicated that: (1) the meaning, causes, and effects of poverty are not only diverse but also relative to context (in terms of both time and place); and (2) poverty in Uganda is linked to vulnerability, low levels of educational attainment, lack of income diversification, illness, regional imbalance, macroeconomic bottlenecks, dysfunctional social practices, political instability, insecurity, displacement, gender disparity, corruption, and indolence. The literature, including the country's poverty reduction strategy papers, affirmed that several governmental, private sector, charitable, civil society, religious, multinational, and diplomatic organizations are trying to address these factors and, at the household level, successive surveys have reported notable improvements in the quality of life (cf. Uganda Bureau of Statistics [UBOS], 2011). Notwithstanding, many households are still stagnating in poverty (Deininger and Okidi, 2003b; Lawson, McKay and Okidi, 2003; Johannes, 2005; UBOS, 2011). Why? In general, related literature links the stagnation to the causes of poverty enumerated above. Moreover, it has also been argued that the country creates more poverty (e.g., through war and bad governance) than it provides opportunities for transformation (cf. Collier, 2011). However, in a context where knowledge of the aforementioned causes of poverty has informed the design and implementation of interventions and some households are transiting from poverty despite the production of poverty at the macroeconomic level, these factors do not seem to satisfactorily account for the stagnation.

Accordingly, the study attempted to account for stagnation in and mobility from poverty in the country—trusting that, although stagnation despite implementation of poverty alleviation programs may not be surprising, accounting for it may enhance the effectiveness of the programs. Data were collected from a random sample of 323 households—drawn from various parts of the country—using a semi-structured questionnaire. The questionnaire was divided into three sections: household identification particulars; status of household (regarding wealth and poverty); and factors accounting for stagnation in or mobility from poverty. The questions on the status of the households were structured as a scorecard aimed at creating a dichotomy of households *transiting* from and *stagnating* in poverty. They touched on attributes of access to healthcare, education, assets, clean water, sanitation facilities, income, food security, land, and quality accommodation—because related literature identified them as key indicators of social status in the area. The third section touched on the respondents' view of wealth and poverty, the status of their households regarding the two, and the things to which they would attribute this status.

The respondents' scores on the household status scorecard were computed into an index codenamed "household welfare index." The households were categorized as rural, semi-urban, or urban, depending on the neighborhood where they were located. For each of the categories, the mean score on the household welfare index was established and the households were further categorized into transiting from and stagnating in poverty thus: household's score on index ≥ category mean score on household welfare index = transiting; and household's score on index < category mean score on household welfare index = stagnating (Table 3).

Table 3: Distribution of Households by Status

Neighbourhood	Transiting	Stagnating	Total
Rural	71	79	150
Semi-urban	53	58	111
Urban	40	22	62
Total	164	159	323

Source: Ssempebwa et al. (2012).

The respondents defined wealth mostly in terms of access to the basic requirements of life, income, and ownership of assets (Table 4).

Table 4: Meaning of Wealth (%)[1]

	Transiting			Stagnating		
	Rural	Semi-urban	Urban	Rural	Semi-urban	Urban
	n = 71	n = 53	n = 40	n = 79	n = 58	n = 22
Access to basics (food, shelter & bills)	59	42	33	40	39	64
Education	1	2	3	-	3	-
Good health	4	5	5	6	8	10
Income 1 (cash)	17	19	28	25	19	18
Income 2 (regular source)	15	13	18	9	7	5
Income 3 (diversified source)	3	9	5	3	7	27
Paid employment	4	8	8	9	10	9
Assets 1 (real estate)	30	36	40	29	43	55
Assets 2 (cars, phones, etc.)	15	17	3	8	10	5
Self-employment	-	-	8	3	7	9
Livestock	15	-	-	11	12	9
Social capital (children, relatives & friends)	3	-	3	1	5	5

Source: Ssempebwa et al. (2012).

However, notable differences were established between the respondents' and researchers' characterization of the statuses of the households (Table 5).

---

[1] Multiple responses elicited.

Table 5: Respondents' and Researchers' Characterization of Households' Status

	Respondents' characterization of their households	Rich	Neither rich nor poor	Poor	Total
Researchers' characterization of respondents' households	Transiting	38	51	69	158
	Stagnating	30	25	101	156
Total		68	76	170	314

Source: Ssempebwa et al. (2012).

The main difference between the respondents' and the researchers' characterization of the statuses of the households surveyed regarding wealth and poverty is that only a few of the respondents the researchers characterized as transiting from poverty concurred with the characterization and vice-versa. Sixty-nine (representing 43%) of the respondents the researchers' scorecard characterized as transiting from poverty characterized themselves as being poor while 30 (representing 19%) of the respondents the scorecard characterized as stagnating in poverty characterized themselves as being rich. In accounting for the status of their households, some of the respondents provided reasons for this disparity (Table 6).

Table 6: Reasons Transiting Households Cited for Feeling Poor and Stagnating Households Cited for feeling *Rich*

Thinking about wealth and poverty, where would you categorize your household among the two? Why?

Transiting Households	**Stagnating Households**
• In between [poverty and wealth] because there is still need for progress	• Wealthy because I have a job
• Middle class ... not yet there	• Wealthy because they have land
• Medium rich: transiting from poverty because the household head is working hard	• Not very poor not rich because [I am] healthy and can work ... [I] own a plot and a house
• Poor because [household heads] not in formal employment	• Moderate because gets food and shelter
• Poor household because [they] have no assets	• I am rich because I have life
	• I am wealthy because I am attending

- In between [poverty and wealth] because [the household is] working hard to deal with changes in the environment and prices
- [A] Poor household because a lot more is still desired
- Middle class because [even if they] have achieved some things, more is yet to be achieved
- ...in the middle because [they] still need *other* things
- Poor [because] they have no car and animals [livestock]
- Medium: I can't meet all my needs however I try to meet some [of the] needs
- Midway between wealth and poverty because in as much as I am able to provide for my family, I am not very wealthy in terms of assets
- I am moving toward riches because I have food, medical care, can pay [school] fees for my children ... I am thinking of buying more land and I have a job so I am working
- In between [poverty and wealth] because I can afford most of the daily needs though I still find difficult in getting others [but] I am self-employed and hard working
- In between wealth and poverty ... though I have not invested much, I am able to attend to my family's needs and [I am] doing some investments
- Poor because we lack a farm and [my] wife is not working
- school
- I am in between the two because I can look after my family
- Not poor because [I] can afford food, rent, etc.
- [We are] wealthy because we have a plot [of land]
- Rich because can self support [sic]
- Wealthy because [he is] working
- Wealthy because owns a house and plot [of land]
- Middle class because can meet the basic needs
- Rich because we can meet all [basic] our needs
- At least I own a house; I do not consider myself poor
- Rich because [I am] not renting
- I am wealthy because I have developed good ideas through training
- Rich because we are healthy
- Rich because they can afford their needs
- Wealthy because [they] have land for cultivation
- Wealthy because is hard working
- Wealthy because I am living [sic]

Source: Ssempebwa et al. (2012).

The respondents who characterized their households as transiting from poverty cited 12 factors for the transition (Table 7).

Table 7: Correlates of Transition from and Stagnation in Poverty[2]

S/N	Reasons for upward mobility	n	%[3]	Reasons for stagnation	n	%[4]
1	Education*	12	7	Low level/ lack of educational attainment	5	3
2	Gainful employment*	29	18	Un/underemployment	43	27
3	Inheritance*	11	7	Inherited syndrome of disadvantage	3	2
4	Access to markets*	32	20	Lack of market	27	17
5	Frugality*	54	33	High [consumption] expenditure	58	36
6	Access to productive resources*	37	23	Lack of capital (money, land, etc.)	120	75
7	Social capital*	44	27	Social and political exclusion	16	10
8	Good health*	8	5	Sickness	33	21
9	Hard work	116	71	Livestock diseases**	24	15
10	Serendipity	11	7	Bereavement**	8	5
11	Mobility	5	3	Taxes**	35	22
12	Remittances	22	13	Climate change**	66	42
13				Poor overhead infrastructure**	44	28
14				Inflation**	51	32

*Contrasts condition of households stagnating in poverty.
**Applicable to households transiting from poverty.
Source: Ssempebwa et al. (2012).

Eight of these factors are traditionally known to be positively related with mobility from poverty. Indeed, eight of the factors the respondents who characterized their households as poor or *stagnating* in poverty cited for the stagnation of their households contrasted the factors direct-

---

[2] Multiple responses were elicited.
[3] Calculated as a percentage of 164 (number of households in transiting category).
[4] Calculated as a percentage of 159 (number of households in stagnating category).

ly. However, five of the factors cited by the households in the *stagnating* category, namely, livestock diseases, bereavement, taxes, climate change, poor overhead infrastructure, and inflation, are also applicable to the households in the *transiting* category. The finding that majority (71%) of the respondents in the *transiting* category cited "hard work" (described in terms of resilience, diligence, innovativeness, and diversification) for the status of their households suggests that the households work hard to overcome these impediments. The "hard work" appears to be supported by the households' members' educational attainment, involvement in gainful employment, inheritance, access to markets, frugality, access to productive resources, social capital, good health, serendipity, mobility, and remittances. However, the finding that majority of the respondents from these households expressed discontentment with the households' statuses (Table 5) gives credence to the view that although their hard work is supported by these factors, they work hard because they are not contented with their situation (Table 6). Conversely, the stagnating households' syndrome of disadvantage is compounded by their contentment with their status (Table 5).

Accordingly, this study demonstrates a basic point: despite their indisputable challenges, many of the *stagnating* households are stagnating because they are contented with their situation. This position appears to corroborate Bird and Shinyekwa's (2005) view that some people stagnate in poverty because they are indolent albeit superficially. Although the finding that households stagnating in poverty were contented with the statuses of their households suggests that these households are complacent, it is the researchers' scorecard that characterized them as stagnating in poverty. Incidentally, there were disparities between the attributes of this scorecard (i.e. access to healthcare, education, asset ownership, quality of water and sanitation, income, food security and dwelling) and some of the things respondents in the *stagnating* category characterized as wealth (e.g., children). It is also notable that these respondents did not simply characterize their households as well-off (cf. Table 5); they possessed the things that they characterized as wealth (Table 6). Although this does not does not necessarily make them well-off, the disparity between their characterization of poverty and the *conventional* characterization of poverty has an implication for the methodology of poverty reduction strategies in the country. In as much as the production of poverty and wealth is rooted in the material production of society and has objective indicators, those fighting to alleviate poverty need to synchronize their definition of these indicators with that of the poor whose transition from poverty they are trying to facilitate. Conversely, review of related literature indicates that the poverty alleviation programs that have been implemented in Uganda focused on attributes of poverty/wealth that are similar to those in the researchers' scorecard—analogous to fixing square pegs in round holes. This appears to account for the *failure* of these programs to positively transform the stagnating households. The finding that the *stagnating* households had access to the things they considered to constitute wealth suggests that the poor are able to pursue and achieve wealth the way they know it. Thus, closing the gap between their perception of development and that of development planners/ practitioners, with the result that the poor perceive development the way those promoting it perceive it, could enhance the effectiveness of poverty alleviation programs in enhancing social transformation. This view is in concurrence with the conclusions from the study of the critical success factors in Caritas Kenya's Self-Help program and aspects of related studies conducted in DRC, Mozambique, and Rwanda.

3.2 Evidence from DRC, Mozambique, and Rwanda

Teams of researchers based at Université Catholique de Graben (DRC), Universidade Catholica do Mocambique (Mozambique), and Universite Catholique de Kabgayi (Rwanda) surveyed the perceptions poor people in their countries hold about their poverty and needs and related their findings to relevant poverty alleviation programs—to account for the performance of the programs. The teams made three common findings that support the case for poor-people-led poverty alleviation programs. As in Uganda, each of the research teams found ostensibly poor people but who felt that they were not poor. Secondly, sizeable proportions of the participants who admitted to being poor indicated that they are endowed with valuable resources, notwithstanding their poverty. Ironically, however, the teams also found that many of the poverty alleviation programs identified in the study areas neither disaggregated the poor by their perception of their poverty nor exploited the resources the poor believed themselves to possess to the poor's advantage, which appears to account for the ineffectiveness of the programs in enhancing social transformation.

4 Implication for the Political Economy of Poverty in the Global South

The foregoing discussion suggests that poverty alleviation programs are more effective if they involve the poor in defining poverty, assessing their needs and in designing and implementing poverty alleviation programs. This proposition rhymes well with literature underscoring the need to contextualize poverty (e.g., Harvey and Reed, 1992; Hashemi, Schuler and Riley, 1996; UMU, 2009; UMU, 2010). Conversely, observable practice in many large-scale poverty alleviation programs (mainly by governments and multilateral development organizations) in Sub-Saharan Africa is at variance with the proposition. This appears to explain the persistence of poverty in the region despite investment of colossal financial resources in a multiplicity of poverty alleviation programs (cf. Collier, 2007; Moyo, 2009). This being the case, it is recommended that organizations working to alleviate poverty from the region elicit and integrate the input of the poor into the design and implementation of poverty alleviation programs. This will not only ensure that poverty alleviation projects/programs reach the people they are intended to reach but also that they do so in an effective, cost-effective, and sustainable way.

5 Acknowledgment

We gratefully acknowledge the financial, administrative, and technical support of the Centre for Coordination of Research (CCR) of the International Federation of Catholic Universities (IFCU). We also acknowledge feedback, and support, received from colleagues at the Catholic University of Eastern Africa, Universidade Catholica do Moçambique, Université Catholique de Graben, and Université Catholique de Kabgayi within the framework of the research project, "The Path of Development: African Catholic Universities and the Challenges of Poverty". We also thank Professor Mariano Féliz for reviewing and commenting on an earlier draft of this chapter. We also acknowledge, with thanks, the comments and suggestions of participants at the Comparative Research on Poverty (CROP) workshop on the Political Economy of Poverty and Social Transformations of the Global South (Cairo, Egypt—December 10-12, 2012). Finally, we gratefully acknowledge the financial and administrative support of CROP and the American University in Cairo, which enabled us to participate in the workshop.

Disclaimer

We wish to affirm that the views expressed in this article are ours and do not necessarily reflect the views of the International Federation of Catholic Universities (IFCU), CROP, the American University in Cairo or their partners

References

Abuka, C. A., Ego, M. A., Opolot, J., Okello, P. (2007) Determinants of poverty vulnerability in Uganda, Institute for International Integration Studies (IIIS) Discussion Paper Number 203, IIIS, Dublin.

Ayako, A. B., Katumanga, M. (1997) Review of Poverty in Kenya: Report prepared for ActionAid-Kenya and the Institute of Policy Analysis and Research (IPAR), IPAR, Nairobi.

Bansikiza, C. (2007) Responding to poverty in Africa, AMECEA Publications, Eldoret.

Bird, K., Hulme, D., Moore, K., Shepherd, A. (2003) Chronic poverty and remote rural areas, CPRC working paper Number 13, Chronic Poverty Research Centre, Manchester.

Bird, K., Shinyekwa, I. (2005) "Even the 'rich' are vulnerable: multiple shocks and downward mobility in rural Uganda," Development policy review, Vol. XXIII, No 1.

Centre for Governance and Development (2007) National Devolved Funds Report: Institutional Structures and Procedures, Research Report 3, Centre for Governance and Development, Nairobi.

Collier, P. (2007). The Bottom Billion: Why the Poorest Countries are Failing and What Can Be Done About It, Oxford University Press, Oxford.

Collier, P. (2011). Wars, Guns and Votes: Democracy in Dangerous Places, Random House, New York.
Crook, C. R. (2000) "Decentralisation and poverty reduction in Africa: Determinants of relative poverty in advanced capitalist democracies," American Sociological Review, Vol. LVIII, No. 3.
CRS (2010) Savings and Internal Lending Communities (SILC): field agent guide, CRS, Kampala.
Daxbacher, L. (2004) The poverty and social impact analysis (PSIA) pilot study in Uganda, DFID, Kampala.
Deininger, K., Okidi, J. (2003a) "Rural households: incomes, productivity and nonfarm enterprises," in Reinikka, R., Collier, P. (eds) Uganda's recovery: the role of farms, firms and government, Fountain Publishers, Kampala.
Deininger, K., Okidi, J. (2003b) "Growth and Poverty Reduction in Uganda, 1999–2000: Panel Data Evidence," Development Policy Review, Vol. XXI, No. 4.
Dorr, D. (1992) Option for the poor: a hundred years of Catholic Social Thought. Orbis, New York.
Due, J. M., Kurwijila, R., Aleke-Dondo, C., Kogo, K. (1990) "Funding Small-Scale Enterprises for African Women: Case Studies in Kenya, Malawi and Tanzania," African Development Review, Vol. II, No. 2.
Ellis, F., Bahiigwa, G. (2001) Livelihoods and Rural Poverty Reduction in Uganda, World Development, Vol. XXXI, No. 6.
GoK (2007) Kenya Vision 2030. GoK, Nairobi.
Harvey, L. D., Reed, M. (1992) "Paradigms of Poverty: a Critical Assessment of Contemporary Perspectives," International Journal of Politics, Culture and Society, Vol. VI, No. 2.
Hashemi, S. M., Schuler, S. R., Riley, A. P. (1996) "Rural Credit Programs and Women's Empowerment in Bangladesh," World Development, Vol. XXIV, No. 4.
Johannes, G. H. (2005) "Measuring Welfare for Small but Vulnerable Groups: Poverty and Disability in Uganda," Journal of African Economics, Vol. XIV, No. 4.
Johnson, S. (2004) "The impact of microfinance institutions in local financial markets: a case study from Kenya," Journal of International Development, Vol. XVI.

Kisekka, J. (2011) "A reflection on the concept of development: implications for Africa," in Lutz, D. W., Shimiyu, P. M., Osengo, G. N. (eds) Rethinking integral development in Africa, Consolata Institute of Philosophy Press, Nairobi.

Lawson, D., McKay, A., Okidi, J. (2003) Poverty persistence and transitions in Uganda: a combined qualitative and quantitative analysis. Chronic Poverty Research Centre (CPRC). Working Paper No. 38, University of Manchester, Manchester.

Lukwata, J., Ogula, P. A., Ryan, P., Ayako, A., Wakah, G., Onsongo, J. (2012) An Assessment of Kenya Government's Revolving Loan Funds Programmes and Catholic Church's Self-Help Group Approach Projects, Unpublished research report, Catholic University of Eastern Africa, Nairobi.

Mehrotra, S. K., Delamonica, E. (2007) Eliminating human poverty: macroeconomic and social policies for equitable growth, Zed Books, London.

Microfinance Support Centre (2007) Organisation's strategic mid review for the period 2005–2009. Microfinance Support Centre, Kampala.

MoFPED (2001) Uganda Poverty Status Report (2001), MoFPED, Kampala.

MoGLSD (2003) The social development sector strategic investment plan (SDIP) 2003–2008: integrating human progress with economic growth for sustainable development, MoFPED, Kampala.

Moyo, D. (2009) Dead aid: why aid is not working and how there is a better way for Africa, Farrar, Straus and Giroux, New York.

Mubiru, A. (2006) "Sh10 Billion Entandikwa Loans Still Unpaid," The New Vision, July 22, 2006. In <http://allafrica.com/stories/200607 240708.html>accessed October 12, 2012.

Muhumuza, W. (2007) Credit and reduction of poverty in Uganda: structural adjustment reforms in context, Fountain Publishers, Kampala.

Mukui, J. T. (2005) Poverty Analysis in Kenya: Ten Years on, Central Bureau of Statistics, Nairobi.

Murori, M. (2010) Linking up and reaching out, <http://www.caritasnairobi.org/index.php?option=com_content&view=article&id=1142:linking-up-and-reaching-out&catid=101:self-help&Itemid=291> accessed October 22, 2012.

Nduhukhire-Owa-Mataze (1999) "Africa: a continent exiting and entering a century in a sickbay. Part one: Africa's development paralysis," Mtafiti Mwafrika. Number 3 UMU, Kampala.

Office of the Deputy Prime Minister and Ministry of Finance (2011) Statement on the MSE Fund: Fund for Financial Inclusion of the Informal Sector, Office of the Deputy Prime Minister and Ministry of Finance, Nairobi.

Ogwang, J. (2007) "Government to probe entandikwa losses," The New Vision, August 19, 2007.<http://www.newvision.co.ug/D/8/19/582192> accessed August 4, 2012.

Ssempebwa, J., et al. (2012) "Overcoming Poverty: Accounting for Stagnation and Upward Mobility in Central Uganda," East African Researcher, Vol. II, No. 2.

Stevenson, L., St-Onge, A. (2005) Support for Growth-Oriented Women Entrepreneurs in Kenya, International Labour Organisation, Geneva.

UBOS (2011) Uganda Demographic and Health Survey, 2011, UBOS, Kampala.

UMU (2009) Nnindye Baseline Assessment Study. Unpublished project report, UMU, Kampala.

UMU (2010) A multidisciplinary, cross-culture and participatory understanding of community needs in Uganda, Unpublished research report, UMU, Kampala.

Chapter 6
SCOPE AND USEFULNESS OF "RIGHT TO INFORMATION" AS ANTI-POVERTY TOOL: THE BANGLADESH EXPERIENCE

Kazi Nurmohammad Hossainul Haque

Kazi Haque undertakes a general overview of the history of Right to Information (RTI) policies in Bangladesh at the same time as he focuses his scholarly attention upon a series of case studies which emphasize both the potential and limitations of RTI as a strategy for both empowering those living in poverty and facilitating their attempts to emerge from such crippling circumstances socially and economically. The information provided does point to the power which RTI programs can furnish to those who seek to demand accountability from those in positions of authority at the local, state, and even national level. At the same time, however, Haque effectively indicates the explicit problems caused in the effective implementation of the program and the realization of its benefits due to the persistence of profoundly institutionalized corruption at numerous sociopolitical levels as well as the lack of adequate education and awareness as to the nature and extent of the program.

1 Introduction

Poverty is a multidimensional human state that has various manifestations. Keeping pace with changing scenarios of poverty in specific contexts, concepts of poverty and strategies to address it have also changed accordingly. Academic thinking related to poverty, which has in some cases had a relevant impact on political thought and policy articulation, has travelled from the decided "narrowness" of what has come to be known as the Basic Needs Approach (see Streeten et al. 1981) to what is frequently referred to as the Capabilities Approach (see Sen, 1985, 1988) which, by many estimates, the present authors included, is a great deal broader in scope and much more flexible in its potential foci. In a related and even analogous manner, anti-poverty strategies have also registered a significant shift: moving from the "needs" orientation (commonly referred to as the Needs Based Approach) and focusing increasing attention on what has come to be labeled the "rights" orientation (Rights Based Approach) in academic and policy discourses. Taking into consideration all of these changes and the increasingly fluid nature of poverty studies in the second decade of the twenty-first century it just may be possible that some time in the foreseeable future we will witness the creation and evolution of something akin to a market-based approach to fighting poverty. According to certain scholars these tendencies feed into at the same time as they respond to the rising tide of a neoliberal revival of sorts which holds as a crucial tenet the centrality of deficit reduction in addressing financial crises throughout the globe, the majority of which are, apparently, taking place in the southern hemisphere (See Watson, 2012).

As a manifestation of rights-based anti-poverty strategies, poverty has increasingly begun to be treated as an essential component of good governance and the promotion of social progress and welfare. This is a radical departure from previous strategies which emphasized to a great extent the overbearing necessity to eliminate or at the very least reduce poverty through the combined intervention of branches of government in the affected areas together with oversight and assistance carried out by representatives of both northern and southern NGOs who are capable of acting with the direct and active support of western donors. In the present investigation we wish to express a lingering uncertainty as to whether or not those anti-poverty strategies which have been undertaken so far have succeeded in eliminating or reducing levels of poverty in those areas where such policies have been initiated. Based upon the evidence which will be analyzed and synthesized, here it seems possible if not likely that in many significant cases these governmental and otherwise official actions have actually (re)produced poverty rather than realizing the goals which they are ostensibly attempting to achieve. If this is indeed the case, then such strategies that have supposedly formed part of the implementation of good governance and progressive development agendas are also suspect and should be reevaluated and carefully investigated in order to ascertain their true natures. In spite of these decidedly problematic aspects of these initiatives historically and in present contexts, the volume of good governance-related anti-poverty strategies is growing continuously with new tools-techniques lining up behind the old ones and vying for an opportunity to cut their teeth on the grim reality of poverty in those communities which are (un)fortunate enough to be considered viable test cases and recipients of these treatments. RTI, among this endlessly proliferating constellation of tools and techniques, is increasingly projected by NGOs as an effective anti-poverty innovation particularly in the contexts of Global South and transition countries where such knowledge might not otherwise be readily available to those disenfranchised members of the society who are largely excluded from centers of power and influence. RTI is often emphasized by development practitioners as a means through which the empowerment of the poorer and marginalized sections of society may be realized. Such a new found status of strength, so the argument goes, is realized by securing these individuals' and communities' access to crucial public services. This capacity to retrieve essential knowledge will, it is felt, result directly in an increased scope being made available to these people which will in turn allow them to graduate out of poverty (MJF, 2011). Despite the seemingly idyllic nature of these propositions and the manner in which they are formulated, sounding as they do rather like the panacea which is capable of painlessly and immediately bringing about the termination of poverty as we know it, RTI literature, the overwhelming bulk of which is technocratic in nature, tends to concentrate on the possibility and application of these policies in areas which include promoting democratic participation, exposing corruption and fostering accountability: all of which might be considered relevant but secondary factors in poverty treatment and reduction.

Therefore, as a result of and in careful consideration of the complex and difficult circumstances in which RTI has been thrust both theoretically and practically, this chapter attempts to adequately respond to two major research questions. In the case of the first, it is our intention to investigate in what manner precisely RTI can contribute toward working in conjunction with the lived experiences and enduring legacies of poverties in those areas most intensely affected by it. The second issue is to assess the real, concrete usefulness of RTI as an anti-poverty tool in the specific contexts which are under consideration here. In order to contextualize and respond to these rather complex research agendas, this study will be based upon an evaluation of eight micro case studies wherein we can observe and begin to understand the exercising of RTI by (and supposedly for the benefit of) persons and communities who are living in conditions of poverty. The topics of the case studies here are generally concerned with government services which are commonly thought to be those which are the most useful for the rural poor of Bangladesh. These are primarily social safety net programs, agricultural supply systems, maternal health care services, and processes through which *khas* land is allocated and utilized. The cases feature women, men, and groups which are comprised of individuals of both genders. We have chosen to limit the scope of our case studies to those emanating from Bangladeshi contexts for at least three salient reasons. First of all, Bangladesh is at present one of the poorest countries in the world according to various means of evaluating poverty. At the same time, however, the country as a whole has made some impressive gains in poverty reduction over the last two decades and has also had some relevant and noteworthy successes, specifically as in the case of the anti-poverty innovation of microcredit which Bangladesh has been instrumental in developing and therefore giving to the world as a whole. In second place, the country has introduced the RTI Act (RTIA) and has been, on the surface at least, aggressively promoting its implementation for a number of years now. It is also worthy of mention that this decision was made in large part as the result of a civil society advocacy movement. One of the major selling points of the movement, which allowed it to gain such momentum and achieve such results, was the compelling idea that RTI would enhance poverty alleviation by further empowering the poor to exercise their rights. With the third year of the RTIA's implementation, it will be good to see how far the law has been capable of living up to its fame as a viable anti-poverty tool. Thirdly, the present researcher is most familiar with the conditions of Bangladesh as it is his home country and he has been observing its RTI developments for the last two years, a period considered adequate for the analysis and assessment of such policies. The chapter's main line of argument is centered upon the idea that RTI is much more likely to become an effective anti-poverty tool should steps be carried out to ensure that poor people can adopt it with full ownership and empowerment. This is not the case if RTI remains closely linked to the participation of such groups in limited and limiting NGO projects.

The chapter is composed of six major sections including this introduction. The core discussion of the chapter starts in the second section where we begin our investigation by exploring the conceptual foundations of the right to information as anti-poverty tool. This analysis will be realized by drawing in large part upon the capabilities approach originally elaborated by Sen (1980, 1985a, 1985b, 1993, 1999) and by taking into consideration the human rights approach to poverty (Hunt, Osmani and Nowak, 2002; Sen, 2004, 2005). The third and fourth sections are designed to shed light on the complex realities behind poverty and RTI scenarios of Bangladesh in the period under consideration. Section 5 analyzes the case studies of RTI application by poor and marginalized peoples in line with the research questions which have been stated above. Finally, the chapter draws its synthetic conclusions based upon these theoretical and practical bases of knowledge.

2 Right to Information as Anti-Poverty Tool: Conceptual Foundations

The idea of RTI is originally not associated with poverty and its association with human rights is also a more recent phenomenon than one might think. RTI as a social imperative emerged in the eighteenth century in Scandinavian countries and started gathering pace in the post-World War II era. As early as 1766, the joint parliament of Sweden and Finland (at that time both of these now distinct entities constituted parts of Swedish Empire) passed the Access to Public Records Act that is commonly regarded as the first RTI law in history. In 1946, the United Nations General Assembly in its very first session adopted Resolution 59(I) that states, "Freedom of Information is a fundamental human right and [...] the touchstone of all the freedoms to which the UN is consecrated." Article 19 of the Universal Declaration of Human Rights (UDHR) further strongly recognized the right to information as an essential part of the fundamental right to freedom of expression.[1] This was reiterated

---

[1] UDHR Article 19: "Everyone has the right to freedom of opinion and expression; this right includes freedom to hold opinions without interference and to seek, receive and impart information and ideas through any media and regardless of frontiers."

in Article 19 (2) of the International Covenant of Civil and Political Rights (ICCPR) in 1966.[2]

While information as a right was considered to be crucial for the articulation of the human rights project as a whole, the concept of inalienable human rights was at that time being increasingly regarded as central to emerging fields of development thinking including attempts at a more profound understanding of the nature and causes of poverty in multiple circumstances. The recognition of this phenomenon comes from Sen (2004: 315) as he observed that:

> Few concepts are as frequently invoked in contemporary political discussions as human rights. There is something deeply attractive in the idea that every person anywhere in the world, irrespective of citizenship or territorial legislation, has some basic rights, which others should respect. The moral appeal of human rights has been used for a variety of purposes, from resisting torture and arbitrary incarceration to demanding the end of hunger and of medical neglect.

Sen (1980, 1985a, 1985b) has pioneered research agendas focusing upon and drawing inspiration from human rights, subsequently applying such ideas in economic thinking by emphasizing the importance of developing human capabilities as opposed to economic growth as the core motivator in the amelioration of situations of poverty globally. The human capabilities concept or the capabilities approach stipulates that human life needs to be considered as a combination of various doings and beings. These are various forms of functioning that range from elementary ones such as the necessity of one's being well-nourished and disease-free extending on up into more complex necessities which might be seen to include such needs as that of having self-respect and participating adequately in community life. The capability of a person refers to the various combinations of functions that a person can choose to have

---

[2] UDHR Article 19 (2): "Everyone shall have the right to freedom of expression; this right shall include freedom to seek, receive and impart information of all kinds, regardless of frontiers, either orally, in writing or in print, in the form of art or through any media of his choice."

or, in other words, the freedom that a person has to choose the kind of life which they desire (Nussbaum and Sen, 1993: 3).

It is this centrality of *freedom* that provides one of the core concepts deployed in order to connect human rights and human capabilities concepts. This is what Sen (2005: 152, 155) is referring to when he points out that "(t)he concepts of human rights and human capabilities have something of a common motivation." This is a point that he later elaborates upon, explaining that, "human rights are best seen as right to certain specific freedoms (and) capabilities can be seen broadly, as freedoms of particular kind." He also equates terrible deprivations with the lack of freedom as demonstrated through an individual's capacity to escape destitution. He argues that people remain poor not only due to indolence and inactivity, as highlighted in numerous examples which might be culled from previous literature on poverty, but also because of a lack of alternative possibilities which are in fact reproduced through social institutions which continue to limit the freedoms of those who are forced to live with poverty.

In laying the guidelines of what has now come to be commonly referred to as the human rights approach to poverty reduction, Hunt, Osmani, and Nowak (2002) found there to be a nearly perfect consistence between this method and the capabilities approach to poverty just mentioned. They heartily accepted and in certain ways adopted the definition of poverty forwarded by those scholars working within the trajectories defined by the capabilities approach such as the absence or inadequate realization of certain basic freedoms often due to a marked lack of access to resources, both economic and political. They have also demonstrated a shared concern with the crucial importance of basic freedoms as the fundamentals of minimal human dignity in conceptualizing poverty.

What ultimately took shape as the result of the work of Hunt, Osmani, and Nowak (2002) is a document entitled "Human Rights and Poverty Reduction: A Conceptual Framework" of the Office of the United Nations High Commissioner for Human Rights (OHCHR). This publication asserts that a human rights approach to poverty reduction stipulates that those measures intended to reduce poverty and reestablish adequate social participation and status should be perceived and treated as an obligation rather than the piecemeal manifestation of sporadic impulses which find their beginning and end in the instability and insufficiency of welfare or charity as carried out in many societies. The main features of this newly defined obligatory systematic policy of poverty reduction include empowerment of the poor, explicit recognition of the national and international human rights normative frameworks, accountability, nondiscrimination and equality, participation, and other human rights (OHCHR, 2004: iv, 13–20).

The new direction in conceptualizing poverty brought to light and explained by the capabilities approach was widely disseminated and fed into a programmatic level of activity through the UN's human rights approach to poverty reduction. Backed by a comprehensive and dynamic understanding of poverty which is based upon the capabilities approach, there was scope for wider strategies, and the development of tools and techniques to be used to attack poverty. Thus, the availability of and access to information in the form of entitlement and rights discourse was also given priority as part of "other human rights of particular importance to poverty reduction strategies (OHCHR, 2004: 20)." Without securing the right to information, poor people will not be empowered; they will be unable to demand accountability and secure participation in any meaningful way. RTI is therefore one among other human rights (that I would like to term as fourth-generation human rights) which takes its place beside what are considered to be more fundamental civil and political rights (first-generation human rights); economic, social, and cultural rights (second-generation human rights); and, third-generation human rights as women's rights, children's rights, minority rights, indigenous peoples' rights, rights of the peoples with disabilities, and so on.

3 The Poverty Situation in Bangladesh

The economic growth of Bangladesh has been accelerating over the last few decades. From the low growth rates which were recorded up to the 1980s, ranging between 3% and 4%, the growth rate has accelerated to 5–6% or higher during the current decade. The country has even successfully managed to steer its way through the last global financial crisis since it has continued to attain the 6.7% growth target in the Financial

Year (FY) 2011–2012 supported by a strong rebound in exports and the consequent expansion of the manufacturing sector (GOB, 2012).

The poverty rate is gradually decreasing in Bangladesh but absolute poverty is increasing with population growth. The recent Household and Income Expenditure Survey (HIES) has shown that while the poverty reduction rate was 8.9% in 2000–2005, poverty reduction was less in 2005–2010, being registered at 8.5%. The size of the country's poor population declined to 31.5% of the population as a whole in 2010. The upper poverty line in rural areas stood at 35.2% in 2010 against 43.8% in 2005, while in the urban areas it was 21.3% in 2010 against 28.4% in 2005. For the previous two decades of 1991–2010, the country's poverty level dropped by 25.2%. Moreover, the poverty gap decreased to 6.5% in 2010 from 9% in 2005 which even surpasses the MDG target of 8% by 2015. While the head of the Bangladesh Bureau of Statistics (BBS) saw this as close to achieving the MDG by nearly halving the poverty incidence by 2015,[3] Unnayan Onneshon, a nongovernment think tank, was skeptical about such a positive assessment. Their report of the country's poverty reduction claims that the average poverty reduction was 2.46% during 1991–2010. They argue that if the poverty reduction rate does not accelerate, then it is likely that the share of the poor as a part of the national population will still be sizable in 2021, at 22.9% (Unnayan Onneshan, 2012).

In many indicators of poverty reduction set under MDGs, which include such factors as life expectancy at birth, infant and child mortality rates, containing the spread and fatality of malaria and tuberculosis, populations having access to drinking water and sanitation, adult literacy rates, and the expansion of primary and secondary education with gender parity, there have been considerable improvements. However, the absolute values of many of the indicators are still high, indicating an enduring legacy of poverty-related problems on large and small scales. Household income for all groups has improved, though the distribution has become more unequal nonetheless.

---

[3] Quoted in *The Financial Express* report titled "Poverty level declines to 31.5pc in 5 years: BBS" published in March 20, 2012.

4 RTI Situation in Bangladesh

An RTI law compels Government Organizations (GOs) as well as other entities as stipulated under its provisions to disclose information of public interest to common citizens. The idea behind these laws is that by accessing and utilizing such information citizens will be able to claim their rightful entitlements from the government and other authorities responsible while making these figures of power more transparent in their actions and more accountable to their citizens and constituencies. By adopting the Right to Information Act 2009, Bangladesh joined 90 other countries in the world that have enacted similar laws to entitle their citizens to exercise their right to information legally and rapidly. The Bangladesh RTIA includes within its purview both GOs and NGOs who use foreign/public funds to carry out their projects.

RTIA begins with a preamble that discusses core constitutional and legal principles underlying the law and a set of concerned definitions. Article 2(g) of the laws defines "right to information" as the right to obtain information from any authority. Article 2(b) gives a detailed classification of such authorities from whom information is to be obtained. Article 2(d) describes information providing units. Articles 4–9 have elaborate provisions for right to, preservation of, publication of and access to information including how to file a request for information and the precise procedures for providing such information. Article 10 of the law stipulates the establishment of designated officers of the information providing units for providing information. Articles 11–23 constitute detailed provisions pertaining to the establishment, financial matters, and officers and employees of information commissions. Articles 24–29 are concerned with those remedies and recourses to be sought under the law when such directives mentioned above are not adequately carried out.

Based on the powers vested in government under Article 33 of RTIA, Right to Information Rules, 2009 was introduced into law on 1 November, 2009. This document lays down administrative procedures for receiving information request, providing information, appeal application, use of internet, information request fees, and information request forms. An Information Commission was established under Article 11 (1) of the Act and a three-member commission was appointed under Article 12. The current members of the Information Commission at the time of the composition of this investigation were: Professor Dr. Golam Rahman, Chief Information Commissioner (CIC), and Nepal Chandra Sarker and Professor Dr. Khurshida Begum Sayeed, Information Commissioners.

The RTI Rules 2009 stipulate a precise application form which is to be used in order to make information requests to designated officers of information providing units. The information requested should be provided to the applicant within the specific time unless that information falls under the provision of Section 7 (information that is not mandatory to provide).

According to the Annual Report, 2011 of the Information Commission, the total number of information requests made in 2011 using the prescribed form was 7,808. Among them, the GOs and the NGOs have received 7,671 (98%) and 137 (2%) applications respectively (Information Commission, 2012: 48). This is a decidedly paltry sum if we take into account the vast size of the country's population and their presumed information needs. There are thirty-six Information Providing Units (IPUs) of government in each upazilla or sub-district, the bottom administrative tier in the country's RTI infrastructure. These are thirty-six different government offices at the *upazilla* level that cover different public services. With 500 *upazillas* in total, there are at least 18,000 IPUs which are government run in the country. Given this information, the number of information requests made in 2011 does not even amount to one information request per each IPU of the government.

One study of the implementation of RTIA has attempted to explain this apparent lack of demand for information:

> There is [sic] no reasonable grounds for the law to be trusted and embraced by the people. As a result, very few people took the law seriously when it was enacted and those who came to know about it did not fully understand the real objectives of the law. As a result, very few applications for information, relevant to the objectives of the Act, were made by citizens to public authorities (RIB, 2011).

Despite such a miserably low demand, the supply side may sound buoyant from the highly responsive IPUs who have fielded the information requests. The Annual Report, 2011 of the Information Commission informs us that, out of all the 7,808 information requests, 7,616 (98%) of these requests have been met, 104 (1%) requests are pending and 88 (1%) have been discarded. But one independent study of RTI implementation was not so optimistic regarding these statistics. It observed that,

> Government officials too are not helping to improve the situation by their lack of awareness about or negative attitude to the law. Most of them are unaware about it, mainly because the Government has done little more than basic publicity about the law and its intents. Those that have heard about the law and sat through awareness-building exercises either did not understand it fully or accept it seriously (RIB, 2011).

5 RTI as Anti-Poverty Tool: Case Studies from Bangladesh

This chapter is now going to illustrate the scope and the usefulness of RTI as an anti-poverty tool through a set of micro case studies taken from throughout Bangladesh. These micro cases will be analyzed in the light of the conceptual foundation of RTI-poverty linkages based upon the capabilities approach and the human rights approach to poverty as discussed earlier. RTI presents anti-poverty potentials for various sections of the poor in a wide range of areas particularly in securing public services that are useful for the poor. The micro case studies discussed here are about the use of RTI with respect to such public services including social safety net programs, agriculture, land and health care. Instead of considering a few large and potentially high-profile case studies, this chapter attempts to make use of a handful of micro case studies in order to capture a broader understanding of the scopes and uses of RTI in fighting poverty.

5.1 Rezia Khatun Gets a VGD Card

Rezia Khatun was a 36-year-old widow who supported herself by begging. She had no valuable asset in the form of cultivable land except the small land holding on which her house was situated. At a certain point, she came into contact with Sabikunnahar, a fieldworker working with

NGO D.Net. As suggested by Sabikunnahar, Rezia joined the village group being organized at that time by D.Net. She learned about government social safety net programs such as that offered by Vulnerability Group Development (VGD) from the weekly awareness sessions of her group which she attended. As a result of this new found awareness she came to the decision that a VGD card would be helpful to her. She established contact with the local Union Parishad (UP) Chairman and filled out the appropriate forms in order to register her application for a VGD card. In spite of the fact that everything appeared to be in order the chairman turned down her application saying that there were no VGD cards left in the UP and that there would not be a single card available until the following financial year.

Rezia made up her mind to pursue the matter further and with Sabikunnahar's help she filed an information request and delivered it to the UP secretary under the RTIA. She requested the following information: how many VGD cards had been allotted to the UP that year, whether she was eligible for acquiring a VGD card or not, and how VGD cards were distributed. The UP Secretary complied with the RTI application and provided the information about the allotment of VGD cards, which showed that Rezia was in fact eligible to receive one. As a result, the UP Chairman was compelled to allot a VGD card to her. After receiving the VGD card, Rezia was able to stop begging and devote herself to other potentially more beneficial activities.

5.2 Shamima Akter Secures VGD Cards for Village Women

Shamima Akter is an 18-year-old high school student from a small village located in the Vimkhali Union of Jamalganj Upazilla in Sunamganj district in northeastern Bangladesh. She is also the local president of Ekota Youth Network, a youth group devoted to civic engagement and participatory local governance which cooperates and coordinates activities with the SHARIQUE project of INGO Intercooperation. As a part of these cooperative endeavors, the group members received training in RTI and learned about their rights from Intercooperation.

At the end of 2010, Shamima came to know that Upazilla administration was preparing a new list for VGD beneficiaries for the Financial Year (FY) 2011–2012. She also noticed that some extremely poor women living in her village who are eligible for VGD did not appear to be included on the beneficiary list. Perceiving this to be a discrepancy she filed an information request about the VGD list on January 2011 with the local UP Chairman who showed a marked reluctance to respond. Later that month, however, Shamima's information request came to notice of the concerned Upazilla Nirbahi Officer (UNO). He set up a committee to review the VGD list. As a result of these more meticulous revisions, several names that were not eligible for VGS cards were removed from the list and the names of four other women, who, in fact, were eligible, were included forthwith. The VGD selection committee, headed by the UNO, approved the report of the review committee as well as the revised list. On February 2011, Shamima finally received the revised list from the Union Parishad. Shamima and her group could then, as a result of the information which they received, verify if the beneficiaries selected were actually eligible according to the established criteria.

5.3 Jobeda Begum is Able to Maximize Benefits from Social Safety Net Programs

Jobeda Begum is a divorcee single mother of two children from a village located in the Bhalukagachchi Union of Putya Upazilla in Rajshahi District. In her search for an adequate livelihood, she came to know about different social safety net programs organized and implemented by the government in order to improve the lot of vulnerable peoples such as women, the poor, and the elderly. She also made contact with Samata Nari Kalyan Samity (SKNS), a local NGO. As a result, she participated in a training workshop on RTI given by SKNS. Jobeda was interested to know about government social safety net programs in her union. She submitted an information request to the secretary of the local UP attempting to gather more information regarding the number of social safety net programs in the area, who was going to benefit from these programs and the details of the procedures which needed to be followed in order to be included on the beneficiary list of the programs for the FY 2010–2011. The secretary provided her with all of the information which she had requested.

Jobeda shared the information with her fellow villagers. They noticed that some of the programs did not appear to be implemented properly according to the pertinent regulations. The villagers set up a Project Implementing Committee (PIC) to ensure a proper implementation of the safety net programs free from corruption and favoritism. Jobeda became one of the nine members of PIC. The committee prepared a list of twenty-one eligible beneficiaries who need to be included in the official beneficiaries list and submitted it to the UP. As the list was prepared through consultation, the UP accepted the list, and as a result, these names were eventually included in the official list. Union Parishad included everyone on the list and these people received different forms of livelihood support from government social safety net programs.

5.4 Rafiqul Islam Secures VGF Allocation

Rafiqul Islam is a farmer who resides in Cox's Bazar district in South East Bangladesh. He formerly ran a salt farm until 1991; that year he was unable to continue managing this business as a result of damage to his properties due to a severe cyclone. Since then, he has been working as a farmer. He also works on a voluntary basis providing social services to the poor. He started volunteering with the NGO Bangladesh Disaster Preparedness Centre (BDPC) in 2009 and learnt about RTI law while undergoing the NGO training program.

When he heard that the government was going to begin distributing rice in his union under the Vulnerable Group Feeding (VGF) scheme, he asked the Project Implementation Officer (PIO) of his Upazilla about the quantity of rice that each VGF card holder would receive. Despite the absolute legality of his request, the PIO initially denied him the information. Being conscious of his rights, Rafiq confronted the PIO asserting his right to know the requested information under RTIA. When he was faced with such incontrovertible facts, the PIO gave in and informed him that 10 kg rice was to be allocated per person within his union. During rice distribution, the UP Chairman advised those present that that 7 kg rice was to be allotted per person. Aware that this was not the correct amount, Rafiq immediately spoke up in protest informing this official that they already know that the allocation is 10 kg. The Chairman insisted that he would have to deduct 3 kg per person to reimburse transportation costs and other related expenses. But faced with people's protest, the Chairman was compelled to give at least 9.5 kg rice per person to those present.

5.5 Mosharef Hossain Majhi Secures Agricultural Supplies

Mosharef Hossain Majhi is a farmer from Barisal District in Southern Bangladesh. The Upazilla Agriculture Officer (UAO) of his home upazilla Banaripara runs the Integrated Pest Management (IPM) club and the Integrated Crop Management (ICM) Farmer's Field School through which pesticide equipments are distributed and farmers are trained in their use. UAO is supposed to allocate these services following specific procedures and guidelines that are not always followed properly. Mosharef learned about RTIA from local journalist Mizanul Islam who earlier attended a workshop on RTIA given by NU.

With the help of Mizan, Mosharef submitted an information request to the UAO in May of 2010. After consulting with his higher authorities, the UAO refused to deliver the requested information categorizing it as confidential in July, 2010. Mosharef then filed an official appeal against this decision of the UAO to the District Agriculture Officer (DAO) in September, 2010 but this official sustained the UAO's decision. Mosharef then appealed to the Deputy Director, Department of Agricultural Extension (DAE) of Barisal region who forwarded it to Additional Director General (DG). The latter also sustained the refusal of information. Finally, Mosharef lodged a formal complaint with the Information Commission (IC).

In March of 2011, the IC held a hearing with the UAO in order to investigate the reasons which had been utilized in order to deprive Mosharef of information and for labeling agriculture-related information as confidential. The Commission found nothing confidential in the requested information and instructed the UAO to provide the requested information by April, 2011. The IC also directed the higher authority of DAE to appear in the second hearing in order to respond to charges of giving misleading instructions.

5.6 Poor Women Get Access to Maternal Health Care

A landless organization associated with NGO Nijera Kori (NK) at Gangni upazilla of Meherpur district in western Bangladesh learned about irregularities in the allocation of cards under the Maternal Health Voucher scheme through which poor pregnant women are entitled to health services for a maximum amount of 8,000 Taka until the child is born. The group members heard from many poor expectant women resident in that locality that the maternal health voucher cards were mainly being distributed to the women of wealthy families. It additionally was brought to light that in the case of twenty poor women who were given the cards, each were charged 200 Taka by the health officials who distributed them. Four members of the landless organization jointly filed an information request to the Upazilla Health Officer (UHO) in July of 2010. They asked the following questions: How many cards are distributed monthly under the Safe Motherhood Health Voucher project? What are the criteria for selection of families for distribution of cards? Who is responsible for selecting the beneficiaries and distributing the cards? What are the benefits and services that card holders would get? What are the registration fees?

In reply to their information request, the applicants were only able to obtain partial information about the number of cards distributed. Instead of appealing against the nondelivery of information, they collected evidence of irregularities in the maternal health voucher project. In July of 2010, the landless organization staged a demonstration attended by 200 men and women, and submitted a memorandum signed by hundreds of people of the locality to the Civil Surgeon (CS), the senior most government health official of the district. They also sent copies of the memorandum to other government high officials in the locality and heads of local governments. The applicants of the landless organization also met with the Mayor of Meherpur town, Chairman of the Upazilla, and Upazilla Health Officer. As a result of these multiple actions, the CS launched an investigation into the allegations and found them to be true. The accused health official was transferred as a penalty. The CS disclosed detailed information about the "Maternal Health Voucher Scheme" including the profiles of the beneficiaries, beneficiary selection criteria, and procedures. The village people came together to identify potential local beneficiaries and proposed the names of twenty pregnant poor women who then received the health card.

5.7 Landless Peoples Secure Access to Land Records

While agriculture is an important sector of the Bangladesh economy, 65% of rural populations are still landless. An important aspect of land reform policy has been the acquisition and distribution of *khas* land, which is government-owned land that includes agricultural and nonagricultural land as well as water bodies. Out of the 3.3 million acres of khas land, only a small fraction has been distributed to the poor, who face problems in both obtaining and retaining the land. In fact, only 11.5% of the agricultural khas land is effectively owned by the landless poor.

On September 2010, a landless organization associated with NGO NK at Ramgati upazilla of Laxmipur district in southern Bangladesh sought information on *khas* land available in the locality and their distribution process. Riaz, a member of the landless organization, submitted an information request to the Assistant Land Officer (ALO) of his union. The ALO expressed his inability to provide the information and suggested to Riaz that he apply to the Assistant Commissioner (AC) Land at Upazilla Land Office instead. Riaz and over a hundred fellow members of the landless organization staged a demonstration in front of the Upazilla Land Office in November of 2010. The AC (Land) met with the group and promised to provide them with the requested information within the specified time as per RTIA should they apply by submitting an information request to him. After Riaz complied accordingly, he received photocopies of the information on December 2010. The information was then used to formulate the action plan of the landless organization.

5.8 Fishermen Win Access to Khas Water Body

Sonaidanga water reservoir of around 57 acres is a khas water body at Raiganj Upazilla in the northwestern district of Sirajganj. Despite the decidedly public nature of this water resource, a part of the Sonaidanga reservoir was illegally purchased by two influential local residents in the 1950s. In connivance with corrupt land officials, they modified the land record by recording the reservoir in their own name and even changed its classification from a water body to an agricultural land. As a result, the water reservoir lost its public categorization in the government land records and ordinary people were denied their access to this water resource. Moreover, the two illegal occupiers started to use the reservoir for commercial fishing, an activity which threatens to deplete and destroy the ecosystems surrounding the reservoir.

In 2007, the local landless organization associated with NK started an advocacy campaign in order to free Sonaidanga of illegal occupation and once again make it universally accessible. Following the formal legal introduction of RTIA, they filed an information request to the AC (Land) of the area on January 2011 requesting data related to records and letters related to the reservoir, and the topography and nature of the land below. The AC (Land) did not accept the application. He argued that the reservoir is the private property of the "illegal occupiers" and gave photocopies of the "false" record.

In this situation, the landless organization adopted strategies of both street agitation and fighting a concentrated legal battle to release the *khas* water body and annul the forged land records. Around 300 fishing families living along the banks of the Sonaidanga reservoir sent a memorandum to the Upazilla Nirbahi Officer (UNO) demanding the release of the *khas* land. The UNO investigated the case and submitted his findings to his superior, the Additional Deputy Commissioner (Revenue), who sent those documents to the Department of Land Records (DLR) in Dhaka for assessment. The findings of the investigation confirmed the complaints of the landless peoples that the land ownership record of the reservoir had been illegally changed. The landless organization also filed a case in the District Sub-Judge Court-2 against the illegal change in land records.

In the meantime, the illegal occupiers of the reservoir tried to turn it into a private fishing farm by installing bamboo enclosures that cut off common people's access to the water. The local people petitioned to the UNO to take steps against these actions and the local police were directed to act accordingly. The local police, however, did not undertake any action in order to rectify the situation. As a result of this inactivity on the part of the police, there was a protest of 400 men and women against the enclosures and police inaction. Then the landless organization themselves removed the bamboo enclosure. The illegal occupiers complained to police against the members of landless organization and NK local staff. Police harassment ensued. The landless organization is continuing with its agitations and a now protracted legal battle backed by advocacy in local civil society.

6 RTI as Anti-Poverty Tool: Analysis of Case Studies

The case studies described above have been discussed here in order to illustrate various aspects of the application of RTI by different types of poor peoples in their attempt to achieve or enhance their capabilities to combat the economic and political symptoms of poverty which they are forced to live with on a day-to-day basis. These poor people come from a variety of backgrounds and are faced with a diverse range of complex problems as they include both men and women: widows, students, divorcee single mothers, farmers, landless farmers, and fishermen. They mainly live in rural and semi-urban areas. They have sought to gain or ensure their access to different public services through RTI: social safety nets like VGD and VGF, agricultural supplies, *khas* land, and *khas* water bodies.

It was discussed earlier in this chapter that the capabilities approach tends to view poverty as the absence of certain freedoms that would otherwise enable people to achieve and retain certain capabilities that ensure that they can enjoy a better quality of life. Additionally, the human rights approach to poverty reduction asserts that each and every society should treat the project of reducing poverty among its impoverished populations as an obligation founded upon legal rather than simply ethical and moral principles. Poverty reduction is deemed possible through empowerment, human rights, accountability, nondiscrimination, equality, and participation. If these are enhanced in the case studies discussed above, then we should as observers consider that these successes are a manifestation of the scope as well as usefulness of RTI as an anti-poverty tool.

The case studies definitely show that RTI can empower the poor if it is used properly. It is in fact most useful for the section of the population who are least powerful in political and economic terms. In the gendered and hierarchical rural power structure of Bangladesh, it is incomprehensible for a widow such as Rezia, a teenager such as Shamima, and a divorcee such as in the case of Jobeda to raise their voices and to be able to secure their rightful share in social safety net programs. Although poor farmers like Rafiq and Mosharef are more empowered than their women counterparts, they are still at the bottom of rural power structures as they are merely small landholders without large asset bases. RTI has enabled them to exercise their citizen entitlements despite the many manipulations carried out by the UP Chairman (in Rafiq's case) and numerous illegal rejections by the local agriculture bureaucracy (in the case of Mosharef). RTI is a source of not only individual empowerment but can also foment what we might call a collective empowerment of the poor as illustrated in several cases of landless organizations' exercise of RTI. While as landless individuals, the members of these organizations were at the bottom of rural power structures individually. However, being organized into issue-based groups, they were more empowered than other landless individuals who were not organized. RTI processes available through RTIA made available channels through which these organizations were able to influence local decision making and therefore have a larger stake in determining the course of actions and circumstances which had great and constant impact upon their lives.

The chapter earlier talked about the idea of human rights which can be usefully divided into first-, second- and third-generation types. The cases described here show that RTI can be instrumental in advancing various human rights particularly those which we should consider to form part of second- and third-generation categories. As Rezia, Shamima, Jobeda, and Rafiq secured their social safety net entitlement through RTI application, they were able to exercise their basic economic and food rights: aspects of their lives which, when improved, brought about a vast change for the better in their situations. RTI also facilitated the securing of women's rights for Rezia, Shamima, and Jobeda. Through securing government agricultural supplies by applying RTI, Mosharef also secured his right to food and a right to livelihood. As poor women of Gangni, Meherpur, gained maternal health care benefits with RTI, their health rights were enhanced. As the landless farmers and fishermen secured access to *khas* land and *khas* waterways, their rights of land, food, and livelihoods were maximized.

RTI is often emphasized as a viable accountability tool. The cases of this chapter show how proper legal RTI application enhances both horizontal and vertical accountability in government services specially those which crucial to the maintenance and improvement of the limited livelihoods and capabilities of the poor. When Rezia asked for information about VGD, she did not initially receive any response meriting the name from the UP Chairman. When Rezia applied legally under RTIA, however, she had to be given answers since rejection would have been unlawful. RTI thus enabled Rezia, a poor widow, to exert horizontal accountability vis-à-vis the local UP and to thus force him to respond in a similar, legally justifiable manner. Shamima's information request initially was not able to generate horizontal accountability due to the UP Chairman's negligence. But this initial request was instrumental in generating vertical accountability when the UNO, the superior of the UP Chairman, responded to her questions and carried out the necessary investigations of relevant data in order to be able to do so. Securing of accountability went much deeper in the case of poor women getting access to maternal health care with revelation and prevention of ongoing corruption and penalization of corrupt officials—all thanks to the proper application and realization of RTI through legal channels.

The micro cases show how RTI can indeed be instrumental in establishing nondiscrimination and equality for the poor especially with regard to their knowledge of and subsequent access to government entitlements. As per constitutional provisions, no citizen of Bangladesh can be discriminated against on the basis of any difference such as race, color, religion, sex, socio-economic situation, and so on. In other words, equality of all peoples is overtly and legally stipulated. Lack of information with regard to government services for poor people creates loopholes which are breeding grounds for underhanded manipulation and widespread corruption. In the case of poor women getting access to maternal health care, the maternal health voucher cards were initially distributed among wealthy women of the locality. This was not just a violation of the law but also anti-constitutional since there was discrimination against the poor at work. The RTI was instrumental in revealing and addressing the discrimination which had previously been taking place. In the case of fishermen winning access to *khas* water body, poor fishermen were discriminated against while the local government officials were unduly favoring two local strongmen through corruption and illegal alteration of records. It was through the processes of RTI and the legitimacy provided by it that the local landless organization could expose this discrimination and corruption.

Participation is an important capability that can make the difference between populations and individuals living above and below poverty lines. Government services intended to realize poverty reduction can be fruitless despite all the good intentions upon which they are founded if at the end of the day the poor cannot participate in them properly. There can be various obstacles to their adequate implementation due to the persistence of corruption, regulatory complexities, and structural barriers against which even well meaning programs and actors may be unable to effectively work in order to support the interests of the poor. RTI can be an effective tool in bridging the oftentimes abysmal gap between policy intention and policy materialization. This is evident from some of the cases discussed in this chapter. The information request made by Jobeda in fact led to a participatory process of preparing the properly composed social safety net beneficiaries list. When the landless organization was trying to ensure poor women's access to maternal health care, being an organized group, they were already seasoned in the thorny process of participation. RTI, however, helped them to purposefully channel their participation toward influencing decision making within local administration and thus aided them greatly in achieving their objectives.

7 Concluding Observations

The analyses so far of the micro case studies from Bangladesh demonstrates the scope and usefulness of RTI as an anti-poverty tool and shows its enabling effects on empowerment, human rights, accountability, nondiscrimination, equality, and participation for the poor. However, the extremely limited evidence of RTI application by the poor from the micro cases is not matched with evidence of information requests carried out under RTIA reported by the Information Commission's annual report of 2011. This is not only due to the fact that a total of 7,808 information requests for one year are to be deemed to be very low. It is also true that many of the information requests were not even actually made by the poor themselves. The eagerness to make information requests under RTI is found to be significantly greater among more affluent sections of society, such as the middle and upper middle classes.

Moreover, many of the information requests submitted cannot be considered fully self-driven. The information requests submitted by the poor are often facilitated by the NGOs and CSOs[4] rather than emerging from the initiative and know-how of impoverished individuals and the organizations in which they participate. This is also made evident from the micro cases discussed in this chapter.

However, NGO-CSO facilitation of information requests does not necessarily mean that there was no demand by the applicants on their own. With lower levels of education and awareness among the country's poor, third party's facilitation is in some cases crucial for their full realization of RTI. Besides, many people still do not know much about RTI and the manner in which it functions; one survey found that 44% people still do not know about RTIA (RTI Forum, 2011: 3) and as noted by one observer, the majority of poor people have no idea how to make information request despite the fact that they require information on a daily basis in order to improve the quality of their day-to-day life.[5] In this circumstance, NGOs and CSOs also have a role to play in order to educate poor people about RTIA and its proper application and potential. Education and facilitation by NGOs and CSOs withstanding, for RTI to realize its full potential as a successful anti-poverty tool, poor people themselves ultimately have to be in the driving seat rather than that of a passive passenger. It should not be allowed to be the case that they will apply the legal rigors of RTI only when they are encouraged by any NGO, CSO, or such third party to do so. Poor peoples have to be educated and motivated about the potentials of RTI as a powerful anti-poverty tool and should thus be capable of using RTIA in exercising their government entitlements.

---

[4] Opinion expressed by Syeed Ahamed, CEO, Institute of Informatics and Development (IID), a Dhaka-based think tank working to bridge information gap in society.

[5] Opinion expressed by Zakir Hossain, Chief Executive, Nagorik Uddog (NU), a Dhaka-based NGO that work on protection and promotion of RTI.

Bibliography

GOB (2012) "Budget Strategy FY 2011–15," prepared by the Ministry of Finance, Government of Bangladesh.

Hunt, P., S. Osmani and M. Nowak (2002) "Draft Guidelines on a Human Rights Approach to Poverty Reduction Strategies," prepared for Office of the High Commissioner for Human Rights (OHCHR), United Nations.

Information Commission (2012) Annual Report 2011, Information Commission, Dhaka.

MJF (2011) RTI Act 2009, Bangladesh: Success Case Stories of Empowering People, MJF, Dhaka.

OHCHR (2004) Human Rights and Poverty Reduction: A Conceptual Framework, United Nations, New York and Geneva.

RIB (2011) "Two Years of Right to Information in Bangladesh: A Review," Unpublished report, Research Initiatives Bangladesh.

RTI Forum (2011) "Review in Progress of RTI Law Implementation: Citizen and Institutional Experience," Unpublished report.

Sen, A. (1980) "Equality of what?" in McMurrin, S. (ed.) Tanner Lectures on Human Values Vol. 1, Cambridge University Press, Cambridge.

Sen, A. (1985a) Commodities and Capabilities, Elsevier Science Publishers, Oxford.

Sen, A. (1985b) "The Standard of Living," The Tanner Lectures on Human Values, delivered at Clare Hall, Cambridge University, March 11–12, 1985.

Sen, A. (1988) "The Concept of Development" in Chenery, H. and T. Srinivasan (eds) Handbook of Development Economics Vol.1, Elsevier Science Publishers, North Holland.

Sen, A. (1993) "Capability and Well-being" in Nussbaum, M. and A. Sen (eds) The Quality of Life, Oxford University Press, Oxford.

Sen, A. (1999) Development as Freedom, Oxford University Press, New York.

Sen, A. (2004) "Elements of a Theory of Human Rights," Philosophy and Public Affairs, Vol. 34, No. 2.

Sen, A. (2005) "Human Rights and Capabilities," Journal of Human Development, Vol. 6, No. 2.

Streeten, P., S. Burki, M. Haq, N. Hicks and F. Stewart (1981) First Things First, Meeting Basic Human Needs in Developing Countries, Oxford University Press, New York.

Unnayan Onneshan (2012) Decelerated Decline? State of Poverty in Bangladesh 2012, Unnayan Onneshan, Dhaka.

Watson, N. (2012) "Private Foundations, Business and Developing a Post-2015 Framework," IDS In Focus Policy Briefing, Issue 25, June.

Chapter 7
PERI-URBAN DWELLING AND SOCIAL TRANSFORMATION IN AFRICA

Innocent Chirisa

This chapter focuses upon one of the most persistent problems facing what are now frequently referred to as "developing" countries, in particular those expanding nations in the Global South. The persistence and incrementing of peri-urbanization, basically a euphemistic term used to refer to the proliferation of slums and informal dwellings in cities and at their fringes, is a topic often swept under the rug at policy meetings or quietly relegated to the nether-realm of the irresolvable ills of development, industrialization, and attendant urban expansion. Chirisa manages to deftly sum up the actual state of such settlements as well as the various reasons behind their proliferation and the continuing basic problems which they experience and represent to the cities and nations where they are found. The author concludes with a well-reasoned call for increased institutional responsibility and transparency in such countries where peri-urbanization appears to be extending beyond the capacities of those in power and the residents of such settlements are now taking matters into their own agile hands.

1 Introduction

Peri-urbanization is pushing Africa toward extreme poverty owing to circumstances associated with the dynamics of politics in peri-urban areas (Muzondo et al., 2004; Jenkins and Andersen, 2011). This is despite evidence of an improving gross domestic product (GDP) in a number of nations across the continent. By way of example, the Kenyan GDP real growth rate for 2011 stood at 4.3%, with a per capita GDP of US$1,700. Rwanda, whose agricultural sector contributes about 40% of its GDP, had a per capita GDP of US$ 355, 66 in 2011. The aforementioned examples show significant economic growth although poverty levels remain high in the same countries.

In most cities of the developing world, the provision of proper infrastructure for sanitation, road access, drainage, and water supply lags behind the growth experienced in such urban areas. Coping strategies used by communities and households in the face of rising peri-urban poverty Africa include vernacular architecture, otherwise known as "architecture without architects" (Vestbro, 2008). There are also self-help strategies toward the provision of water and sanitation (Kulabako, Nalubega and Thunvik, 2007; Pangare and Pangare, 2008), street vending, informal peri-urban farming (FAO, 2011), peri-urban mining, and managing the "politics" of the place. This includes claiming space through slum-lordism, negotiating for land tenure and resisting planning.

Peri-urbanization, the settlement of populations beyond the boundaries of urban centers, is a reality in Africa (Simone, 2003; Agbola and Agunbiade, 2009). It manifests itself when households of different income levels are pushed to the city margins largely as a result of the high cost of living in the cities (Melesse, 2005; Paulo, Rosário and Tvedten, 2007; UNHABITAT, 2008a; Mels et al., 2010; Ndugwa et al., 2010; Fieuw, 2011; Jenkins and Andersen, 2011; Mutisya and Yarime, 2011; Mkula, 2012). Peri-urbanization is usually accompanied by both personal and environmental health constraints, owing essentially to inadequate infrastructure provision (Merkel and Otai, 2007, Yongsi, 2009; cf. Kalimba and de Langen, 2007). In Africa, it is largely an expression of poverty (Muzondo et al., 2004; Barry and Rüther, 2005; Arimah, 2010). This chapter critically analyzes peri-urbanization as both a theoretical and practical aspect of survival in an increasingly urbanized world. The purpose of the chapter is to demonstrate that people are adapting to poverty by capitalizing on opportunities that certain spaces offer (Al-Khayat, 2008; Kipper and Fischer eds. 2009). Most African peri-urban dwellers are often used by politicians in their bid to stay in power as they constitute a "market" for political promises (Nabutola, 2004; Kudva, 2009).

2 Theoretical and Analytical Framework

A complex relationship exists between poverty and politics (Murowe and Chirisa, 2006). Politics is especially manifest in public spending on slum-upgrading processes. Public spending is distorted, as some areas are clearly favored over others, for political expediency. Using the interest group model to explain this phenomenon, Annez and Linn (2010: 23) have observed that

> [i]n order to understand better how political processes support or impede urban poverty reduction ... the "political agency of the poor", [being] the capacity of the poor to "select, reward and sanction the leaders, institutions, policies, formal rules and informal norms that directly affect their lives" matters.... [A] key reason for the persistence of urban poverty and the inability of the poor to bring about conditions that improve their lives substantially, is that they lack in political agency. This is despite the fact that in many countries the poor are perhaps the single largest interest group (if seen as a cohesive group) and that they may have in principle democratic or representative political means to pursue their collective interest.

The excerpt shows that poverty and politics are closely intertwined. Paradoxically, however, although the poor are in the majority, they fail to change their destiny. Slum dwellers are motivated to solve their own problems without much external support. Hooper and Ortolano (2012: 111), referring to Kurasini in Dar es Salaam, argue that there are three explanations for this, namely "...the nature of payoffs from participation; owners' greater belief in their efficacy of action; and owners' greater connection to place." It is this connectedness to a place that Chirisa (2010) defines as the "stewardship of place." The ensuing paragraphs try to expose the reality of the peri-urban dwelling using theories of vulnerability, resilience, capability and functioning, and clusters of disadvantage. These theories show how poverty is both an asset and a liability for politicians, who seek votes through it and the poor, who have to live with it every day.

Using the vulnerability theory, one can see how the majority of poor peri-urban dwellers live on the margins of life, making them extremely vulnerable. Jenkins and Andersen (2011) call this phenomenon of gross vulnerability "bottom-end churning" (Mabughi and Selim, 2006: 6). According to this theory, particular social groups are at risk of impoverishment due to discrimination based on class, ethnic, or related factors such as disability or area of residence. Vulnerability complexes are usually determined by the nature of household headship, such that women or child-headed households are strongly linked with poverty. These complexes are compounded by external risks, shocks, stresses, and deprivation. The vulnerability theory has been criticized as being generalized, oversimplified, and of doubtful validity. The theory's inability to account for subgroup variations in the central characteristics associated with poverty partly explains why David (1970) dismissed it as offering little guidance with regards to strategies in managing it. Despite this criticism, evidence on the ground shows that there is an ongoing battle being waged against vulnerability and poverty in urban and peri-urban settlements, where the poor resort to built-in mechanisms of resilience.

The resilience theory shows the extent to which poor households confront and manage poverty. Resilience is the expression of "...positive adaptation despite significant life adversity" (Strumpfer, 2003: 70; cf. Luthar, 2003; Lemay, 2004). Resilience initially applied to ecological phenomena, but has been extended social circles. In social analysis, the theory holds that all people have the ability to overcome adversity and succeed in spite of it. In this respect, it is a strengths-based model, which argues that support and opportunities lead to success in individual and group life. James Garbarino has argued that the coping theory is superior to resilience, given that the capacity to withstand adversity is not absolute. For Clarke and Clarke (2000), extant differences in the way individuals experience adversity and overcome it explain how resilience decreases as risks increase. Cultural contexts and the location of individuals are of great significance (Luthar and Zelazo, 2003). Narrowness in focus, limited attention to broader structural dynamics in society and ethnocentrism have been cited as obvious weaknesses in the resilience theory (Iwasaki, Bartlett, MacKay, Mactavish, and Ristock, 2005). Despite the weaknesses mentioned, the theory provides a critical frame through which to analyze the resilience of peri-urban dwellers in Africa vis à vis the vagaries of life. They usually lack the necessary facilities and resources to lead a meaningful life but continue to thrive in (spite of) adversity.

The Capability and Functioning Theory by Amartya Sen will shed some light on how they manage to cope. This theory was coined in 1980 by

Amartya Sen, the 1998 Nobel laureate in economics. It focuses on what people are effectively competent to do (Robeyns, 2005). It is a broad normative framework used to evaluate and assess individual well-being and social arrangements, policy design, and proposals for social change within a society. Sen has argued that capability is such that development has to enhance lives as well as the freedoms enjoyed by individuals and groups (Todaro and Smith, 2003). In Sen's view, poverty is not accurately measured by income but by what a person is or is not capable of doing (Robeyns, 2005). To scholars like Robeyns, the capability approach is not a theory to explain poverty, inequality or well-being. Rather, it is a tool and a framework within which to conceptualize and evaluate these phenomena. Thus, people's ability to function in terms of what they want to engage in, and to be who they want to be is what Sen terms functionings (Robeyns, 2005). The capability approach does not a determine well-being in terms of utility but capabilities and functionings. The approach is criticized for being too individualistic, failing to consider individuals as part of their social environment, socially embedded and connected to others, and paying less attention to groups and to social structures (Robeyns, 2005). Sen generally fails to supplement his framework with a coherent list of important capabilities (Clark, 2005), simply noting that capabilities are valuable. Nevertheless, evidence points to peri-urban poor groups as enjoying quite a number of freedoms and capabilities, which have seen the poor becoming innovative in a bid to sustain themselves without being dependent on the government.

Another way of viewing the peri-urban poor is through Robert Chambers' (1983) clusters of disadvantage, which explains poverty as a trap and a vicious cycle. In Chambers, poverty is multidimensional and entails clusters of disadvantage that are poverty proper (that is, in financial terms), physical weakness, isolation, vulnerability, and powerlessness. These five clusters of disadvantage interact with each other to trap people in a situation of disadvantage, leading to deprivation. This poverty trap is a self-perpetuating condition in which an economy and the people that define it are "caught in" vicious cycle, leading to persistent suffering and underdevelopment. The main criticism leveled at the Chambers deprivation trap is its rural centrism, which means that it cannot be fully applied in an urban and peri-urban setting. However, in Africa, the challenges of poverty have, of late, been concentrated in peri-urban areas. It is possible to socially transform the peri-urban areas of Africa, provided that the tenets of theories advanced by Sen and Chambers and others are fully grasped and the people are empowered to shape their destiny with resilience and determination based on effective poverty-fighting strategies.

3 The Path of Unsustainability: Constraints and Opportunities

This section explains the ecological, institutional, economic, and political challenges bedeviling peri-urban settlements in Africa. Sustainability in peri-urban living is a complex issue dependent on ecological, economic, social, political, and technological factors (Muzvidziwa, 2005).

3.1 Ecological Challenges

Rapid population growth in peri-urban areas coupled with inadequate resource capacity and resources lead to serious environmental degradation. This manifests in the form of pollution, deforestation, and uncontrolled development on fragile land such as wetlands. Most informal settlements in Africa, as elsewhere, lack adequate basic services and are usually located in the peri-urban and environmentally sensitive areas such as flood-prone areas (Muzvidziwa, 2005) which then suffer ecological disturbances. Most housing units in the informal settlements of Cape Town, for instance, are located on disused landfills and wetland areas that are ecologically fragile and prone to flooding. Large amounts of fecal waste are discharged directly into the environment, and a lot of refuse is dumped in wetland areas, causing serious ecological problems such as the depletion of biodiversity. Practices such as deforestation are associated with expansive brick molding as households seek to fire and strengthen bricks. Moreover, most of the peri-urban poor rely on wood-fuel for cooking and other domestic uses. As households pursue peri-urban agriculture, the uncontrolled application of pesticides and organic waste often results in soil and water table contamination. The high usage of pit latrines results in high levels of pollution of underground water sources. High concentrations of pollutants from the burning of waste and gaseous and liquid industrial emissions in the peri-urban zone result in environmental deterioration of and squalor in peri-urban areas. The inadequacy of waste treatment and management systems in the informal settlements of Kigali, for example, explains the vulnerability of the places and their inhabitants (cf. REMA/UNEP/UNDP, 2007).

There are also ecological opportunities, however. In Nairobi, for example, there are a good number of environmental resources for development. These include forests, freshwater systems and biodiversity (City Council of Nairobi, 2007), which have development potential in the form of tourism and agriculture, which are vital carbon sinks for the entire city. In peri-urban Kinshasa, organic waste has been converted into high-quality organic fertilizer through mechanical composting, and the poor are at the forefront of managing the processes. Recycled and treated wastewater has been used to irrigate fruit orchards and ornamental plants. Moreover, peri-urban areas with their biodiverse landscapes can contribute to the livelihoods of the residents. In South Africa, Cape Town is ecologically and strategically located within an area of globally significant biodiversity and unique conservation value. The peri-urban poor have learnt to tap into the ecological asset and make a livelihood out of it.

3.2 Institutional Constraints

In most African cities, the urban sector lacks the powers necessary to effectively plan and manage investment in urban infrastructure and service delivery. Various municipal structures are ill-equipped in the face of rapid demographic expansion and growing urban informality. In Kampala, for instance, of the 1,500 tons of solid waste generated in the city daily, only about 35% is collected and disposed of by the Kampala City Council (KCC). The rest is disposed of or managed indiscriminately by the private sector. Institutional obstacles in the informal peri-urban settlements normally include skills deficiencies in administering informal areas and corrupt tendencies, compromising competence, performance, and delivery (Misselhorn, 2008). In addition, there is a serious erosion of capacity in the private sector and NGOs and declining levels of effective cooperation with the state in projects aimed at improving conditions in the peri-urban settlements. Limited administrative capacity and financial resources, weak institution, poor governance, and lack of capacity to enforce laws and bylaws explain why institutions fail to improve services in peri-urban areas, particularly in informal settlements (UNHABITAT, 2006). This is further compounded by the high turnover of experienced managers, bureaucracy and corruption in local authorities, which is crippling the capacity to meet the demands of ever-growing populations. Although civil society organizations often assume responsibility for the provision of services in the peri-urban areas, a good number of them lack the capacity to adequately fill the huge gap left by the government in these settlements. This is largely because of the piecemeal and project approach that they use. Effective operation by nonstate organizations is usually hampered by erratic funding, nonrepresentation at various levels of governance and lack of technical support. Less than half (43%), for example, have received technical support from other organizations in Nairobi. In Ethiopia, peri-urban areas are managed by sub-city administrative units such as the "kebeles," institutions which are faced with a number of challenges such as lack of capacity to effectively perform their duties. These include inadequate working procedures, institutional facilities, and manpower (UNHABITAT, 2008a). The institutions are also not fully empowered especially in terms of revenue collection, planning systems, and expenditure, and central city administration rarely supports them in terms of planning and services.

In city of Kigali, NGOs, the private sector, community associations, and district authorities are operating with limited technical and financial means. There is no institutional umbrella for the implementation of certain projects (Republic of Rwanda, 2010). Institutions such as the Giza Beautification and Cleaning Authority (GBCA), which is responsible for garbage collection, are failing to cope with the daily rate of garbage production in the peri-urban areas of Cairo. The Lilongwe Water Board (LWB) and the Electricity Commission of Malawi (ECM) are so weak that they cannot extend their services to peri-urban areas.

Nevertheless, there are also some institutional opportunities. The Greater Cairo region has endeavored to strengthen local administration and urban planning legislation to enable it to prepare its own detailed plans, which are different from the master plan. These plans dispose of public land and use the proceeds to finance local service delivery, especially in informal areas where service delivery is lagging behind (Cities Alliance, 2008). Municipalities are outsourcing service delivery, which should provide a window of opportunity to stimulate local economic development (Pedley, 2010). A remarkable sign of good governance by the state is the involvement of peri-urban dwellers in the management of their own affairs, as advocated for by many international institutions.

3.3 Socioeconomic Challenges

In most cases, the most vulnerable groups in peri-urban areas are denied access to microfinance to start or boost their micro-enterprises (Tsinda, 2011). This creates a vicious cycle of poverty, as no or low levels of investment in informal businesses result in low capital growth. In peri-urban Lilongwe, for example, the informal sector does not have adequate infrastructure, including markets and credit facilities. Such a dearth in basic infrastructure and services has also hampered the development of adequate entrepreneurial skills among the poor (Fransen and Dijk, 2008; UNHABITAT, 2011). This, in turn, explains the high unemployment rates in the city and its periphery (Alder, 1995; Mathare Zonal Plan, 2012). When households live on the margins because of low income and are confronted with high land prices and construction costs, they are forced to live like paupers in slums (Batran and Arandel, 1998). Notwithstanding, informal settlements, especially those in South Africa, provide several economic opportunities through which residents can improve their socioeconomic status. The peri-urban areas generally provide low-cost access to the city, with few barriers of entry to operations. Home-based industries have been noted as having the potential to improve the average household income and general welfare of the household. Several creative and innovative small enterprises have received full empowerment, improving economic conditions in some peri-urban areas. The education of peri-urban dwellers is also significant and quite a number of them have received adequate education in basic entrepreneurship (Abdelhalim and Samra, 2010; Lawanson and Olanrewaju, 2012). Responsible authorities can also use this opportunity to formalize illegal activities to raise revenue for upgrading measures. Informal urban areas can also be targeted with programs that raise the support of youth and extend credit to existing and newly formed small and microenterprises. In Nairobi and Cairo, some youth have developed competencies in information technologies to make themselves more attractive in the competitive job market (Piffero, 2009).

3.4 Political Challenges

Political power and authority in informal settlements is often vested in powerful individuals or groupings—the slumlords or warlords. Moreover, control and access to power and economic opportunities are consistently linked to a ruling party. This promotes incidences of conflicts in informal settlements (Piffero, 2009). Political interests in informal areas are manifest in the level of infrastructure supply connections to electricity, water and sewer, which become topical issues during election periods, when infrastructure is a highly saleable good. Peri-urban informal settlements lack public sector and law enforcement agencies, leading to chaos, rampant vandalism to public property, further entrenching levels of poverty. Nonetheless, a functional approach to slum challenges reveals a number of opportunities that even the donor community can exploit (Dafe, 2009; Struyk and Giddings, 2009; Annez and Linn, 2010). Sometimes land is informally and illegally allocated by politicians as a way of rewarding people loyal to them. Land allocation defines patron-client relations, and is normally done along ethnic lines. In a multi-ethnic society such as Kenya, this has the ripple effect of ethic divide and mistrust. This, in turn, results in violence in certain communities (cf. UNDP, 2007).

4 Evidence of Peri-urbanization and Related Phenomena in Africa

Following are case studies drawn from different regions in Africa, namely North Africa, East Africa, West Africa, Central Africa, and Southern Africa.

4.1 North Africa

In Sudan, Khartoum is expanding at a tremendous rate, with significant environmental health problems being observed in its peri-urban areas, where a host of informal settlements have emerged. These informal settlements are characterized by crowdedness, squalor, unpaved roads, scanty water, as well as poor sanitation and waste management, which are usually associated with an increasing incidence of communicable diseases. Most peri-urban Khartoum dwellers have embarked on peri-urban agriculture to supplement their food requirements. High-value crops are grown. The farmers thus raise significant income through the sale of their farm produce while providing the city with a reliable supply of perishable vegetables. Besides urban farming, the informal sector also thrives, as residents are involved in a range of activities including car repairs, blacksmithing, and vending at the local markets and the most vulnerable groups scavenge for food from rubbish dumps.

Approximately 70% of urban dwellers in Egypt—some 12 million people—live in informally built homes on privately owned or public land, which are sprawled haphazardly around major urban centers. The fact that over 6 million of the informal home dwellers live in peri-urban Cairo has been viewed as evidence of the failure by the Egyptian Government to provide affordable housing (Kipper and Fischer, 2009). The informal structures come in various forms—makeshift stone houses, wooden shacks, and crumbling brick structures, all evidence of unregulated construction of houses. As in Khartoum, settlements are inadequately serviced with poor roads and means of public transportation. The dwellings are poorly ventilated and garbage collection is inadequate, threatening public health. In most cases, basic infrastructure (sewerage, piped clean water) is conspicuously absent. There is little or no formal connection to electricity in these settlements. As a livelihood coping mechanism, peri-urban dwellers sell food informally, collect steel from demolished homes, or sort garbage, hunting for anything of value to salvage or sell. Small businesses serve the community and bring significant income to those who run them (Jenkins and Andersen, 2011).

4.2 East Africa

Like Cairo, Kampala in Uganda has a large percentage of its population (about 60%) residing in informal settlements in poor living conditions. The houses built by inhabitants are sub-standard, and made out of such materials as mud blocks, clay blocks, mud and wattle, and burnt clay or earth bricks (Musana, 2011). Inadequate formal housing delivery has forced large numbers of people to settle in the city's peri-urban areas where land is cheap and controlled by traditional leaders. It would be inaccurate to say, however, that only poor people live in this zone. Members of the well-to-do classes are also resident in this area, which benefits the poor, who they employ as gardeners, nannies, and housemaids.

In the slums of Kampala, the dearth of basic social amenities such as potable water, electricity, education, health care service, and adequate shelter is a common phenomenon. The 2005 National Household Survey indicated that a large proportion of households occupy single rooms, in crowded conditions, their incomes are generally low, and that many of the city's residents are employed in the informal sector, mostly in small businesses and on a subsistence basis (Musana, 2011). Besides, there are also home-based enterprises that contribute significantly to household incomes and offer some level of social protection. In the informal settlements, 80% of the inhabitants are classified as low-income earners.

In Ethiopia, the unplanned and uncontrolled expansion of cities has led to several problems, including the increased cost of infrastructural provision. Informal housing in Addis Ababa has been perceived as having some ecological consequences, since most informal housing units occupy wetlands and hilltops. Some of these areas are susceptible to flood risks, exposing the residents of such areas to serious environmental hazards. In Addis Ababa, for instance, squatter settlements are located mainly in city margins (Ambaye, 2011) and their number and size have increased over time. A study conducted by the Urban Development and Works Bureau in 2000 indicated that the total area covered by squatter settlements in Addis Ababa is 2,000 hectares. Over 300,000 people in 600,000 squatter housing units were living in this place. A large percentage (84.8%) of the housing units were walled in wood and mud but in the new squatter settlements, more than one-third of the housing units were made of block walls; 82.2% of the households were using electricity for lighting, and 17.8% were using lanterns (Melesse, 2005). 48.3% of the housing units had individual kitchens, while 0.4% had shared kitchens. More than half (51.3%) of the housing units had no kitchen facilities at all. 36.5% of the housing units had private toilets, 1.3% had shared toilets, and the majority (63.2%) had no toilet facilities at all. Moreover, about 64.8% of the households obtained water supplies from water vendors, while 33% of the household obtained it from both vendors and unprotected rivers. Only 2.2% of the household heads reported having access to piped water supply. These statistics reveal that households were living under adverse conditions and in abject poverty.

Irregular daily wage labor and informal activities are the bedrock support for 92.3% of households. Cotton spinning, straw plaiting, washing laundry, hairdressing, serving as traditional birth attendants, pruning, brewing local beer, and preparing food are sources of income for the majority of women. A few young females are employed as servers or cleaners in private hotels. Other sources of revenue such as peri-urban agriculture and horticulture have been instrumental in shaping the livelihood status of residents. Products from such activities include fruits, herbs, vegetables, and mushrooms. Urban horticulture meets about 30% of the total vegetable requirements and 60–70% of the leafy vegetable requirements of Addis Ababa (Bahir, 2010). This has been a source of income and nutrition as well as promoting peri-urban food security.

In Kenya, the rapid urbanization of Nairobi has increased the demand for housing land, forcing the poor to settle in areas characterized by lack of proper housing and public services (Nabutola, 2004). The inhabitants also face numerous hazards such as floods, landslides, and environmental contamination. They live in overcrowded conditions characterized by poor sanitation, inadequate and unclean water, makeshift shelter, and very unstable social networks. The bulk of the houses is made of mud and wattle with iron sheets. Between 60% and 93% of slum households rely on water vendors for water. Sewerage and human waste disposal in informal settlements pose a major threat to health. Municipal services do not cover most of these areas due to the shortage of refuse collection vehicles. Other inhabitants of the informal settlements obtain water from illegal water line connections, while others use sewage-contaminated water from nearby rivers (APHRC, 2002). Effluent and fumes from the nearby industrial areas seriously pollute informal settlements, as seen in Embakasi and Kasarani in Kenya. About 94% of the residents rely on charcoal as a source of energy, which increases the risk of fire and environmental degradation (Alder, 1995). Water, sewage, and other pollutants drain into the valley from surrounding communities and facilities. Moreover, irregular solid waste collection also results in large, exposed dumpsites (Lawanson, Yadua and Salako 2012). In Kibera, the use of rainwater is unhealthy as "...it is mixed with the stool that people throw anywhere even on the roof" (APHRC, 2002: 7), a phenomenon otherwise known as flying toilets. In 1995, there were 134 informal settlements with 77,589 inhabitants in and around the city. By 2007, the combined population of these informal dwellers was estimated at 1,886,166 (City Council of Nairobi, 2007). Rents in the informal settlements are pegged between KShs 500 and 700 per month for a house with significant water supply and toilet facilities (UNHABITAT, 2005). Peri-urban Nairobi is often targeted by politicians, especially during election periods, in their quest for support and votes (Nabutola, 2004; Dafe, 2009).

Only one-third of the people living in Kenya's informal settlements are employed in the formal sector; two-thirds work in the informal sector (UNHABITAT, 2005). To cope with adversity and poverty, residents in the informal settlements build their livelihoods on their resource endowments, namely skills and abilities, land, savings, equipment, and formal or informal support groups and networks (APHRC, 2002). A nutritional survey conducted in 2009 by Oxfam GB, Concern Worldwide and Care International in two villages of Kibera in Kenya revealed that 90% of the residents faced severe food shortages as a result of unstable sources of income. They were resorting to reducing the quantity of meals they consumed, thereby reducing diet diversity. Informal sector practices include, among other things, firewood collection or charcoal burning, petty trade, repairs, carpentry, and metalwork.

4.3 West Africa and Central Africa

In Lagos Nigeria, the growth of informal settlements is attributed to rapid urbanization in the city (Jibril, 2006), and the fact that two-thirds of the population living in slum neighborhoods. The slums have been built on fills or perched on stilts over open water. Sewage and solid waste management systems in the city's informal settlements are practically nonexistent. Residents rely on pits or dispose of human waste and garbage directly into surface waters. The influx of people to peri-urban areas and the lack of affordable formal housing have resulted in the emergence of informal settlements, which are an eyesore. Lagos' informal settlements range in size from clusters of shacks to entire districts, which are scattered across the city. In 1984, 42 settlements were identified as blighted and by 2004, the number had increased to approximately 100 (UNHABITAT, 2008b).

In Central Africa, the Rwandan capital of Kigali is characterized by the massive peri-urban informal settlements, which have degenerated into slums. Prodigious urban development in Kigali occurred in 1980. It was slum-like in shape and now covers around 70% of the city (Kalimba and

Langen, 2007). Inhabitants of the peri-urban areas of the city face different challenges including lack of basic urban infrastructure with exception of electricity (+/–80% are connected) and water distribution (+/–60% connected). There is a huge backlog in terms of infrastructure with access, drainage, and sanitary conditions in most parts of the city margins recorded as bad.

4.4 Southern Africa

In Mozambique, Maputo has been described as an urbanized "cement city" with informal peripheral neighborhoods inhabited by the majority of the population (UNHABITAT, 2010). Conditions in peri-urban areas are characterized by disorderliness, making it difficult to provide essential infrastructure and other municipal services. The majority of residents rely on pit latrines and have a poor solid waste disposal system. Woody biomass consumption dominates the areas where there is limited electricity. Public lighting is scanty and compromises the security of the residents. Informal economic activities thrive in the peri-urban informal settlements, taking the form of street vending, petty trade and waged labor in privately owned peri-urban farms (FAO, 2011). A large number of women are also involved in marketing their agricultural produce.

In Malawi, Lilongwe's rapid urbanization process is pegged at about 4% per annum (UNHABITAT, 2011). This rapid urban expansion explains the city's failure to provide basic services and the development of informal settlements. In 2008, about 76% of the population were informal dwellers (UNHABITAT, 2011). Low-income areas and informal settlements make up 73% of the residential land share. Residents have little or no access to social infrastructure and basic urban services. Houses are in poor condition and prone to fires and floods. Basic urban services such as water and electricity are supplied. In informal settlements, water is supplied mainly through Communal Development Committees (CDCs) and Water Users Associations (WUAs) (Devereux, 1999).

Cape Town in South Africa has, in recent times, experienced a huge increase in its informal settlements (cf. Muzondo et al., 2004). More than 220 informal settlements with an estimated of 900,000 people are faced with a number of challenges summarized by the Mels et al. (2010: 2) as the "...[l]agging behind of sanitation coverage, with container and buckets being the systems ... [S]ettlements are located on unsuitable land and are difficult to access for water and sanitation servicing....[Only], 36.5% of the population in the informal settlements are serviced with basic infrastructure." Livelihood and survival strategies in the informal areas of Cape Town are very diverse and include employment as casual labor, scrap collection, begging, selling petty commodities and running plaza shops and shebeens and making repairs. Home industry entails baking, hairdressing, dressmaking, and children day care centers (mainly done by women). Households in the informal settlements of Cape Town are characterized by women who generally lack economic security, with the majority generating income in the informal sector. Informal workers are not protected by labor legislation and lack access to credit facilities due their very low incomes. Informal settlements are far from commercial centers, such that residents are economically disadvantaged (City of Cape Town, 2007).

Urban local authorities are generally struggling to provide services to rapidly expanding informal settlements. Poor strategic planning, inadequate oversight, and misleading official statistics further exacerbate the capacity of urban authorities.

5 Conclusion and Policy Options

The foregoing discussion reveals that Africa and its cities are moving along a very unsustainable path, as evidenced by examples drawn from the sub-regions of North Africa, West Africa, Southern Africa, and East Africa. Peri-urban informalization typified by poverty of households, institutions, and the state at large has produced unplanned and disorderly spatial settlements. Substandard and overcrowded housing, inadequate electricity, water and sanitation, road, solid waste management services, and deteriorating urban livelihood options are the hallmarks of peri-urban informal settlements. Mega-slums are mainly located in the peri-urban areas. Failure by the state to provide infrastructure and investment opportunities and its incapacity to implement housing, environmental, and urban policies are the chief reasons for this. Innovative solutions and strategies developed by the urban poor to improve their living environments can lead to the gradual expansion of informal settlements. Such innovations include informal small businesses, and other diverse coping strategies such as peri-urban farming. Relevant authorities need to integrate the innovations of peri-urban informal dwellers into city management systems (Beattie, Mayer and Yildirim, 2010) with a view to the social transformation of these areas. This implies capitalizing and improving on the innovations by the poor to ensure sustainability. Evidence from elsewhere shows that an integrationist model that combines ideas from two or more actors provides a more sustainable framework for development. Africa needs to embrace the realities of its current poverty through discourse, reflection, and informed action. It is important to create platforms on which local communities, local authorities, central governments, the private and voluntary sectors come to share ideas and contemplate a more sustainable future together, so as to transform communities and enable them to escape poverty.

References

Abdelhalim, K. and Samra, M. A. (2010). Participatory Upgrading of Informal Areas: A Decission makers' Guide for Action. Cairo: Participatory Development Programme in Urban Areas (PDP) in Egypt.

Agbola, T. and Agunbiade, E. I. M. (2009). Urbanization, Slum Development and Security of Tenure: The Challenges of Meeting Millennium Development Goal 7 in Metropolitan Lagos, Nigeria. De Sherbiniin, A. A. Rahman, A. Barbieri, J. C. Fotso, and Y. Zhu (eds.). 2009. Urban Population-Environment Dynamics in the Developing World: Case Studies and Lessons Learned. Paris: Committee for International Cooperation in National Research in Demography (CICRED). URL: http://www.populationenvironmentresearch.org/workshops.jsp#W2007

Alder, G. (1995). Tackling Poverty in Nairobi's Informal Settlements: Developing an Institutional Strategy. Environment and Urbanization 7(2): pp. 85–107.

Al-Khayat, N. A. (2008). Self-Help Urban Services in Informal Settlements: The Case of Water and Electricity Services in Raml Al-'Ali Informal Settlement, Unpublished Thesis, Department of Architecture and Design of the Faculty of Engineering. Beirut: Architecture, American University of Beirut, Lebanon.

Ambaye, D. W. (2011). Informal Settlement in Ethiopia, the Case of two Kebeles in Bahir Dar City, FIG Working Week 2011, "Bridging the Gap between Cultures," Marrakech, Morocco, May 18–22, 2011.

Annez, P. Clarke and Linn, J. F. (2010). An Agenda for Research on Urbanization in Developing Countries: A Summary of Findings from a Scoping Exercise. URL: http://www-wds.worldbank.org/servlet/WDSContentServer/WDSP/IB/2010/11/15/000158349_20101115101056/Rendered/PDF/WPS5476.pdf

APHRC (African Population and Health Research Center) (2002). Health and Livelihood Needs of Residents of Informal Settlements in Nairobi City. Nairobi: African Population and Health Research Center.

Arimah, B. C. (2010). Slums as Expressions of Social Exclusion: Explaining the Prevalence of Slums in African Countries. Nairobi: UNHABITAT.

Bahir, A. L. (2010). Human Induced Disaster and the Socio economic Capitals of Squatter Settlers: The Case of Kore Community in Addis Ababa, Ethiopia. Journal of Sustainable Development in Africa 12(6): pp. 217–232.

Barry, M. and Rüther, H. (2005). Data Collection Techniques for Informal Settlement Upgrades in Cape Town, South Africa. URISA Journal 17(1): pp. 43–52.

Batran, M. E. and Arandel, C. (1998). A Shelter of Their Own: Informal Settlement Expansion in Greate rCairo and Government Responses. Environment and Urbanization 10(1): pp. 217–232.

Beattie, N., Mayer, C. and Yildirim, A. B. (2010). Solutions to Meet the Global Urban Housing Challenge. Paper presented at the UN World Urban Forum, Brazil, March 2010.

Chambers, R. (1983). Rural Poverty: Putting the Last First. London: Longman.

Chirisa, I. (2010). An Analysis of the Environmental Stewardship Concept and Its Applicability in Peri-urban Towns: Lessons from Epworth in Zimbabwe. Journal of Sustainable Development in Africa 12(4): pp. 41–57.

Cities Alliance. (2008). Slum Upgrading Close: Exprience of Six Cities. Washington: The Cities Alliance.

City Council of Nairobi. (2007). City of Nairobi Environmental Outlook. Nairobi: CCN.

City of Cape Town. (2007). Sustainability Report: Informal Dwelling Count. Cape Town.

Clark, D. A. (2005). The Capability Approach: Its Development, Critiques and Recent Advances. Manchester: Global Poverty Research Group.

Clarke, A. M. and Clarke, A. D. (2000). Early Experience and the life path. London: Jessica Kingsley Publishers.

Dafe, F. (2009) No Business Like Slum Business? The Political Economy of the Continued Existence of Slums: A Case Study of Nairobi. London: Development Studies Institute. URL: http://www2.lse.ac.uk/internationalDevelopment/pdf/WP/WP98.pdf

David, E. (1970). Poverty Theories and Income Maintenance: Validity and Policy Relevance.

Devereux, S. (1999). Making Less Last Longer: Informal Safety Nets in Malawi. Lilongwe: Institute of Development Studies.

FAO (Food and Agricultural Organization) (2011). The Place of Urban and Peri-urban Agriculture (UPA) in National Food Security Programs. Rome: FAO.

Fieuw, W. V. P. (2011). Informal Settlement Upgrading in Cape Town's Hangberg: Local Government, Urban Governance and the "Right to the City," Unpublished Master of Philosophy Thesis, Faculty of Economics and Management Sciences: Stellenbosch University.

Fransen, J. and Dijk, M. P. (2008). Informality in Addis Ababa. Rotterdam: IHS.

Gondo, T. (2009). Urban Land Informality: An Evaluation of Institutional response options to land Informalization in Ethiopian cities. University of Venda.

Hooper, M. and Ortolano, L. (2012). Motivations for Slum Dweller Social Movement Participation in Urban Africa: A Study of Mobilization in Kurasini, Dar es Salaam. Environment & Urbanization 24(1): pp. 99–114.

Iwasaki, Y., Bartlett, J., MacKay, K., Mactavish, J. and Ristock, J. (2005). Social Exclusion and Resilience as Frameworks of Stress and Coping among Selected Non-dominant Groups. International Journal of Mental Health Promotion 7(3): pp. 14–17.

Jenkins, P. and Andersen, J. E. (2011). Developing Cities in between the Formal and Informal. Paper presented at the 4th European Conference on African Studies, African Engagements: On Whose Terms? Uppsala June 15–18, 2011.

Jibril, I. U. (2006). Resettlement Issues, Squatter Settlements and Problems of Land Administration in Abuja, Nigeria's Capital. Paper prepared for the 5th FIG Regional Conference, Accra, Ghana, March 8–11, 2006.

Kalimba, I. and de Langen, M. (2007). Infrastructure provision as part of Slum Upgrading: the case of Kigali, Rwanda, Paper presented at ENHR 2007 International Conference "Sustainable Urban Areas".

Kipper, R. and Fischer, M. eds. (2009). Cairo's Informal Areas Between Urban Challenges and Hidden Potentials—Facts, Voices, Visions. Cairo: GTZ Egypt/Participatory Development Programme in Urban Areas (PDP).

Kudva, N. (2009). The Everyday and the Episodic: The Spatial and Political Impacts of Urban Informality. Environment and Planning A 41: pp. 1614–1628.

Kulabako, N. R., Nalubega, M. and Thunvik, R. (2007). Study of the Impact of Land Use and Hydrogeological Settings on the Shallow Groundwater Quality in a Peri-urban Area of Kampala, Uganda. Science of the Total Environment 381: pp. 180–199.

Lawanson, T. and Olanrewaju, D. (2012). The Home as Workplace: Investigating Home Based Enterprises in Low Income Settlements of the Lagos Metropolis. Lagos: ISOCARP Congress.

Lawanson, T., Yadua, O. and Salako, I. (2012). Environmental Challenges of Peri-Urban Settlements in the Lagos Megacity.

Lemay, R. (2004). Resilience versus Coping. Child and Family Journal 8(2): pp. 11–15.

Luthar, S. S. (2003). Resilience and Vulnerability: Adaptation in the Context of Childhood Adversities. London: Cambridge University Press.

Mabughi, N. and Selim, T. (2006). Poverty as Social Deprivation: A Survey. Review of Social Economy 64(2): pp. 181–204.

Mathare Zonal Plan. (2012). Collabour Ative Plan for Informal Settlement Upgrading. Nairobi.

Melesse, M. (2005). City Expansion, Squatter Settlements and Policy Implications in Addis Ababa: The Case of KolfeKeranio Sub-City. Working papers on population and land use change in central Ethiopia, nr. 2, Acta Geographica—Trondheim.

Mels, A, Castellano, D., Braadbaart, O., Veenstra, S., Dijkstra, I., Meulman, B., Singels, A., Wilsenach, J. A. (2010). Sanitation services for the informal settlements of Cape Town, South Africa. Desalination 251: pp. 330–337.

Merkel, S. and Otai, J. (2007). Meeting the Health Needs of the Urban Poor in African Informal Settlements: Best Practices and Lessons Learned. Washington, DC: USAID/Urban Institute.

Misselhorn, M. (2008). Position Paper on Informal Settlements Upgrading. Urban Landmark.

Mkula, C. (2012). Urban Explosion Threatens Lilongwe's Mchezi Township. Lilongwe: Weekend Times, Saturday, April 14, 2012.

Murowe, S. R. and Chirisa, I. (2006). Sally Mugabe Heights: The Tale of an Incidental Zimbabwean Peri-urban Housing Scheme Seeking Legitimation. Zambezia XXXIII(i/ii): pp. 71–89.

Musana, A. N. (2011). An Analysis of Housing Typologies in the Informal settlements of Kampala: A Case study of Kitintale and Mbuya. URL: www.infra.kth.se/bba/IAPS%20papers%20pdf/full%20paper_066.pdf

Mutisya, E. and Yarime, M. (2011). Understanding the Grassroots Dynamics of Slums in Nairobi: The Dilemma of Kibera Informal Settlements. International Transaction Journal of Engineering, Management, & Applied Sciences & Technologies 2(2): pp. 197–213. URL: http://www.TuEngr.com, http://go.to/Research.

Muzondo, I. F., Barry, M., Dewar, D. and Whittal, J. (2004). Land Conflicts in Informal Settlements: Wallacedene in Cape Town, South Africa. Paper prepared for the FIG Working Week, Athens, Greece, May 22–27, 2004.

Muzvidziwa, V. N. (2005). Informal Settlement Dwellers and Environmental Problems, in UNISWA Research Journal of Agriculture, Science and Technology, Special Volume No.1: pp. 25–37.

Nabutola, W. (2004). Upgrading Informal Settlements in Kenya: Rural and Urban. Paper prepared for the FIG Working Week, Athens, Greece, May 22–27, 2004.

Ndugwa, R. P., Kabiru, C. W., Cleland, J., Beguy, D., Egondi, T., Zulu, E. M., and Jessor, R. (2010) Adolescent Problem Behaviour in Nairobi's Informal Settlements: Applying Problem Behaviour Theory in Sub-Saharan Africa. Journal of Urban Health: Bulletin of the New York Academy of Medicine 2010: pp. 1–20.

Robeyns, I. (2005). The Capability Approach: A Theoretical Survey. Journal of Human Development 6(1): 93–114.

Oxfam GB, Concern Worldwide and CARE International in Kenya (2009). The Nairobi Informal Settlements: An emerging food security emergency within extreme chronic poverty.

Pangare, G. and Pangare, V. (2008). Informal Water Vendors and Service Providers in Uganda: The Ground Reality. URL: http://www.waterdialogues.org/documents/InformalWaterVendorsandServiceProvidersinUganda.pdf

Paulo, M., Rosário, C. and Tvedten, I. (2007) "Xiculungo"—Social Relations of Urban Poverty in Maputo, Mozambique. Report 13, URL: www.cmi.no/publications.

Pedley St. (2010). Catalysing self-sustaining sanitation chains in informal settlements (3K-SAN): Application to: SPLASH.

Piffero, E. (2009). What Happened to Participation? Urban Development and Authoritarian Upgrading in Cairo's Informal Neighbourhoods. Bologna.

REMA/UNEP/UNDP (2007). Bugesera Pilot Integrated Ecosystem Assessment; Final Report. Kigali: Rwanda Environmental Management Authority, United Nations Environmental Programme, United Nations Development Programme.

Republic of Rwanda (2010). National Policy and Strategy for Water Supply and Sanitation Services.

Sen, A. K. (1992). Inequality Re-examined. Oxford: Clarendon Press.

Shouyu, C., Qin, Z. I. and Eric, M. M. (2010). Sustainable Urbanization's Challenge in Democratic Republic of Congo. Journal of Sustainable Development 3(2).

Simone, A. M. (2003). Moving Towards Uncertainty: Migration and the Turbulence of African Urban Life. URL: http://time.dufe.edu.cn/wencong/africanmigration/2Simone.pdf.

Strumpfer, D. J. (2003). Resilience and Burn-out: A Stitch that Could Save Nine. South African Journal of Psychology 33(2): pp. 69–79.

Struyk, R. J. and Giddings, S. (2009). The Challenge of an Urban World—An Opportunity for U.S. Foreign Assistance. URL: http://www.intlhc.org/docs/The_Challenge_of_an_Urban_World.pdf

Todaro, M.P. and Smith, S. C. (2003). Economic Development. Harlow: Pearson Education Limited.

Tsinda, A. (2011). A Review and Analysis of the Situation Pertaining to the Provision of Sanitation to Low-Income Settlements in Kigali city (Rwanda): Adiagnostic Report. Kigali.

UNDP (2007). More Slums Equals More Violence: Reviewing Armed Violence and Urbanization in Africa. URL: http://www.genevadeclaration.org/fileadmin/docs/regional-publications/Armed-Violence-and-Urbanization-in-Africa.pdf

UNHABITAT (2005). Situation Analysis of Informal Settlements in Kisumu: Cities without Slums Sub Regional Programme for Eastern and Southern Africa. Nairobi.

UNHABITAT (2006). Nairobi Urban Sector Profile. Nairobi: UNHABITAT.

UNHABITAT (2008a). Ethiopia: Addia Ababa Urban Profile. Nairobi: UNHABITAT.

UNHABITAT (2008b). The State of African Cities Report: A framework for Addressing Urban Challenges in Africa. Nairobi: UNHABITAT.

UNHABITAT. (2010). Mozambique Cities Profile. Nairobi: UNHABITAT.

UNHABITAT. (2011). Malawi: Lilongwe Urban Profile. Nairobi: UNHABITAT.

Vestbro Dick Urban (editor) (2008). Are Architects and Planners Obstacles to Slum Upgrading? URL: http://arcpeace.org/NewARC-Peace/Publications/EnablingBook3.pdf

Yongsi H. B. Nguendo (2009). Human Settlement, Land Management and Health in Sub Saharan Cities. International Journal of Human and Social Sciences 4(1): pp. 10–17.

Chapter 8
ANALYSIS OF WOMEN'S ORGANIZATIONS AS DRIVERS OF GENDERED SOCIAL TRANSFORMATION: EXPERIENCES FROM ZIMBABWE

Manase Chiweshe

Poverty in Zimbabwe is gendered in ways that have ensured women are the majority of the poor with 70% located in the rural areas. Rural women constitute the bulk of marginalized people, yet their life conditions remain unproblematized at the policy level. What sort of social transformation is required for these women? Who should lead this transformation? This chapter explores the theme of social transformation as it relates to structural poverty and gender issues. It questions whether women's movements and grassroots organizations in Zimbabwe can act as catalysts for this social transformation. Through a nuanced analysis of the nature, activities, capacities, and ideologies underpinning women's movement, the author present a complex picture of contradiction, collusion, differentiation, success, and failure of the women's movement in poverty alleviation in Zimbabwe. This highlights the different actors within women's activist movements while narrowing the focus on various grassroots agencies that offer opportunity and hope for a truly transformative process.

1   Introduction

Poverty is an enduring legacy of human histories. The majority of Africans have long lived in abject poverty. After decades of development aid and neoliberal-led projects designed to promote poverty alleviation, Africa's poorest are found further at the margins. Poverty in Zimbabwe, however defined, is highly gendered in ways that have ensured women remain the majority of the impoverished. This chapter explores the theme of social transformation as it relates to addressing gendered dimensions of structural poverty. It questions whether the women's movements and grassroots organization in Zimbabwe can act as social catalysts and change agents for this social transformation. Through a nuanced analysis of nature, activities, capacities, and ideologies underpinning women's organizations, this chapter presents a complex picture of contradiction, collusion, differentiation, success, and failure of the women's movement in aiding poverty alleviation. In analyzing the women's movement in Zimbabwe, the chapter begins with Eerdewijk's and Mugadza's assertion that:

> The contemporary status, and the future, of the women's movement in Zimbabwe has been the subject of much discussion and debate. In the early 2000s, a returning concern was that "women's movements have lost their vibrancy and resilience, and are no longer as effective in representing women's interests in their counties, as they were in their formative years" (Masvaure and Wamwanduka 2008, p. 1).

Essof also positioned her 2013 book *Shemurenga* in relation to discussions in the early 2000s, when "some questioned whether women's organizing actually constituted a movement," others argued that the movement had been "weakened ideologically," whereas others "recognised a movement but saw it as weak and dismantled".

Women in Zimbabwe are marginalized from mainstream economic activities despite the fact that they are 52% of the population. This is because the majority of women are domiciled in rural areas and as such isolated from policy-making processes. Contributions made by women should be understood within the social and cultural governance system of rural areas, in which patriarchy plays a key role in determining how and to what extent they should be involved in the processes of development.

2 History of Women's Organization

The history of women organizations in Zimbabwe can be directly linked to the Christian missionary movement in colonial Rhodesia. The very first documented women's organizations were Christian groups as Ziyambi (1997: 7) notes:

[...] [The] earliest women's groups in Zimbabwe were linked to missionary activity and the church. The Wesleyan Women's Groups and the Media in Zimbabwe Methodist Church women's Ruwadzano (fellowship) movement had taken hold in the then Southern Rhodesia by 1919... The primary aim of these groups was to teach African women about God. Secondary aims included instructions on how to maintain a home that measured up to Christian standards of cleanliness... The Victorian ideal of virtuous wife, selfless mother, and tidy, industrious housekeeper was the goal for which all African women should be taught to strive.

While these groups were conservative in their approach, they provided spaces for women to meet and interact on their own. The concern of the organization was limiting women to the private sphere and these groups have continued in postcolonial Zimbabwe. Women are taught about cooking, home design, sewing and involved in various health and entrepreneurial activities in church groups. It is only around 1923 that the first signs of women organizing within the public sphere begin to emerge. Chiweshe and Bhatasara (forthcoming) note that in 1923 women were part of the Southern Rhodesia Bantu Voters Association and they successfully organized a boycott of the beer halls in 1934. Colonial structures in many ways suppressed women from actively organizing within the public sphere. Under colonial rule in Zimbabwe, Gaidzanwa (1992) illustrates how patriarchy and white colonial capital colluded to institutionalize gender inequalities. Colonial government required male labor in the cities and mines but wanted women to stay in the rural areas to reproduce labor and care for the old, sick, and injured men. African men on the other hand wanted women to remain in the rural areas to safeguard their land claims, which they would use after retiring. As such laws were put in place to curtail women's movement in the urban areas where most accommodation was for single men in flats.

As Zimbabwe's fight for independence intensified during the 1970s, women became an important part of the armed struggle. This had an impact on gender as women fought and participated in the war with their male counterparts. Women fighters were viewed as equals during the war and there was an assumption that independence from colonial rule would usher in gender equality. In understanding gender and the liberation movement in Zimbabwe, Groves (2007) argues that:

> Gender politics appeared increasingly institutionalised within ZANU, allowing the party's Women's League to declare publicly that "for the revolution to triumph in its totality there must be emancipation of women" (in Seidman, 1984: 419) ... Nhongo-Simbanegavi reports that "it carried pictures of formidable-looking women, often in situations defying traditional notions of femininity" (2000: 1). The emancipation of women was possible, Weiss argued, "thanks to the social change that was set in motion by the armed revolution"; women were playing a "dynamic role in the national liberation movement....[1]

Mojubaolu Olufunke-Okome (2003: 82) argues, "In both its colonial and post-colonial forms, the African State has discriminated consistently against women." At independence in most African states, women were simply co-opted into the structures of the new ruling elites. Gaidzanwa (1992) shows how in Zimbabwe, women simply became appendages of the partriachial ruling classes without any fundamental changes in their conditions. The postcolonial state in Africa has thus largely been partriachial and co-opting women through gender mainstreaming programs which do little to transform structures that place women in inferior positions. The liberation struggle did not yield the benefits it had promised for women.

The Zimbabwean state took a paternalistic view toward women's organizations and issues as the benefits of independence did not lead to women's emancipation. The government implemented some progressive measures such as the Legal Age of Majority Act, which gave women adult status at the age of 18. Overall women's organizations were largely organized around the state with very little being done to challenge the patriarchal status quo. What the liberation struggle had done however was to provide opportunities for some women to gain education outside

---

[1] http://www.e-ir.info/2007/12/13/the-construction-of-a-%E2%80%98liberation%E2%80%99-gender-and-the-%E2%80%98national-liberation-movement%E2%80%99-in-zimbabwe/[accessed 23 June 2014]

the country, lead in various spaces of the struggle, and show that they could do what men can do also.

Women's organizations post independence were thus largely subdued by the state. Until the 1990s such organizations focusing upon women's issues would shy away from making more radical demands on the state, preferring instead to work with and in the state, more often than not as an expression of the personal/ class interests which the dominant leadership bring into the movement structures. It is only in the 1990s were the emergence of civil society organizations that we see a radical change in the women's movement as organizations such as Musasa emerged. Such organizations defied the paternalistic and partriachial structures of the state and demanded radical change in the situation of women. In 1983, however, women activists had already began to challenge the state with the formation of a Women's Action Group to protest the arrest of women moving on the streets alone at night (Makanje, Shaba and Win 2004: 10). The increased education for women and access to international spaces where feminism and gender issues were discussed such as 1985 United Nations Women's Conference in Nairobi, Kenya, led to important milestones within the movement. This was however met with a "backlash against the pioneers of the women's movement soon after independence was quite severe, especially for those who advocated for women's emancipation. This backlash was more vicious from fellow females than males" (Kwinjeh, 2010: 8).

3 Gendered Social Transformation: Theoretical Grounding

This chapter looks at social transformation from a gendered perspective. It questions whether gender as defined, organized, and advocated for in Zimbabwe holds any promise for poor and marginalized women. It highlights the challenges facing women's movements and how they can ultimately be mobilized as vehicles for gendered social transformation. Only when women on the continent began to speak on their own experiences without copying and pasting theoretical assumptions alien to their existence will we begin to see the women's movement bearing fruit for millions of suffering people on the continent. Social transformation is a fundamental shift in how a society is organized. Such shifts are radical in nature, altering sociocultural systems and relations. Mukaramurenzi (2011) argues that the best process of social transformation is one that eradicates all kinds of inequalities and hierarchies that have been established between men and women throughout history. To understand better how social transformation can lead to gender equality, I adopt Spannos's theory of complimentary holism which is an "alternative to historical materialism, which would keep in possession the effort to understand the historical forces of change but also bring the attention to the totality of social relations and the core factors that shape people and society as a whole, not only by class struggle, but through all aspects of life" (Mukaramurenzi, 2011: 5). The theory of complimentary holism provides for four spheres of social life: economic, kinship, community, and political. Social transformation depends on what takes place in the four spheres of life mentioned above. There is a complementary and holistic orientation, which does not a priori assume the primary dominance of any of the spheres over any of the others, but instead seeks to understand how the parts of the whole are interdependent and relate to one another.

Gendered social transformation thus focuses and depends upon changes in the four spheres of life articulated by Spannos (2008). This, however, requires us to understand what gender means and what it signifies in those four spheres. Transforming multiplicity of relations of subordination that women find themselves under requires an understanding of gender inequalities in all spheres of society. To better illuminate this idea, the paper invokes the concept of intersectionality, which allows for a better analysis of how the spheres interact and intersect to create women's subordinate position (Crenshaw, 1991). Intersectionality accepts that women carry multiple and conflicting identities mainly based on class, religion, caste, and ethnicity, which affect their involvement and action in women's groups. Ramtohul (2012) argues that the concept of intersectionality and identity has shown that identities are complex, comprising multiple intersections of class, gender, race, nationality, and sexuality, causing individuals to react differently at different times. She adds that women's political actions do not solely depend on their feminine identity, but are also influenced by other social traits with which they identify. In a study of women in the United States and South Africa,

Bahati Kuumba (2002: 504) notes that "activism of women and their organizations sprang from their particular positioning within systems of multiple oppressions simultaneously experiencing racial/ethnic, class, and gender oppression." Emergence of women's organization in Zimbabwe thus has to be understood using intersectionality theory which recognizes that women are often positioned and intersected within system of multiple oppressions such as racial, patriarchal, and class inequalities.

Categorization of Women's Organizations and Their Activities

Women's organization in Zimbabwe can be categorized in different ways. In terms of size, there are national, regional, and community-based women's organizations. National organizations such as Women in Politics Support Unit have a wider reach and focus on issues at a national scale. Operations of national-level organizations are geared toward achieving a higher level impact at policy level while community-based organizations are oriented toward particular needs at the grassroots. Regional organizations operate at ward, district, or provincial level. Such organizations are based, operate, and work within specific areas. Women's organizations can also be formal and informal. Formal organizations are registered, legally recognized entities which are funded and have written constitutions with rules and regulations. Such organizations have paid staff and are usually founded by individuals or groups of women and even men. They go into communities and start projects most of which are determined by donor funds and interventions. These organizations are more visible and their sphere of influence is greater. Informal organizations are usually started by women at the grassroots as spaces for women to meet, socialize, share, teach each other, and initiate projects such as revolving groups. Such organizations are based on trust and are limited to women who know and live near each other. They are not registered and are not recognized by the state. The groups are ephemeral in nature, depending on continued social capital.

Women's organizations are located in different locations namely urban, peri–urban, and rural areas. The majority of organizations are urban based though they still have programming within rural areas. Some have offices in the rural areas they operate in but these face challenges in terms of electricity, communication, and networking access. Location is important in terms of visibility and access to donors and it also determines the type of programming as programs differ in urban and rural areas. Women's organizations in Zimbabwe are mainly involved in policy and advocacy work. Organizations such as the Women's Lawyers Association for example are involved in understanding how inheritance and customary laws affect women. Few organizations are involved in women empowerment yet a change in policy or laws alone will not lead to equality in other spheres of life. With sexual violence being a prevalent problem, especially domestic and gender-based violence, it is disheartening to see very few organizations involved in such work especially supporting rape victims. Another way to categorize women's organizations is by focusing on the age group they work with. There has been an increase in youth-based organizations while those focusing on children such as the Girl Child Network have operated for years.

There are also organizations, especially at donor and international level, that are not necessarily women's organizations but do a great deal to promote gender equality. Such organizations are involved in either funding women's organizations or implementing women related programs. One example are organizations such as SIDA and USAID which have largely funded women's organizations operating in various parts of the country. There are, however, complex challenges involved with such donor agencies, as Diana Jeater (2011) argues:

> The perception amongst workers who are trying to make a difference at the grassroots in Zimbabwe is that big aid agencies such as UNICEF and DfID don't engage with communities to find out what they need; they deliver to them. Jeannie Sinclair described turning up for a session with her care-givers one day, to find the village filled with DfID Land Cruisers and people from the district whom she had not met before. Apparently this was the "˜delivery' of DfID's gender-based violence programme. The DfID team swooped in, gave everyone free Coca-Cola and a text to keep about GBV, and then swooped out again. The free drink and the hoohah attracted scores of participants, who could be recorded on the programme report. Job done? A combination of tight auditing and external agenda-setting influences the evaluation of projects, and this in turn affects the project design. In order to be reportable, outcomes must be measurable. In order to be measurable, they

must be tangible. There is a common complaint is that aid agencies only recognise "things" as outcomes, not relationships.[2]

There are also international organizations which come in two broad categories working within the women's sector in Zimbabwe. Firstly, are the UN agencies working in various ways to promote women's interests. UN Women is directly involved and can be categorized as an international women's organization. UN Women's mandate in Zimbabwe is, however, aided by other agencies such as UNDP, UNFPA, and UNICEF. The major challenge with UN organizations is apparent when one considers the uncoordinated nature of their programs. This may be because they operate as separate entities and issues of control may lead to conflicts. Secondly, are those international NGOs such as CARE International, World Vision, Plan and Goal. All these organizations have gender- or women-focused programs of one form or another. The major challenge, however, is that these programs tend not to question or challenge patriachial norms but rather focus upon piecemeal activities such as gardens, revolving funds, and projects. Another problem is the limited reach of such organizations that work in only a few districts in the country.

4   Class and Ideological Basis of Women's Organizations

Women's organizations are a kaideloscope of differing interests and ideologies. It can be argued that differences of education, job opportunities, and cultural possibilities also get filtered through the lenses of class and ethnicity which structures the individual experiences of women and as such their organizing. Thus, it is mainly educated, middle-class, and career women who initiate and run women's organization. We could also argue that the women's movement in Zimbabwe allowed access for women into the middle class which has both advantages and disadvantages for the movement. The disadvantage is that this severely undermined its political viability and effectiveness as a movement while it also created new sources of identity for women in the public which fur-

---

[2]   http://africanarguments.org/2011/08/08/parasites-of-the-poor-international-ngos-and-aid-agencies-in-zimbabwe-by-diana-jeater/ (accessed May 12, 2013).

thered their cause for equality. Like other middle-class-led movements, women's organizations in Zimbabwe face a severe disconnect with the grassroots. There is a lack of understanding of gender-related concepts by a significant number of civic organizations working in the "gender sector" in Zimbabwe. The concept of gender is widely used in Africa but what this concept precisely denotes remains fraught with contestations. We have to question the essentializing tendencies of much feminist scholarship which tends to promote binary views of gender that reduce women to their vaginas and generalize these individuals into an underclass of victims under the overwhelming oppression of patriarchy. The existence of patriarchy in many societies in Africa is not disputed and that it subjugates women and relegates them to the private sphere is well documented. What is missing is a nuanced understanding of how gender interlinks and interplays with various other forms of identity such as class, age, ethnicity, religious affiliation, nationality, and status to determine our lives. To proclaim gender as the overarching factor in all situations is to hide various fascinating and crucial modes of identities which are constantly being created and recreated by active agents in their everyday lives.

Ramtohul (2012) argues that women's organizations need to mobilize a feminist consciousness if they are to transform unequal gender relations. There are thus many contested feminist positions. For some feminist consciousness is the awareness by women that they belong to a subordinate group and that, as members of such a group, they have suffered wrongs. It is recognition that their condition of subordination is not natural, but societally determined. This will lead to the development of a sense of sisterhood; the autonomous definition by women of their goals and strategies for changing their condition; and the development of an alternate vision of the future. This consciousness needs to be steeped in the everyday lived experiences of women on the continent. Feminist consciousness calls for sisterhood and unity among women through transcending their intersectional identities. Nzegwu (in Oyewumi, 2004: vii), however, is suspicious of this as she argues that there is a myth of sisterhood among women, yet what pertains is actually a "sisterarchy." Any talk of solidarity among women has to avoid recreating other forms of inequality among them. For example, rural women and educated middle-class activists with exposure from travel across the world already face distinct differences despite their similar gender.

In a blog narrating her personal experiences, Delta Ndou highlights how the mainstream women's movement in Zimbabwe is mainly Harare-based (capital city). Other areas have sub-offices but remain outside the mainstream. She outlines how for young women outside Harare the movement remains inaccessible and hopelessly out of touch with the grassroots. Women who have been at the helm of the movement do not invest in training the next generation; transferring skills, knowledge, wisdom and fostering a culture of continuity. Without mentoring the next generation of leaders, the work done by these women activists will be interred with them.[3] This is what Murungu (2008) has described as a lack of succession plans in most organizations where competition over resources or survival has led to older members closing doors for young members.We can propose a serious critique on the radical and transformative nature of urban-based civil society in Zimbabwe. Civil society in Zimbabwe (which includes women's organizations) has been thought of as progressive, yet "...civil society itself is in various ways a site of domination, inequality and conflict: the moment of social domination inscribed within civil society is ignored" (Helliker, 2012: 11). Women's organizations fall prey to problems that generally affect all other civil society groupings, for example upward accountability and urban bias. They are answerable to donors and women at the grassroots have little say in how or what happens with programming. There has been a growing literature denouncing the undemocratic tendencies within the civil society in Zimbabwe (Makumbe, 1998; Mhlanga, 2008). Women's organizations are sadly part of this civic context in which people have created cults and protection around positions and spaces.

5 Challenges Facing Women's Organizations

Ziyambi (1997) argues that women's groups in Zimbabwe have historically operated within a tight resource base as they have always existed outside government support. In Zimbabwe, funding flow from interna-

---

[3] http://itsdelta.wordpress.com/an-open-letter-to-the-womens-movement-in-zimbabwe/ (accessed August 12, 2012).

tional donors to local civic organizations has gradually declined from around US$2.6 million to just over US$1 million since 2007 (Joint Donor Steering Committee, 2010). Most formal women's organizations depend on international donor funding which has its own serious pitfalls: for example, such funds are usually tied to short-term projects which might not necessarily help in the long-term battle against inequality. With the reduction of donor funds there is also increased competition for donor resources as various organizations battle for relevance. This has led to a lack of coordination and at times outright confrontation among organizations.

The space for organizing in Zimbabwe has shrunk and the material conditions (infrastructure, political space, capacity) that support organizing have been severely eroded (Jones, 2008). Post 2000, women's organizations turned to survival mode as they faced multiple threats and challenges from a state and its agents who became more violent and an economic context which made it difficult to operate. With many arrests of female activists, most women's organizations have to be apolitical, and to be more service oriented and hence keep in a safe space (Jones, 2008). Another problem is that politically the women's movement remains weak. Major political parties remain male dominated and patriarchal in orientation. Women are represented in the two biggest parties, the MDC and ZANU PF, yet the women's wings of these parties remain oriented toward the political goals of leaders. Without women-centered political party the efforts of women within these patriarchal structures will achieve very little as women's activist Thoko Matshe notes, "Zimbabwe will still be a patriarchal state no matter who wins [the elections] currently, so for women it is 'Aluta Continua'—the struggle continues" (Jones, 2008).

One of the biggest challenges for the women's movement has been the question of the state. The state in this instance is not simply the government but rather the whole authoritarian structure based on partriachial and masculine control of and over women: their bodies and identities. The period following the 2000 crisis made this question more pertinent as Win (2004) notes, "The crisis has left the women's movement in disarray... A major blockage for the Women's Coalition is its lack of a clear position on its relationship with the State." Pietrzyk (2009) argues that the women's movement remains problematically betwixt and between this issue of relating to the state. Complicating matters here are the individual relationships of some activists with the state. As Pietrzyk (2009) points out, the women's movement in Zimbabwe has never really rebounded from Operation Clean Up of 1983 when the state violated the rights of ordinary citizens by arresting thousands of women for the "crime" of being on the street alone. As noted earlier, this led to the birth of Women's Action Group (WAG) which was followed by many other organizations some of which challenged the state, others remained apolitical and yet still others were co-opted and captured by the state. This confrontational approach to the state by WAG meant that it remained isolated from the growing women's movement and they were disowned by some women's organizations in public. Even for other women their confrontational approach to state and patriarchy was untenable. Present-day women's movement is still riddled with this problem in relation to state and patriarchy. The differences in approach and worldview toward the state and patriarchy have often seen divisions between organizations. Thus we have organizations all working for the development of women but yet miles apart on what this really means and the extent to which they will challenge entrenched power relations.

Political polarization in Zimbabwe makes it difficult for many organizations to operate. Organizations working in governance and human rights issues are often seen as representatives of positions of support or condemnation of ZANU PF or its opponents. It is not only political parties that carry this perception but also, media, donors, and women's organizations themselves. This has brought about attacks on many organizations especially the "silencing" of the women's movement on Prime Minister Morgan Tsvangirai's (leader of the Movement for Democratic Change) treatment of women in his personal life. Different women's organizations have over the years found ways to make strategic and selective linkages with the state and various other political movements such as National Constitutional Assembly (NCA), Movement for Democratic Change, and other women's organizations. It remains, however, an important issue going forward for the women's movement to analyse, outline, and strategize how they relate to the state and various other agencies. Essof (2005: 13) notes that, "Whether women should organise within the state or stay outside of it has been the subject of much debate internationally. Some commentators believe that effective reform can only come via state instruments, while others argue that the state co-opts women's issues."

6   Is There a Women's Movement(s) in Zimbabwe?

This question is based on an ongoing internal conversation within Zimbabwean women's organizations. In my view, the particular concern is whether there is unity of purpose and general agreement toward similar goals and outcomes. A women's movement presumes a coalition, a coming together of different minds, forces, groups, and organizations working toward fulfilling women's interests. Shareen Essof (2005), in analyzing the outcomes of a meeting in 2001 of women's organizations that was meant to discuss the question, asks the question, "does Zimbabwe have a women's movement?" and notes three responses. Firstly, there were those who questioned whether the activities of Zimbabwean women's organizations constitute a movement; secondly, those that suggested that the movement had been so ideologically weakened that it was reduced to perpetuating the patriarchal status quo; and lastly, those that recognized a movement, but described it as weak, paralyzed, and in disarray. What is interesting at that time is how unsure women's organizations were about being a movement. When concentrating on their differences, these organizations appear as a loose collective.

In answering the question of whether there is a women's movement in Zimbabwe.

Shaba (2001) argues that the women's movement can be explained as being a loose formation of development organizations and individuals who apply a feminist ideology to development activities aimed at uplifting the status of women in Zimbabwe. There are those who stress the divisions and challenges that paralyze the movement. For them the movement is at best weak and polarized. Political polarization in the country has caught up with women's organizations in Zimbabwe. Women's movement in Zimbabwe is a collection of fragmented sections caught up in politicking at the expense of people's welfare. The constitution making process has provided another space to spell out the differing.

Win (2004: 19) asks "...if the Zimbabwean women's movement can rise above the challenges of the current context, and coalesce once more around shared interests, with our sense of these interests made stronger by an awareness of the differences between us." This question arises from the need to understand whether being a woman is reason enough to join others. Why privilege gender at the expense of all other forms of inequalities? Women's interests diverse depending with where they are located in space and time. Building coalitions of people with diverse interests and values requires further understanding of diversity and finding common ground. Musonza (2012) then asks a pertinent question: What are women's issues anyway? One of the interesting aspects within the Zimbabwean context is the issue of sexuality. Zimbabwe has a hegemonic discourse of heteronormality based on the power-constructions of male-domination, political interference, and the rise of religious fundamentalism. Sexual rights are a contentious issue within the women's movement. For women who are lesbian or transsexual, their interests mainly revolve around earning their rights in a country were queer and alternative sexualities are repressed and stigmatized. Most women's organizations, especially those based on religious philosophies, do not support the fight for sexual rights; politically based organizations such as ZANU PF Women's League follow the party line, thus being outright hostile to homosexuality. Gays and Lesbians Zimbabwe (GALZ, 2012: 5) argue that:

> During the Committee on the Elimination Discrimination against Women (CEDAW) reporting planning meetings held in Harare in October 2011, GALZ was not invited to participate in the process and this has resulted in the organisation producing this report independently. The exclusion of LBT people in the women's rights space is a challenge as issues that are presented by women's organisations and coalitions fail to reflect abuse and violations experienced by this "minority group" and serve to highlight homophobia within the women's human rights space.

Women find themselves at different intersections and thus their experiences differ with respect to class, ethnicity, race, sexuality, religion, education, location, age, and physical attributes. For example, women in rural Matabeleland live in a dry region that has historically faced marginalization and thus face severe food insecurities. There interests do not necessarily correlate to those of most organizations that are located in the capital city Harare, far away from their everyday lives. Women's interests are not unitary but we can try to transcend these differences and intersectionalities. How this process of transcending should happen when issues that are divisive, such as sexuality, politics and ethnicity, are involved is highly contested. McFadden (2002) narrates her own experiences with the women's movement in Zimbabwe where she did not get any support when deported for "betrayal of 'Zimbabwean culture' and 'family values' and identified as a lesbian." Even though she was heterosexual, her feminist stance and views against homosexuality as inauthentic and criminal were deemed dangerous. Yet none of the women's organizations came out to her support. As she notes: "The deafening silence with which this was greeted by the Women's Movement in Zimbabwe spoke volumes about the hegemony of patriarchal nationalism, of the deeply ingrained right-wing definitions of alternative sexual choices as culturally alien, and of the political and discursive silencing of women through the surveillance of their sexuality" (Macfadden, 2002).

In discussing this question of whether a movement exists in Zimbabwe, I think it is pertinent to discuss one such effort by various actors to build a coalition based on women's interests. The Women's Coalition (WC) was set up in 1999 as a way to push women's demands in the constitution. This was around the time where a coalition of diverse organizations under the banner of National Constitutional Assembly (NCA) was formed. Among the commendable work they have done, one is to fight for the increase in participation of women in the constitution-making processes in Zimbabwe. WC had members within the NCA which successfully campaigned for a "No" vote on the government promoted constitution in 2000. The authors of the new constitution were chosen by government under what was known as the Constitutional Commission (CC), which co-opted some members of the NCA and WC and this created crisis and mistrust within wider civil society and the women's coalition. WC was faced by a crisis of divergent interests and questions, which Win (2004) succinctly outlines:

Was confronting the State a desirable tactic? What kind of alliance would the women's movement have, if any, with the opposition political parties in this process? Was a good constitutional document all the women wanted, or was it critical that this should emerge from an inclusive process? What exactly would constitute "good enough" participation, by and for women? How would the question of race and racism be tackled both within our own ranks, and in the wider political discourse?

Yet going forward any talk of a women's movement in Zimbabwe needs to deal with this pertinent issue. It is about managing the diversity of interests' and tactics of different organizations while maintaining a common goal.
Commodification of Resistance: Women's Movement and Donor Funding in ZimbabweWhile it is not advisable to generalize with regard to all civil society organizations, post 2000 Zimbabwe has shown increasing complications when dealing with donor funding. Zeilig (2008), in explaining the evolution of the student movement in Zimbabwe, outlines an interesting concept introduced by the International Socialist Organization (ISO). He notes that:

> The term commodification of resistance was coined by the ISO to describe how resistance was privatized (or perhaps a better term is "bought") by NGOs in Zimbabwe. This is, perhaps, a symptom of the frustrated transition, and the decline in the movement that gave birth to the MDC, which is regarded as having distorted grass roots activism by the introduction of donor money (Zeilig, 2008: 230).

This phenomenon is apparent across all civil society sectors in Zimbabwe. Donor funding while necessary and helpful to building up civil society organizations has led to serious problems at the grassroots. At a time when the country was suffering a serious economic crisis (2000–2008), activists in different organizations with access to foreign currency and trips outside the country became an elite class. This class was in many ways divorced from the realities of many people at the grassroots especially in the rural areas. Competition increased in attracting donor funding as fundraising and not grassroots mobilization became the business of the day for many organizations, some of which had mushroomed in response to the crisis. Zeilig further notes that:

> John Bomba captures these distortions and the effect the "commodification of resistance" has on the student movement: [I]t brings in the question of how the international community has been able to assist us in advancing the cause and in some sense, there has also been an element of misplaced international support that has actually drawn us back…. With the crisis in Zimbabwe … there has been massive monies coming into Zimbabwe. You find a plethora of NGOs … that do nothing that is relevant to the plight of Zimbabwe but none the less they are getting massive financial support. So there is this element … [with] people now selling the ability to resist (Zeilig, 2008: 230).

As activism becomes more embroiled in careerism, it loses contact with the grassroots, the very people that it claims to speak for. The women's movement in Zimbabwe has been caught up in this process. Without women at the helm of efforts of women's organization, a gendered social transformation will not succeed.

Gender activism and scholarship has been co-opted into global processes which has stifled the movement fighting against the impoverishment of the poor, especially rural women, by a global system which favors powerful multinational corporations. The hegemony of global imperialism is increasingly eroding feminism and radical cultural expression and discourses in civil society at an international level. In many ways gender activism has become a career path for many educated middle-class women within academia and NGOs who are using the experiences of rural women and poor urban women as a platform to build careers and make a living. Feminist scholarship has become a market commodity within research houses and organizations where knowledge about and for poor rural women is used for fundraising and project making without fundamental challenge to the structures that keep these women in poverty. Gender activism as promoted currently does not speak to the needs and experiences of a differentiated class of women on the continent. It can be argued that the present context of limitless information, globalized power relations, transnational media oligarchies, and commoditized academic knowledge mystifies patriarchal and neo-imperial injustice through the rhetoric of "liberalisation" and "legitimate" paternalist protection and patriotism. Feminist demands under such a framework are easily and readily co-opted, dismissed, and marginalized.

7 Women's Organizations and Gendered Social Transformation in Zimbabwe

In this section I invoke Spannos (2008) theory of complimentary holism to understand how women's organizations can effectively institute gendered social transformation. As noted, the theory of complimentary holism provides for four spheres of social life: economic, kinship, community, and political. In Zimbabwe, women's poverty and gender inequality is rooted in these four spheres yet women's organizations have rarely challenged them in a holistic manner. Only through a coalition can concerted efforts by organizations working in these various sectors be properly orchestrated and directed. What Spannos's theory shows us is that without complementarity the individual work of organizations will not achieve transformation of existing partriachial systems that have entrenched women in poverty. The theory of complimentary holism thus recognizes the need for coalitions. In Zimbabwe, sharing a gender may not be enough for coalition building (Win, 2004). Yet despite intersectional differences of women, there is a common thread of partriachial control and domination. Building a complimentary network requires embracing all these various interests, manage diversity, and respect differences. This has to be based on the equality of people or groups within the various organizations by avoiding creating sisterachies and promoting certain positions at the expense of others. The political sphere has seen organizations such as WiPSU working toward increasing the number of women in political positions. Increasing numbers without a fundamental shift in the policy framework will not achieve much for the majority of women. The goal should be to change politics and promote women's interests in their diversity. Gendered social transformation begins at the grassroots with the investment of communities in the eradication of structural constraints that leave women poorer than men.

Within the Zimbabwean context, the women's movement as presently operating offers little hope for a holistic transformation of women's lives. What is required is an internal reengineering based on the knowledge, needs, and lived experiences of all women despite their class, ethnicity, religion, or creed.

The important lesson to be learned from the Zimbabwean context is that being women is not the only prerequisite for coming together and building a coalition for transformation. Privileging biology over other identity markers and talk of a women's movement solely based on sharing similar organs only creates hierarchies between women. Rather, a frank assessment of where women are located, who they are and their politics is important in order to build a common interest. Spanno's theory thus provides an important recommendation for women in Zimbabwe: complementarity and not competition. Discord, turf wars, ideological differences, and generational gaps all weaken the movement and thereby affect the achievement of a society in which gender or class can be used as the basis of discriminating against another. Yet Eerdewijk and Mugadza (2015) highlight women's organizations' positive contribution to communities' development. They note that "the history of the women's movement in Zimbabwe is not only about engagement with the state, but also in community-based organizing. The positive effects of community-based organizing in terms of improving livelihoods or facilitating access to services are widely acknowledged, in diverse domains, such as entrepreneurship, savings and credit and HIV/AIDS" (Eerdewijk and Mugadza, 2015: 37).

8 Conclusion

Gendered social transformation remains a work in progress in Zimbabwe. This chapter has explored the women's movement in Zimbabwe as a potential source for this transformation. It has examined the historical evolution of the movement, noting its weaknesses, challenges, successes, and opportunities. There is need for new forms of engagement with people, especially vulnerable groups, based on mutual camaraderie and not top-down approaches utilized by mainstream civil society. Women's organizations need to break from the mainstream ways of conducting business and engage with rural spaces where the majority of the women are located. Competition and contestations achieve very little for the ultimate cause of emancipating women from poverty. While there are many challenges facing women's organization, what is important is that there is already a starting point to allow for network building and began to grapple with sustaining a movement for social change. African feminist scholars, activists, and policy makers need to be steeped in the practices of women's organizations as way to promote action research. As such, in Zimbabwe women's organizations require an ideological basis nourished from below. For long, women's organizations have mirrored the top-down approach and vertical accountability of other civil society organizations, being answerable to donors and not to communities. Engaging with the grassroots as equal partners remains a priority. The movement cannot afford to be urban centric and concentrated within the capital city. Their constituency is relegated to rural spaces as such organizations should respond and concentrate their work in these areas. The realities of most middle-class, urban-based, and university-educated activists and scholars are totally different. Overcoming these important intersectionalities is possible if members of these groups and organizations focus upon transcending differences and concentrating upon their shared needs and objectives.

References

Bahati Kuumba, M. (2002) "You've Struck a Rock" Comparing Gender, Social Movements, and Global Action against Zim's Political Rape Horror, The Zimbabwean, August 22, 2011. Available at: http://www.thezimbabwean.co.uk/news/zimbabwe/51981/global-action-against-zimrsquos-political.html (accessed July 6, 2012).

Crenshaw, K. (1991) "Mapping the Margins: Intersectionality, Identity Politics and Violence against Women of Color," Stanford Law Review 43 (6), pp. 1241–1299.

Essof, S. (2005) "She-murenga: Challenges, Opportunities and Setbacks of the Women's Movement in Zimbabwe," Feminist Africa, Issue 3. Available at: http://www.akinamamawaafrika.org/index.php/publi

cations/more-publications/52-17-essof-shemurenga/file (accessed May 24, 2013).

Gaidzanwa, R. (1992) "Bourgeois Theories of Gender and Feminism and their Shortcomings with Reference to Southern African Countries," in Meena, R. (ed.), Gender in Southern Africa: Conceptual and Theoretical Issues. Harare: SAPES Books.

GALZ (2012) Report on Discrimination against Women in Zimbabwe based on Sexual Orientation and Gender Identity, submitted to the Committee on the Elimination Discrimination against Women on January 6, 2012 for the 51st session, to be held in Geneva.

Groves, A. (2007) The Construction of "Liberation": Gender and the "National Liberation Movement" in Zimbabwe. Available at: http://www.e-ir.info/2007/12/13/the-construction-of-a-%E2%80%98liberation%E2%80%99-gender-and-the-%E2%80%98national-liberationmovement%E2%80%99-in-zimbabwe/ (accessed August 4, 2012).

Jeater, D. (2011) Zimbabwe: International NGOs and aid agencies—Parasites of the Poor? African Arguments. Available at: http://africanarguments.org/2011/08/08/parasites-of-the-poor-international-ngos-and-aid-agencies-in-zimbabwe-by-diana-jeater/

Jones, R. (2008) The Crisis in Zimbabwe: A Gender Perspective, AWID. Available at: http://www.kubatana.net/html/archive/gen/080509awid.asp?sector=gen&year=2008&range_start=31

Kwinjeh, G. (2010) "Thirty Years after Political Independence—Creating Political Space for Zimbabwean Women," in van Reisen, M.E.H. et al. (eds), Zimbabwe: Women's Voices: Report of the European Parliamentary Hearing. Brussels: EEPA.

Makanje, R., Shaba, L.M. and Win, E.J. (2004) "Linking Rights and Participation: Zimbabwe Country Study," Participation Group-Institute of Development Studies, Sussex.

Makumbe, J. (1998) Democracy and Development in Zimbabwe: Constraints of Decentralisation. Harare: SAPES Books.

Masvaure, T. and Wamwanduka, L. (2008) The State of the Women's Movement in Contemporary Zimbabwe. Harare: Friedrich Ebert Stiftung, Zimbabwe Office.

McFadden, P. (2002) Becoming Post Colonial: African Women Changing the Meaning of Citizenship. Paper presented at Queens University, Canada.

Mhlanga, B. (2008) "Civil Society's Double Standards Inimical to Change in Zimbabwe." Available at: www.kubatana.net

Mukaramurenzi, C. (2011) "Education for Social Transformation." Unpublished Master's thesis, University of Peace.

Murungu, G.N. (2008) Women's Movements during the Crisis. Presentation at 2008 AWID.

Olufunke-Okome, M. (2003) "What Women, whose Development? A Critical Analysis of Reformist Evangelism," in Oyewumi, O. (ed.), African Women and Feminism: Reflectingon the Politics of Sisterhood. Trenton: Africa World Press, pp. 66–98.

Pietrzyk, S. (2009) Betwixt and between the State. Available at: http://www.kubatanablogs.net/kubatana/?p=1471 (accessed May 12, 2008).

Ramtohul, R. (2012) Globalization, Intersectionality and Women's Activism: An Analysis of the Women's Movement in the Indian Ocean Island of Mauritius. Paper presented at Rhodes University, September 2012.

Schmidt, E. (1992) Peasants, Traders and Wives, Shona Women in the History of Zimbabwe, 1870–1939. Harare: Baobab.

Shaba, L. (2001) "Keeping Score: Achievements and Constraints of Women's Movement, Women's Plus Final Issue." Available at: http://www.aletta.nu/ezines/email/WomenPlus/11-201.pdf (accessed April 23, 2012).

Win, E. (2004) "When Sharing Female Identity is not Enough: Coalition Building in the Midst of Political Polarisation in Zimbabwe," Gender and Development, 12 (1), pp. 19–27.

Zeilig, L. (2008) "Student Politics and Activism in Zimbabwe: The Frustrated Transition," Journal of Asian and African Studies, 43 (2), pp. 215–237.

Ziyambi, N. (1997) The Battle of the Mind: International New Media Elements of the New Religious Political Right in Zimbabwe. Oslo: University of Oslo.

Chapter 9
CIVIL SOCIETY MOVEMENTS AND RIGHTS DISCOURSE IN POST-APARTHEID SOCIOECONOMIC TRANSFORMATION

Christopher G. Thomas[1]

South Africa's political transition of 1994 promised to transcend colonial and apartheid legacies of poverty and disenfranchisement. Two years into its rule, the African National Congress government dropped the populist participatory transformation policy framework of the Reconstruction and Development Program for the neoliberal orientation of the Growth, Employment and Redistribution (GEAR) macroeconomic policy. GEAR worsened unemployment, social inequality, and poverty. It has been in this context that the rights-based transformation project of the negotiated transition has been pressed to effect changes in the quality of life of the marginalized black majority.

The central question driving this chapter is: Can a philosophy of rights inspire policies and actions which effectively procure significant socioeconomic transformation in the lives of the now enfranchised black majority with a constitutionally legitimated claim to the full scope of citizenship rights? He then looks at how post-apartheid economic policy making followed globally hegemonic neoliberalism and worsened unemployment, inequality, and poverty, consequently increasing dependence on welfarist state support. Constitutionally recognized socioeconomic rights are to be realized under this neoliberalist framework. Social movements have developed in opposition to government's neoliberal policies and contemplated whether socioeconomic rights adjudication creates opportunities for reforms which bring relief to impoverished subordinate classes.

---

[1] Senior Lecturer in Department of Sociology, University of South Africa.

1 Introduction

Rights discourse of the "Age of Rights" emanating in European modernity and its arguably global hegemony following the formation of the post–World War I and II League of Nations and United Nations influenced the struggle against colonialism and four decades of apartheid in South Africa. Discourse about equal enjoyment of all citizenship rights was prominent in the struggle against the misery visited on the disenfranchised black majority,[2] and has been influencing social, political, and economic transformation projects since a political transition in 1994. A new constitution[3] recognizing the rights all citizens may equally claim is the overarching legal framework of rights-based transformation projects.[4] Negotiations for a new constitution and incorporating rights discourse transcended a legacy of previous governments and constitutions by including a bill of justiciable human rights.[5] Constitutional recognition of first-generation and redistributivist second-generation rights,[6] however, has not satisfactorily delivered housing, water, and employment prompting community protests, organized mobilization by social movements and courtroom contestation for the realization of such rights.[7]

---

[2] Odendaal (1984) writes about a mission educated African elite and trading class that expressed their anti-colonial struggle in the language of "national rights," "African rights," "civic rights," and "political rights"; Dugard (1978) analyzes how apartheid policies were a denial of internationally reknown "human rights"; and Asmal et al. (2005) write about how the language of rights were prominent in the various documents of the premier liberation movement, the African National Congress.

[3] The "Final" or "New" constitution, namely, Republic of South Africa, 1996, Constitution of the Republic of South Africa, 1996, Act No. 108 of 1996, replaced the political transition's Interim Constitution. It was adopted by the Constitutional Assembly on 8 May 1996. An amended text was passed on 11 October and signed by President Mandela in Sharpeville on 10 December.

[4] Klare (1998: 150), sees South Africa's rights-based constitution as "transformative" because it entails a long-term project of "constitutional enactment, interpretation and enforcement" to transform social and political inequalities in a democratic, participatory manner.

[5] See Kotze (1996: 138).

[6] TH Marshall's 1949 address, Marshall and Bottomre (1992), "Citizenship and social class," is the seminal argument about the evolutionary emergence of different generations of rights and the welfarist, redistributivist intent of second generation rights which deal with the social class inequalities produced by capitalist social relations.

[7] See Forrest (2003), Habib (2003), and Bearak (2009).

This reality, two decades into post-apartheid, is in tension with optimism about the constitution's transformative framework.

In some circles, and in a "post-socialist world",[8] rights discourse is deemed an ideal strategy to redress a legacy of social inequality. Nonetheless, African scholars are uneasy about rights discourse in Africa's socioeconomic development and transformation projects. Makau wa Mutua sees rights discourse as inappropriate for addressing asymmetric power between citizens and generally for Africa's struggles to undo social inequality, particularly in South Africa,[9] which has vaunted its rights-based constitution as the most advanced in the contemporary world. Protagonists contend the constitution's legitimation rests on its unique inclusion of justiciable socioeconomic rights which the poor may claim to improve their living conditions while simultaneously not promising too much. The European Union's Charter of Fundamental Rights is parsimonious compared to the "avant garde" explicit inclusion of socioeconomic rights in the constitution.[10]

Rights discourse privileges a prominent role for organs of the modern state in the realization of rights that effect transformation in the lives of citizens. Impatience about the realization of socioeconomic rights fuels erratic protests and poses a challenge to the place of rights discourse in post-apartheid transformation projects. In addition, anti-statist mobilization spurns dependence on state institutions to effect liberation.[11]

The central question driving my research in this sphere of struggles against economic globalization and worsening poverty is: Can a philosophy of rights inspire policies and actions which effectively procure significant socioeconomic transformation in the lives of the now enfranchised black majority with a constitutionally legitimated claim to the full scope of citizenship rights? I look at how post-apartheid economic policy making followed globally hegemonic neoliberalism and worsened un-

---

[8] Francis Fukuyama (1989) is a preeminent non-marxist account of the decline of socialist alternatives and a "post-socialist" world characterized by a contemporary convergence to capitalist liberal democratic social orders, an institutional arrangement girded by the language of rights.

[9] See respectively, Makau wa Mutua (2008), Human rights and powerlessness; 1997, Hope and despair for a new South Africa: the limits of a rights discourse; and, more generally, 1996, The ideology of rights.

[10] Hogan (2001: 7) and Heyns and Brand (1999).

[11] John Holloway emerges as a leading proponent of this position in "Change the world without taking power."

employment, inequality, and poverty, consequently increasing dependence on welfarist state support. Constitutionally recognized socioeconomic rights are to be realized under this neoliberalist framework. Social movements have developed in opposition to government's neoliberal policies and contemplated whether socioeconomic rights adjudication creates opportunities for reforms which bring relief to impoverished subordinate classes.

2 Post-apartheid Transformation and Development Strategies and Poverty Trends

The constitution's welfare state aspirations[12] and acquiring the fiscal resources for state social spending are constrained by how much it may actually acquire from its tax revenue base, the economy's performance, and the actual social spending regime embarked upon.[13] The political setting of South Africa's elite-pact[14] has certainly been effected by the present era of globalized capitalism and the hegemonic shift toward neoliberal economic policies which force the decline of welfare state social spending.

The African National Congress (ANC) overcame a major political hurdle by securing a 63% majority in the National Assembly following the 1994

---

[12] The specific sections of the Bill of Rights recognizing such rights are: Section 3 on labour relations, Section 26 on the progressive realization of the right of the right of access to adequate housing, Section 27 on the progressive realization of the right of access to health care services, food and water, and social security, Section 28 on children's rights to basic nutrition, shelter, health care and social services, and Section 29 on the right to education. "Third generation" environmental rights are included in Section 24.

[13] Marxists political economists O'Connor (1973) and Offe (1984) argue that the state's attempts to increase its social spending capacity through tax increases negatively impacts upon individual citizens and the profit motivations of corporations. Gough (1979), shows how social spending came to consume almost half of all state expenditure.

[14] Political scientists Guillermo O'Donnell and Philippe Schmitter (1986) popularized the term "elite pacts" as a mode of transition to an enduring and consolidated democracy. Its defining element is the agreed-upon compromises made between elites that lean toward conservative policies and result in protecting the property interests and economic policy preferences of the ruling elite. A variety of analysts document how this transpired in South Africa, namely, Alexander, 1993; Ginsburg, 1996; Bond, 2000, and 2006; Terreblanche, 2002.

elections, but the challenge to redistribute income remained. A prominent indicator of the ANC's cautious approach to reconstruction is its approach to property relations. Although it is the majority party, it has not embarked upon a drastic alteration of property relations shaped by three centuries of colonial conquest and race domination.[15]

While political parties negotiated the mechanics of the political transition, economists debated economic policies to ensure income redistribution necessary to achieve a stable and democratic society. Prominent themes in the debate about effecting growth and redistribution in a model that accommodated local political and social interests entailed choices between economic growth with persistent class inequality as opposed to growth accompanied by redistribution, as well as eclectic emulation of the capitalist orientations of developed industrial nations with some state intervention, European welfare state economies and Third World and Soviet bloc socialism.[16] The persistent challenge to realize the constitutional redistributive promises must be understood against the background of the ANC government's choice of development strategies and the outcomes of the latter. The ANC adopted the Reconstruction and Development Program (RDP) policymaking framework guidelines for post-apartheid reconstruction and economic policy shortly prior to the transitional elections of 1994. Its trade union ally, the Congress of South African Trade Unions (COSATU), which had endorsed the ANC's Freedom Charter in 1987, played a major role in drafting the RDP.

The RDP's "people-centred" participatory development strategy saw state, civil society, and private sector partnerships addressing the structural problems of decades of isolation of a pariah economy and a legacy of socioeconomic inequality, making promises that an ANC government would build 1 million houses for the poor in five years.[17] Its Keynesian orientation emphasized the state's leading role in the economy and employment creation to facilitate growth, development, reconstruction, and redistribution.[18] In this paradigm, growth and development are the products of a policy emphasizing reconstruction and redistribution. The

---

[15] Marx (1997, 477–478).
[16] Kaplinsky (1991) and Moll (1991: 1, 57–70).
[17] African National Congress (1994).
[18] Adelzadeh (1996: 66) and Le Roux (1997).

RDP acknowledged: demand for raw material and mineral exports central to the apartheid economy did not guarantee a significant income for the state in a global economy with pressures for free trade and competition in manufactured goods; demand for such goods stagnated; and, domestic manufacturers faced international competition in the production of manufactured goods.[19] The ANC soon realized it would have to spurn rhetoric about nationalization of economic assets and socialism in order to attract international investors.[20]

Makau wa Mutua is apprehensive that the permeation of the RDP with rights talk and blind optimism about correcting the apartheid legacy does not identify concrete measures and policies to that effect and is "romantic" about its egalitarian goals, but steers clear of explicitly declaring where the resources for such goals would come from, and the impact it may have on the stock-pile of white privilege.[21] The RDP framework must be judged in terms of the actual provision of houses, jobs, safe water, health care, nutrition, relevant education, and safety and security to citizens. Between 1994 and 1996 the RDP fund controlled R15.5 billion, but many political leaders were soon convinced that it was not the optimal approach to solving South Africa's problems.[22] Its "mass-participation" discourse rejected the "delivery from on high approach." The ANC faced criticisms of nondelivery especially of the promised one million houses in the five years. Closure of the RDP Office in the Cabinet on March 28, 1997 encouraged rumours that the RDP was "dead," and, along with it, the "people-driven" development strategy. Nonetheless, the ANC retorted that its macro-economic policy shift would make the RDP sustainable. Minister of Finance Trevor Manuel stated that although the separate RDP allocation was withdrawn, government's view was the budget as a whole was now directed toward the RDP goals, making a separate allocation unnecessary.[23] Despite criticisms, toward the end of the first term of a post-apartheid government, analysts noted "impressive" achievements, in a short space of time, on delivery of housing, clean water, electrification, land reform, primary

---

[19] African National Congress (1994, 10).
[20] See Sogoni (1990, 13) in the ANC's main policy journal, Sechaba and Hirsch (2005: 29–30).
[21] Makau wa Mutua (1997).
[22] Bond and Khosa (1999: 61–62).
[23] Republic of South Africa, Debates: Index (1996a: 1760).

health care, and public works.[24] The RDP's critics[25] contended that the allocation to housing was only about 1.5% of the national budget; key role players, such as banks, were not eager to extend loans to subsidy recipients to make "top up" improvements and extensions to their basic houses; contractors were not matching the expected housing standards; confusion prevailed about how many houses were actually delivered; constitutional protection of property rights restricted peri-urban land acquisition for low-income housing projects; and pushed such projects away from the cities.

In 1995 the ANC contended that the economy's growth rate of 3% curbed government's delivery on RDP promises.[26] This contextual factor abetted the drift from state interventionism to a convergence with the old white elite's own drift to neoliberal policies before entering into a negotiated political transition. President Mandela's opening of parliament address in 1996 acknowledged modest economic growth and little job creation,[27] called for a "new patriotism" to accept the challenges of structural changes to the economy, and advocated neoliberal ideas about achieving international competitiveness in a new macro-economic policy. In 1996 the ANC dominated Government of National Unity (GNU) announced its preference for an open economy and adopted Growth, Employment and Redistribution: a Macroeconomic Strategy (GEAR), which the ANC elite leadership claimed would realize RDP objectives.[28] The ANC leadership did not engage its alliance partners about the policy change, thus adding to COSATU's criticisms of GNU's privatization strategy over the RDP's preference for a greater state role in coordinating economic growth.[29]

Marais (2001) argues that the evolution of ANC political thought entailed the view that seizure of state power would facilitate the easy remedying of a legacy of social and economic inequalities. The Freedom Charter contained some formulations on the restructuring of a post-apartheid economy, but while in exile the ANC did not refine any post-apartheid economic policy and was not in a strong position to argue the

---

[24] Lodge (2002: 57).
[25] Bond and Khosa (1999: 10–13).
[26] African National Congress (1997).
[27] Mandela (1996).
[28] Mandela (1996a).
[29] Davenport and Saunders (2002: 569–570, 583–584).

structure and workings of a post-apartheid economy.[30] Adopting GEAR was a dramatic change of economic policy and promises of eventual redress. Effectively, the ANC's elite leadership followed the advice of big business think tanks and the elite beneficiaries of black economic empowerment ventures, and converged with principles of the National Party's reform period neoliberal paradigm evident in The Key Issues in the Normative Economic Model of 1993, as well as a document by the Macro-Economic Research Group which advised against state spending, and models developed by big business associations, the Development Bank of SA, the Bureau of Economic Research, the WB, and the SA Reserve Bank.[31]

GEAR recognized the population growth was faster than the economy's growth rate (GDP grew by 1.3% in 1993, 2.7% in 1994, and 3.5% in 1995), and the unemployment rate at GEAR's inception was between 38 and 40%.[32] It emphasized "a competitive fast-growing economy which creates sufficient jobs for all workseekers," in order to achieve "a redistribution of income and opportunities in favour of the poor."[33] An export-oriented economy was expected to attract investment and create jobs as a means of effecting redistribution. GEAR's lofty expectations entailed: an average growth rate increase of 4.2% for four years, then 6% by 2000; creating 1.35 million jobs or 400 000 jobs per annum by 2000; increasing exports by an average of 8.4% per annum, and improving infrastructure.[34] A shift away from reliance on raw materials exports to promoting exports of manufactured goods and an end to tariff protection of local industries was expected to force firms into restructuring for international competitiveness. The plan to put the economy into a new growth path through restructuring industries and increasing their openness to international competitiveness was expected to have long-term benefits of increasing employment opportunities, and with some later redistribution gains through wages.[35]

GEAR's critics dubbed it "trickle down" economics with flawed projections of employment increases and economic growth increases of 6%

---

[30] Marais (2001: 85, 123–124).
[31] Adelzadeh (1996: 66–68) and Marais (2001: 160–163).
[32] African National Congress (1997: 6, 10).
[33] African National Congress (1996, 1997: 16).
[34] African National Congress (1996: 2) and Marais (1996: 31).
[35] African National Congress (1996), Appendix 1.

and then 12%; it was misguided in its privileging of growth first and redistribution later after a period of some sustained economic growth redistribution.[36] In hindsight, low economic growth rate has been apparent along with increased unemployment in the economy's modern and agricultural sectors, and, generally, most seriously affecting the potential Black labor force. The Treasury Department and the International Monetary Fund acknowledged in 2007 that the economy was unlikely to reach the 6% growth rate targeted for 2010 and beyond. The IMF predicted that the growth rate will persist at 4.8% up to 2012, while the Treasury Department revised its projections to a 5.1% growth rate. The thrust of criticisms of economic policy has been that it followed the Washington consensus principles of international financing institutions prescriptions for reform or liberalization of financial movement policies as a means of attracting foreign direct investment, only to see the outflow of capital. Investment has not materialized in the proportions the policy's architects hoped for.[37] The National Economic Development and Labour Council (NEDLAC) [38] a corporatist economic policy advisory council made up of labor, business, government and development organizations, links the high unemployment rate to liberalization of the economy about investment and outflows, and non-realization of expected domestic and foreign investment rates because of the volatility of global financial markets: gross domestic investment as a percent of GDP was expected to increase to 26% but did not exceed 14.9%; between 1999 and 2000 foreign direct investment declined from R9.2 billion to R6.1 billion[39]; portfolio investment into South Africa declined from R83.9 billion in 1999 to R11.8 billion in 2000; overall, a net inflow of R52.4 billion shifted to an outflow of R13.8 billion in 2000. Foreign direct in-

---

[36] See Terreblanche (2002).
[37] Bond (2001: 141).
[38] National Economic Development and Labour Council (NEDLAC) (2001: 7).
[39] Ankie Hoogvelt, 2001, sees the current phase of the globalization of capitalism as characterized by processes of "exclusion" and "implosion" where industrialized countries prefer to invest among themselves and there is a decrease in foreign direct investment from industrialized counties in the economies of the global "South".

vestment decreased by 78% in 2010 to $1.3 billion from $5.7 billion in 2009.[40]

GEAR predicted, under prevailing economic structures and policies, an unemployment growth trend reaching 37% by 2000. In 1995, in the strict definition of unemployment, which treats workers who are discouraged from seeking work as outside of the labor force, it stood at 16.5%, but the expanded definition put unemployment at 29.3% that year.[41] In a total national population of 44.8 million (the 2001 figures, but 50 million according to the 2011 census), and with a national poverty line of R569 per month per adult equivalent, about 21 million people still live below that line; income inequality, when measured by the Gini coefficient worsened; it increased from 0.596 in 1995 to 0.635 in 2001.[42] Despite excitement about constitutionally entrenched socioeconomic rights with expected redistributive effects, as well as government spending on the social wage as President Mbeki's Advisor, Vusi Gumede, contends, countervailing forces produced increased inequality when using the Gini coefficient as an indicator.

Putting brakes on increasing the state's role is contrary to many other expectations and to the state's "positive" role in the realization of socioeconomic rights. Increasingly, the dominant trend in the broad reconstruction, growth, and redistribution debate, marginalized the role of the state in favor of market-led solutions, and increased disappointment and criticism by those still seeking solutions within the framework of reforming capitalism. Activists in post-apartheid social movements regard developments in the economy on employment, the subsequent inability to pay bonds, as reducing many households from fairly good circum-

---

[40] Loyiso Langeni (2011) draws these figures from a United Nations Conference on Trade and Development report.

[41] South African Institute of Race Relations (1996/1997: 358–359). The United Nations Development Programme's (UNDP) (2003: 19–20) discussion of the disastrous outcomes of South Africa's macro-economic policy highlights the figures of the expanded definition of unemployment; it reported unemployment in March 2003 reached 31.2% (5.2 million), but in an extended definition of unemployment the figure stands at 42.1% (8.4 million) in a work force of 29.6 million (UNDP 2003:19–20). Neva Seidman Makgetla (2004), pp. 264–265, notes the expanded definition includes workers who are discouraged from seeking work, and claims the unemployment figure for 2003 is more than 40%, and affects mostly youth, blacks, and women.

[42] United Nations Development Programme (2003).

stances to surprising destitution, a levelling impoverishment that is the source of disharmony. Concern about developments on the volatile issue of housing rights, access to health care, employment, and food are prominent in the statements of critical opinion-makers. The realization that socioeconomic rights is not occurring in line with the expectations of a large segment of the public, even if these masses do not explicitly use the language of rights to demand such services. These ambiguous outcomes from macro-economic policy, which suggest certain positive indicators, but simultaneous signals of further exclusion of segments of the population because of the worsening of poverty and unemployment levels, and the diminished capacity of many households to complement state assistance on realizing housing rights can only possibly contribute to the intensification of social conflict.

The adoption of the Accelerated and Shared Growth Initiative for South Africa (AsgiSA) in February 2006 promised to halve poverty and unemployment by 2014. Achieving that goal remains out of reach given an economic growth rate of 2.5% for 2012 as reported by Finance Minister Pravin Gordhan. Unemployment for 2012 hardly changed from its 25% rate through 2011.[43]

3   Post-apartheid Civil Society Movements

Trade unions and civics movements were major forms of civil society mobilization and opposition to the apartheid state and by endorsing the Freedom Charter they ideologically aligned themselves with the ANC.[44] This likely contributed to civil society organizations being poorly prepared for their role in a democracy. The RDP spoke of a major role for civil society structures in the reconstruction and development after the political transition; however, it turned out that civics seemed useful to the new government only insofar as they could end bond, rent and service boycotts, and get communities in line with government's drift to market policies for the provision of services by accepting the neoliberal disciplining of paying for services. It appeared that social movements whose actions were vital to bringing about a political transition in South

---

[43]   Statistics SA (2011: 4).
[44]   See Seekings (2000).

Africa were to be demobilized in a fashion similar to that observed in other contexts in the corpus of "transition theory," once political elites drifted to neoliberalism.[45] Some civic organizers anticipated being watchdogs that were included in the policy-making process[46] but the ANC government avoided consulting with them and it implemented its own projects.

Following the unfolding of GEAR's neoliberal logic of the privatization and the cost recovery approach to the provision of social services, several "new" social movements have arisen in an environment enabled by democratization processes and are largely animated by the consequences of neoliberal economic policies. Several combinations of relationships are evident between civil society organizations and the post-apartheid state: some organizations operate in marginalized communities assisting them in their daily survival struggles; others are openly adversarial and challenge the government's neoliberal policies.[47] Organizers in the new social movements point to government's ditching of the RDP for GEAR, as a prompt for the growth of an adversarial relationship between government and civil society organizations, as well as the growth of new social movements opposed to the thrust of the neoliberalism, for instance, the Anti-Privatization Forum.[48] Some new social movements draw from class-based ideologies calling themselves "socialist movements" with explicit counter-hegemonic projects against the state; others have formal relationships or partnerships with the state; in some cases, there is vacillation between these strategies; in some instances, the movements use the constitution's socioeconomic rights framework to further their goals.[49] The fortune of the latter strategy is explored in order to answer the paper's research question.

In the field of the right of access to adequate housing, it may have been that the South African National Civics Organisation (SANCO), which once played the premier role in opposing apartheid housing and rent policies, if not moribund, had succumbed to more of a partnership role with the

---

[45] Ginsburg (1996: 74–76).
[46] Ndletyana (1999: 34).
[47] Habib (2003).
[48] Ngwane (2003).
[49] Ballard, Habib and Valodia (2007: 17, 400, 402).

state, whereas it could have used rights discourse to mobilize about slow or nondelivery of housing. It lost cadre to the state and its apparent decline created space for organizations drawn to an adversarial approach on housing issues. Participation in the state subsidised low-income RDP housing scheme remains out of the reach of many households that cannot afford the necessary deposit. The vacant space for mobilizing on housing rights has sometimes been filled by spontaneous actions and ephemeral organizations, as well as those proving to last longer such as the Landless People's Movement (LPM) and Abahlali baseMjondolo ("the shackdwellers").[50] Both organizations are independent of the ANC and have an "adversarial" strategy of engagement with the state animated by an opposition to neoliberal economic policies, which have worsened unemployment and poverty.

The LPM's main concerns include land rights, land reform, and realizing the right of access to adequate housing. Its name misleadingly suggests they are concerned predominantly with rural land reform in the interests of people seeking agricultural livelihoods; however, its campaigns have linked the urban housing shortage to a need for urban land reform too. Press releases of LPM marches and campaign demands in Gauteng Province involving squatters in Protea South and Kliptown (Soweto), Thembelihle (Lenasia), and Thembisa (Kempton Park) reveal a concern with issues of an urban nature, namely, the issues of the urban homeless with an interest in securing permanent urban livelihoods in opposition to the plans of city authorities to clear out informal settlements and prevent land occupations.[51] Slogans announcing the claims behind a specific march read: "HOUSING! LAND! WATER AND ELECTRICITY! AN END TO FORCED REMOVALS! AN END TO POLICE BRUTALITY AGAINST THE POOR!".[52] Although the LPM was formed after a prominent land occupation, where access to housing was one of the underlying issues, it has yet to use the strategy of litigation about constitutionally guaranteed housing rights.

Abahlali baseMjondolo (AbM) has undertaken a well-reasoned struggle over slow delivery of housing and the enduring plight of shackdwellers.

---

[50] "Shackdwellers" in Zulu, see Gibson (2008).
[51] Greenberg (2004: 12).
[52] Landless People's Movement (2007).

Its statements[53] reveal an adversarialism distrustful of notions of rule of law underlying the constitution as well as of left-wing intellectuals: "When Abahlali marched ... a number of left intellectuals declared them criminal in the national press ... it was clear that competing elites in the state and the institutionalised left were united on the position that the poor should not think their own politics and that doing so rendered the movement 'out of order' and even criminal. Abahlali's intellectual project is founded on the decision that 'when order means the silence of the poor then it is good to be out of order'".[54]

4 Landmark Socioeconomic Rights Adjudication

The *trias politica* principle of the statemaking process of the negotiated political transition saw agreement on the institution of a bill of rights and a constitutional court. Against the background of GEAR's poor performance on economic growth and rising unemployment, landmark cases prompted the Constitutional Court to interpret the realization of socioeconomic rights.[55] The constitution, the international human rights agreements that South Africa signs, parliament and the legislation that passes through it, rulings made in the Constitutional Court, the functions of the South African Human Rights Commission (SAHRC), and the activities of NGOs as well as civil society organizations make up a configuration of institutions and structures that impact contestation of the meaning of rights and state obligations, in nurturing a culture of rights, and ultimately redressing the legacy of inequality. The position of the Constitutional Court's justices possibly has effectively positioned them in terms of the rarefied speaking subject that Foucault spoke of where certain agents are elevated to speak authoritatively, a practice that excludes or silences other discourses.[56]

---

[53] Abahlali base Mjondolo (2006).
[54] Their strategy of not engaging the state is arguably akin to that advocated by John Holloway.
[55] Although these cases may not be argued to have been initiated by civil society organizations as such, the cases nevertheless form the basis of landmark rulings that in the litigation strategy of Critical Legal Studies are vital to reformist victories for subordinate classes.
[56] Foucault (1972: 50).

The rituals and reverence associated with the Court and the selection of its highly experienced judges, acting as an independent judiciary as prescribed in a separation of powers of doctrine, still may not prevent the Court from subjecting itself to the dominant discourse on social and economic rights and the capacity of states to act in ways that citizens may enjoy these rights. Hirschl (2004) says democratization in South Africa followed a similar worldwide process, namely, the transfer of significant powers from representative institutions to judiciaries; however, the global swing to "juristocracy" was because the "juristocracy" would protect the neoliberal framework that economic elites are comfortable with. These types of constitutional outcomes preserve and protect the interests and hegemony of three types of elites who favor a trend to "juristocracy" in connection to a preference for neoliberal economic policies. These elites include the old ruling elite that wishes to retain its political hegemony from democratization, the economic elites who see constitutions as a means of promoting a neoliberal economic agenda, and the judicial elite that wished to increase their political influence.[57]

Contestation in courts is crucial in a context where the obligations of government in the realization of rights are not always concrete. A repository of Constitutional Court decisions about socioeconomic rights as well as disputes between organs of state has evolved over two decades since 1994 and a few notable cases frame the basis for the interpretation of the realization of socioeconomic rights. The Soobramoney case preceded Grootboom, but the Grootboom judgment emerges as the foundation of future socio-economic judgments.

4.1 Soobramoney: The Right of Access to Health Care Services[58]

Mr Thiagraj Soobramoney, an unemployed 41-year-old diabetic with heart disease, developed chronic renal failure, and required dialysis treatment. His multiple diseases condition disqualified him for a kidney transplant in terms of the resource-rationing policy of a state hospital in KwaZulu-Natal, which consequently discontinued his state-funded renal services. He exhausted his financial resources and could not pay for dialysis treatment. Although he wished to present his case for state-funded

---

[57] Hirschl (2004: 43).
[58] Soobramoney v Minister of Health, KwaZulu-Natal.

dialysis treatment as an "everyone has a right to life" issue as held by section 11 of the constitution, the Constitutional Court heard the issue as a section 27 matter—a "right to health care" matter.

Soobramoney argued that terminally ill persons whose life could be prolonged were entitled to emergency medical treatment in terms of s 27(3), which held: "No one may be refused emergency medical treatment." His view of the state, its obligations, and capacity to create the funds or resources to be of service to people in his situation led him to believe the state must make additional funds available to the renal clinic. The court determined it as 27(1) and 27(2) matter and asserted that the state's obligations are qualified by the preceding clause s 27(2), "within its available resources." Soobramoney's claim required that s 27(3) "be read as meaning that everyone requiring life-saving treatment who was unable to pay for such treatment was entitled to have the treatment provided at a State hospital without charge."[59]

The justices' majority judgment acknowledged that the constitution sought to address a legacy of disparities in wealth but the state's obligations were constrained by the extent of its resources:

> We live in a society in which there are great disparities in wealth. Millions of people are living in deplorable conditions and in great poverty. There is a high level of unemployment, inadequate social security, and many do not have access to clean water or to adequate health services. These conditions existed when the Constitution was adopted and a commitment to address them, and to transform our society into one in which there will be human dignity, freedom and equality, lies at the heart of our new constitutional order. For as long as these conditions continue to exist that aspiration will have a hollow ring.
>
> What is apparent from these provisions is that the obligations imposed on the State by sections 26 and 27 in regard to access to housing, health care, food, water and social security are dependent upon the resources available for such purposes, and that the corresponding rights themselves are limited by reason of the lack

---

[59] Butterworth's Constitutional Law Reports, 1997 (12), p. 1697.

of resources. Given this lack of resources and the significant demands on them that have already been referred to, an unqualified obligation to meet these needs would not presently be capable of being fulfilled. This is the context within which section 27(3) must be construed.[60]

The justices accept that even if the right were not qualified, the state would still not be able to meet the obligation, and there is a rationality about which state organs use their resources. The provincial health department's resources position about the rationality behind the use of its available resources swayed the High Court judge and the Constitutional Court supported that ruling. The justices were mindful of the state's fiscal position; they were wary of the pressures on the provincial health department's resources; it had overspent its current budget with the expectation of future overspending.[61]

> President of the Constitutional Court, Justice Chaskalson remarked: "One cannot but have sympathy for the appellant and his family, who face the cruel dilemma of having to impoverish themselves in order to secure the treatment [Soobramoney] seeks in order to prolong his life. The hard and unpalatable fact is that if [Mr Soobramoney] were a wealthy man he would be able to procure such treatment from private sources; he is not and has to look to the State to provide him with the treatment. But the State's resources are limited..."[62]

The justices noted that extending the availability of the dialysis machines meant additional costs in overtime wages and putting stress on machines that were showing signs of wear. The penurious Mr Soobramoney's appeal was unsuccessful; he died three days after the Constitutional Court handed down judgment.

The issue dealt with a provincial health department's reasoning about its rational use of its available resources but also the Court's views on the state's national budget allocations. It refrains from challenging the state

---

[60] BCLR, 1997 (12), pp. 1700–1701.
[61] BCLR, 1997 (12), p. 1704.
[62] BCLR, 1997 (12), p. 1706.

on the rational allocation of resources because it accepts the argument that state resources are limited. If judges force a state to realize one right, it comes at the expense of other services and of other people seeking to enjoy the same right. Furthermore, judges do not have the expertise to decide on the state's priorities. Following the trias politica principle, the Constitutional Court justices declined to probe the state's rationality about the use of its resources.

4.2 Grootboom: The Right to Have Access to Adequate Housing[63]

Mrs Irene Grootboom was among a group of indigent squatter camp inhabitants numbering 390 adults and 510 children who applied for low-cost municipality housing but remained on waiting lists for years. They moved out of an overpopulated squatter settlement to occupy an area they believed was vacant land renaming it "New Rest." They were evicted and appealed to the High Court, which referenced the Constitutional Court's ruling in Soobramoney about the provincial health authorities' rational use of available budget resources; it ruled that the local authorities did have a rational housing program within the means of its available resources and the courts should not judge on the suitability of such rational programs.

Some temporary relief came for the squatters because the High Court made a ruling in terms of s 28(c), that children have an unqualified right to shelter. The judge ruled that the children being protected thus could not be separated from their parents; this compelled the authorities to provide emergency relief for these homeless people. In turn, the various branches of government later appealed to the Constitutional Court basing their appeal on the grounds that s 26 is about the right of "access to" adequate housing and the obligation on the state is to take reasonable legislative and other measures to ensure the progressive realization of this right within its available resources. The case made an issue of whether the state was solely responsible for this obligation, or more of a facilitator of the conditions for the realization of the right:

> The right delineated in subsection (1) was a right of "access to adequate housing" as distinct from the right to adequate housing en-

---

[63] Government of South Africa and Others v Grootboom and Others in 2000.

capsulated in terms of the International Covenant on Economic, Social and Cultural Rights. ... Access to adequate housing also suggested that it was not only the State which was responsible for the provision of houses, but that other agents within society, including individuals themselves, had to be enabled by legislative and other measures to provide housing. The State had to create the conditions for access to adequate housing for people at all economic levels of society.[64]

The Constitutional Court decision in 2000[65] was based on a deliberation of s 26; it ruled the homeless people's appeal in terms of the right of access to adequate housing provided through the state's resources unsuccessful. Some relief was found through a creative interpretation of s 28, the children's right to shelter. Nevertheless, eyewitness accounts report that one year after receiving materials for such relief, the community still lived in deplorable conditions and with a sense of being abandoned by the Court.[66] Irene Grootboom died in 2008, still living in a shack and waiting for an RDP house.[67]

Jurisprudence on these rights is still developing but the Court revealed its deliberations and decisions are cognizant of fiscal limits to social spending, which influenced the constitution's architects when choosing language about the state's positive obligations on the realization of positive rights. The Soobramoney ruling clarified the Court's understanding of the "within its available resources" clause of s 26(2):

> [T]he obligation does not require the State to do more than its available resources permit. This means that both the content of the obligation in relation to the rate at which it is achieved as well as the reasonableness of the measures employed to achieve the result are governed by the availability of resources.[68]

Justice Yacoob also pointed out that, although South Africa had signed the International Convention on Economic, Social and Cultural Rights

---

[64] BCLR, 2000 (11), pp. 1171, 1189.
[65] Government of the Republic of South Africa and Others v Grootboom and Others.
[66] van Huyssteen (2003: 295).
[67] Joubert (2008).
[68] BCLR, 2000 (11), p. 1192.

(ICESCR), there was a difference in the wording of the ICESCR and South Africa's constitution on the obligation of states toward the realization of socioeconomic rights. The ICESCR provided for an absolute and unqualified "right to housing." However, the South African constitution acknowledged "the right of access to housing." This qualification of the right is dependent upon the state demonstrating that it was taking "reasonable legislative and other measures" which would enable it "to achieve the progressive realisation" of the right to housing, and that this was dependent on its "available resources."

It was apparent that while the state progressively built up its resources, claims by the homeless to the right to housing and the actions they resorted to encroached on other people's right to private property and land. In 2004, the case of Port Elizabeth Municipality v Various Occupiers and, in 2005, the case of President of the Republic of South Africa and Another v Modderklip Boerdery and Others were about the eviction of squatters from private property. Judgments here were guided by s 27(3) of the Bill of Rights and the Prevention of Illegal Eviction from an Unlawful Occupation of Land Act of 1998 (also called the "PIE Act"). Arguably, these judgments affect the approach to socioeconomic rights since the issue of the pace of the state's use of its resources to provide adequate housing was raised again and the manner in which the constitution approached the interrelationship between land hunger, homelessness and respect for property rights. In the latter two cases, the Court upheld the protection of private property rights, and that homeless people or evictees could not demand of the state immediate fulfilment of the right to adequate housing. Furthermore, the Court would not demand such action by the state. The constitution was an instrument developed in a particular social, political, and economic context that required transformation and achieving equality, and would have to be reinterpreted as these conditions themselves changed.

4.3 The Treatment Action Campaign: The Right of Access to Health Care Services[69]

One of the most well-organized civil society organizations, the Treatment Action Campaign (TAC), initiated the case of Minister of Health and Others vs. Treatment Action Campaign and Others in 2002. TAC opposes the national health department's policy on the link between the Human Immunodeficiency Virus (HIV) and Acquired Immunodeficiency Syndrome (AIDS). It has challenged the government's neoliberal approach to health care policies, and has used both protest and litigation to realize constitutionally guaranteed rights.

This case was about the right of access to health care services (s 27), which TAC had earlier brought to the Transvaal High Court. Specifically, TAC demanded that government make available in state hospitals the drug, Nevirapine, which is used by pregnant women in the prevention of mother-to-child-transmission of the Human Immunodeficiency Virus. The High Court ruled that state health authorities must make the drug available to pregnant women with HIV who gave birth in public health facilities, as well as to their babies. The matter of the separation of executive and judiciary powers became an issue. Government departments felt TAC was asking the Court to make a policy choice whereas it should only rule on whether that department's policy to gradually realize the enjoyment of the right was reasonable. Wesson[70] sees the TAC case as transcending the Grootboom case because it extended individual rights to a particular group. Furthermore, with regard to the state's fiscal limits, there were limited cost implications to extending this entitlement, and the Court was guided by the Grootboom approach in the sense that the state takes reasonable measures in availing this service.

In hindsight, TAC organizers reflect on their involvement in the HIV/AIDS medicines issue and the court ruling victory places that struggle in a larger social structural context.[71] Their struggle for medicines and improved access for health care services for the poor is seen in the context of global austerity trends and decreases in state spending on health care services, and growing poverty and inequality trends and how these exac-

---

[69] Minister of Health and Others vs. Treatment ActionCampaign and Others in 2002 (CCT8/02).
[70] Wesson (2004), p. 296.
[71] Heywood (2010).

erbate the vulnerability of the poor to illness and HIV. TAC found that the constitution and its rights ethos played a major role in facilitating its mobilization and legal victory despite the prevailing despondency of South Africa's left-wing thinkers about using rights discourse as well as right-wing views opposing the broadening of the notion of rights to the realm of social and economic rights.

4.4 Khosa: The Right to Have Access to Social Security[72]

In 2004, the cases of Khosa v Minister of Social Development and Mahlaule v Minister of Social Development were about the rights of persons who are not citizens but "permanent residents" to claim social security inscribed in s 27, as well as the equality of such persons with other citizens in the enjoyment of rights held in the "Equality" clauses of s 9 of the Bill of Rights. These judgments contended omission of the words "or permanent resident" in the Equality clauses was inconsistent with the constitution. Although the challenge concerned one of the constitutionally guaranteed socioeconomic rights, it was not about the meaning of the right, rather, it was about who may enjoy the right.

4.5 Mazibuko: The Right to Water[73]

Mrs Lindiwe Mazibuko and five other residents of Phiri, Soweto, challenged the City of Johannesburg's installation of prepaid water meters as a violation of their s 27 (1) b right to sufficient water. The proceedings from the local court to eventually the Constitutional Court interrogated the notion of "sufficient water" which the Constitutional Court asserted it was not appropriate for the courts to decide, nor was the notion of minimum core content apt in this instance, or in the Grootboom and TAC cases too. The Court asserted it could enforce obligations on the state if it did not make provision for those in desperate need. Nevertheless, it upheld its position that it would respect the policymaking of other arms of government. Its views on the positive aspects of episodic litigation about social and economic rights assert that it is a way of getting government to account to citizens as to whether its policies are indeed "reasonable" or should be reconsidered. Furthermore, the Constitutional Court praised

---

[72] Khosa and Others vs. Minister of Social Development and Others.
[73] Mazibuko and Others vs. City of Johannesburg And Others.

the prominence of NGOs assisting in such litigation in the service of the poor.

4.6 What Choices Remain for Further Socioeconomic Rights Litigation?

The constitution's weak statement of the state's social rights obligations feeds conclusions that the judiciary's adjudication of these rights still functions to protect the hegemony specifically of the economic elite, despite the latter's outwardly transformed nonracial appearance. It may be possible to pronounce on the outcomes of adjudication in terms of the consequences of rulings on the class interests of affected parties. The class, income, and indigent circumstances of the appellant in the Soobramoney case, the community in the Grootboom case, and the intended beneficiaries in the TAC case raise questions about the qualitative changes a constitutional order has meant for poorer segments of society and their dependence on positive state actions. Unfortunately for Mr Soobramoney, there was no creative interpretation of the law to bring him emergency medical relief as happened in the Grootboom case, where similar issues of a rational use of available resources could be proven, but a creative interpretation of the law found emergency relief for a number of homeless people not immediately targeted to enjoy the right of access to housing. The Grootboom judgment made it clear that people were not entitled to demand housing, or any other socioeconomic right, from the state. Wesson[74] feels the interpretations of the law in Soobramoney and Grootboom still leave society' most vulnerable members unprotected, and to advance from this, it is for the courts to incorporate the notion of "minimum core" in their judgments as used in the ICESCR which entails the minimum essential levels a state must attain in allocating resources toward the realization of socioeconomic rights. However, Justice Sachs recalls[75] that when the amicus curiae ("friend of the court") in the Grootboom case, the SA Human Rights Commission, begged the judges to make a decision based on the ICESCR's concept of a minimum core, the judges did not reject the notion; they merely declined because they felt the language of the constitution expresses itself sufficiently and is an adequate

---

[74] Wesson (2004: 297–299, 305–307).
[75] Sachs (2003).

guide; furthermore, there was no clear evidence of what such a minimum core entailed.

Partisans in the "new" social movements offer unsympathetic appraisals of the Constitutional Court and its decisions. Bond's appraisal of the Court is a social structural approach tied to a critique of the ANC-led government's neoliberal policies and accepts no excuses resorting to the trias politica idea of separating the powers of the state where judges accept the executive performs its task in terms of a rational use of available resources. He feels, despite the fact that South Africa has a constitution promising socioeconomic rights, the judges are afraid to challenge the state's neoliberal policies.[76]

5   Taking Socioeconomic Rights Seriously

Foucault's notion of discourse captured the capacity of humans to resist power and avoids the notion of ideology and its representation of subjects in a homogenized fashion. To see rights simultaneously as discourse implies rights are an object of knowledge, statements are made about the truth of that object, and processes about their nature exclude subordinate groups from challenging that truth. Subordinate classes' struggles are advanced by including strategies for an alternative discourse. In pragmatic approaches to rights discourse, this is seen as a Gramscian counter-hegemonic project.[77] Class domination is achieved through coercion as well as consent, and the struggle for liberation must challenge dominant beliefs, values, law, myths, and so on, bringing forth the counter-hegemonic worldview of subordinated classes. Counter-hegemonic projects of subordinate classes entail developing concepts and ideological weapons in ways which challenge the prevailing intellectual and moral order. Subordinate classes must challenge those intellectuals and "rarefied speaking subjects" who dominate the discourse on the nature of rights and who complement the hegemony of dominant classes by defin-

---

[76] See Bond (2004).
[77] Purvis and Hunt (1993: 483–484). Bartholomew and Hunt (1990: 52) partly draw on Foucaultian notions of "discursive struggles," but opt more explicitly for similar Gramscian notions of struggles for hegemony, Bartholomew and Hunt (1990: 55–56), which are more attentive to the commonsense of subordinate classes about political issues.

ing the nature of rights. To achieve this "counter-hegemony" we must ask whether the ideas and practices about rights of the major interpreters, and social agents and institutions dealing with their realization are flexible when encountered with each challenge.

Noting how the University of Witwatersrand Legal Aid Clinic became involved in a case which reached the Constitutional Court, namely, *Occupiers of 51 Olivia Road, Berea Township and Others v City of Johannesburg and Others*, and the subsequent optimistic statement of one of its public interest litigation activists about the role rights discourse played in the case about evicting the illegal occupants of an inner city building: "We are absolutely delighted. This is a victory for human rights and a vindication for the rights of the poor people to housing,"[78] I investigated the possible build up of a momentum about socioeconomic rights litigation and how other similar organizations have become involved in assisting the public with such rights. My optimism was however dealt a blow following discussions with the director at the University of South Africa Law Clinic.[79] Upon querying their involvement in the provision of 1, 372 community legal aid services including litigation, it turned out that the seventeen "Evictions" matters for 2011 were largely disputes between family members who wish to evict other family members following disputes over informal agreements about occupying homes that have been inherited. This distressing revelation caused me to ponder whether the situation may be the same with legal aid clinics at other universities. In conversation with the director of the legal aid clinic at the University of Western Cape it was clear that evictions of illegal occupants of inner city buildings are not an issue in the Cape Town metropolis. However, an area where they do have a considerable caseload of assisting indigent people is in that of divorce which has further ramifications for the realization of the right to housing. The RDP house that divorcing indigent people acquire can only pass on to one former spouse and the other spouse will not receive a subsidy for another RDP house.[80] The director of the University of Cape Town (UCT) legal aid clinic shared the view that the metropolis

---

[78] Cox and Seale (2008).
[79] Interview with Hadley Saayman, University of South Africa Law Clinic, June 7, 2012.
[80] Interview with Shamiel Jassiem, University of Western Cape Legal Aid Clinic, February 23, 2016.

does not have an inner city illegal occupation and eviction issue. However, the UCT clinic has become involved in an ongoing action supporting the legal struggle of the residents of Hangberg, using the *Prevention of Illegal Eviction from an Unlawful Occupation of Land Act of 1998* (also called the "PIE Act"), against the city's and provincial officials' resort to the courts to have them evicted from about 2010.[81] The Hangberg residents are reluctant to move from their informal settlement dwellings while there is slow development about low income housing; they also resort to an indigenous peoples' land claim to an area which has a majestic view of the Hout Bay harbour and surrounding mountains and with nearby upmarket housing.[82]

Except for the case involving the Treatment Action Campaign, organized civil society groups do not appear to have been prominent rights action protagonists in the abovementioned landmark cases. The TAC continues to be active with regards to health services and conditions in state hospitals. The emergence of a new public interest law center in 2010, namely, SECTION 27, marks a new direction in terms of civil society groups foregrounding litigation as a strategy to "change the socio-economic conditions that undermine human dignity and development, and prevent poor people from reaching their full potential."[83] Despite taking its name from the section of the constitution on the right of access to health care services, food, water, and social security, it has a commitment to "a broader focus on socio-economic rights." In 2012 it became very prominent in its litigation action against the Limpopo Province's Education Department's maladministration of the delivery of primary schools textbooks, a matter which it successfully got the North Gauteng High Court to rule as a violation of the right to basic education, a section 29 right of the Constitution.[84] Non-realization of the right, largely due to the state's maladministration, continues to marginalize poor black learners, constrains upward social mobility, and reinforces inequalities in society. The ruling created an opportunity for a civil society organization to have a close relationship with a state organ about its progress with delivery of a ser-

---

[81] Interview with Yellavarne Moodley, University of Cape Town Legal Aid Clinic, February 23, 2016.
[82] See Daneel Knoetze, Hangberg: "a view too good for poor people," 2014, http://mg.co.za/article/2014-10-08-hangberg-on-a-knife-edge.
[83] SECTION27, About us, at http://www.section27.org.za/about-us.
[84] See John (2012), Still no textbooks.

vice, nonetheless, the relationship soured once it was apparent that the state organ remained delinquent about its obligations and SECTION 27 took the matter to court once again.

In addition, the Socio-Economic Rights Institute of South Africa (SERI) emerged as a nonprofit, public interest law center assisting in the fields of housing and evictions, access to basic services and political space, and has provided legal assistance in prominent cases such as the evictions of inner city residents challenging the courts' interpretations of the "PIE" Act.[85] SERI also provides legal assistance to the families of miners killed by police at Marikana mine in 2012.

6 Taking Rights Seriously: Africa's New Constitutions

While it may be apparent that South Africa's rights-based transformation and its pioneering constitutional protection of socioeconomic rights has stalled the pace of socioeconomic transformation, one must add that the neoliberal framework in which it operates exacerbates this. The optimism of the new ruling elite has been that its transformation project would offer lessons worth emulating for other countries undergoing political transformation. Establishing the lessons to be learned from the South Africa may be too difficult to make in this chapter; however, I considered it important to look at the incorporation of rights discourse in the constitution-making of some of the recent state-making and political transitions in selected parts of Africa.

In the Constitution of the Republic of Somaliland approved by referendum in May 2001, a series of articles under Part Three explicitly organizes the spectrum of first- and second-generation rights relating to: Rights of the Individual, Fundamental Freedoms and the Duties of the Citizen; Political, Economic, Social and electoral Rights; Freedom of Movement and Association; The Right to Life, Security of the Person, Respect for Reputations, and Crimes against Human Rights; The Right to Liberty, Guarantees and the Conditions of Rights and Freedoms; The Right to Own Private Property; The Rights of Women. The statement of the Political, Economic, Social and electoral Rights in Article 22 is, however, neither

---

[85] See Occupiers of Erven 87 & 88 Berea v De Wet and Another ("Kiribilly").

elaborate nor ambitious as in the South African constitution. It runs as follows:

> Article 22: Political, Economic, Social and Electoral Rights
> 1. Every citizen shall have the right to participate in the political, economic, social and cultural affairs in accordance with the laws and the Constitution.
>
> Following episodic internal conflict and unrest, Kenya's constitution reform in 2010 produced a Bill of Rights which included social, economic and cultural rights and a range of civil society actors are active in the realisation and safeguarding of these rights.[86]

In the Transitional Constitution of the Republic of South Sudan released in April 2011, Part Two is a Bill of Rights explicitly recognizing socioeconomic rights such as public health (s 31) and housing (s 34). The latter bears similarities to the SA Constitution and opens an avenue for research about what civil society mobilization and litigation processes may unfold toward the realization of the right:

> Right to Housing
> 34. (1) Every citizen has the right to have access to decent housing.
> (2) The State shall formulate policies and take reasonable legislative measures within its available resources to achieve the progressive realization of these rights.
> (3) No one shall be evicted from his or her lawfully acquired home or have his or her home demolished save in accordance with the law.

When looking at constitution-making in the aftermath of the "Arab Spring" in North, locating an English version of Morocco's draft constitutional proposals of June 2011 have proved difficult and more attention is given to those of Egypt and Libya. A search for terms such as "right/s," "housing," "health," "education," and "water" in the 2011 Provisional Constitution of Egypt reveals minimal commitment to the notion, that is, the emphasis is on first-generation rights of association and equal appli-

---

[86] Interactions (s.a.).

cation of law. Article 14 can be regarded as referring to housing rights, but not in the manner anticipated:

> Article 14: It is not permitted for any citizen to be denied residence in a particular area, nor requiring him to reside in a particular place, except in cases designated by law.

Following a period of no official constitution for almost forty years, Libya's Draft Constitutional Charter for the Transitional Stage of August 2011 commits itself to the rights discourse of international declarations and evokes commitment to socioeconomic rights:

> Part Two
>   Rights and Public Freedoms
>   Article (7) Human rights and basic freedoms shall be respected by the State. The state shall commit itself to join the international and regional declarations and charters which protect such rights and freedoms. The State shall endeavor to promulgate new charters which shall honor the human being as being God's successor on Earth.
>   Article (8) The State shall guarantee for every citizen equal opportunities and shall provide an appropriate standard of living. The State shall also guarantee the right of work, education, medical care, and social security, the right of intellectual and private property. The State shall further guarantee the fair distribution of national wealth among citizens, and among the different cities and districts thereof.

Such promising developments inspire trust in a process where increased civil society input is urged—health care professionals have urged thus: "[D]iscussion of the right to health deserves to be featured in sociopolitical discourse, through conventional media, through social media, and through appropriate government forums".[87]

Also prompted by the Arab uprisings, Tunisia's constitutional reform has brought forth a new constitution which includes first- and second-

---

[87] Salhin and Elkhammas (2014: 296).

generation rights; however, concern remains that "[T]he majority of these rights is expressed in just a few words each, and says very little about how these rights are to be exercised."[88] Egypt's revolution has brought forth a constitutional reform expanding the state's obligations toward socioeconomic rights in Article 11, yet enthusiastic civil society engagement with the constitution is skeptical about its vague formulations and the privileging of private sector interests.[89]

Contrary to the pessimist dimension of wa Mutua's appreciation about rights discourse, these developments indicate that rights discourse is far from being dispatched to the trashcan of history in Africa's quest for socioeconomic justice and democratic, participatory institutions.[90] Citizens seeking socioeconomic justice in these new states will go through their own trials of mobilizing and litigating for the realization of rights, and likely push for fresh interpretations thereof by their respective courts and state organs committed to their realization. An upsurge of critiques of Eurocentricism and rights philosophy needs to be cognizant that while rights philosophy may have facilitated the emergence of capitalism and its attendant social and economic inequalities, rights philosophy evolved in a manner to safeguard the interests of capitalism's subordinate classes, and it is in this global system of inequality that capitalism has turned into, where subordinate classes in societies outside of Europe can include rights philosophy in their struggles against the inequalities which capitalism has produced in their own territories.[91]

7 Conclusion

Pessimism prevails about whether rights discourse can effect significant socioeconomic transformation in Africa. Contrarily, Africa's new states and their respective constitutions reveal an imminent jettisoning of

---

[88] Al-Ali and Romdhane, Donia (2014: 5).
[89] Taha (2013).
[90] Wa Mutua's oeuvre in this field is critical of the Eurocentric genesis of rights, its links with the ideologies of liberalism and political democracy, emphasis on first-generation rights and realization of socioeconomic rights through free market institutions, but appreciates that rights philosophy can be adapted and beneficial to Africa's social and economic reconstruction. See wa Mutua (2009).
[91] Amin (1989) offers this appreciation of European paradigms which have been beneficial in struggles against social and economic inequality.

rights discourse is unlikely. The critical legal studies approach of North American pedigree that underlaid my research question was a concern about whether rights discourse limits the aspirations of the black working classes or is it significantly positively impacting the gradual transformation from the apartheid legacy of race and class inequality and improving the socioeconomic conditions of poorer classes. Succinctly, does the experience about rights contestation as promised in South Africa's "avant garde" constitution hold lessons for Africa's new political dispensations? Clearly, it is a reformist strategy about episodic and piecemeal amelioration of the poor's access to and realization of housing, food, water, education, and health care services. Global hegemony of neoliberal policies and austerity about social spending, and the privatized provision and commodification of the latter needs have forced communities into protest and, where legislatively possible, to explore litigation as a means of accessing these.

Rights discourse remains a means of protecting the interests of the powerful and privileged and adjudication by the highest courts hardly steps outside of the bounds of neoliberal thinking about how socioeconomic rights are to be progressively realized. Nevertheless, it does serve to mobilize and empower subordinate classes to bring short-term relief, which is consistent with critical legal studies' advocacy that it is a strategy that must be explored "until the uprising of the masses comes."

Bibliography

Abahlali baseMjondolo. (2006) University of Abahlali baseMjondolo. 6 November. http://www.abahlali.org/node/237

Adelzadeh, Ashgar. (1996) "From the RDP to GEAR: the gradual embracing of neo-liberalism in economic policy," Transformation, Vol. 31:66–95.

AFP. (2012) Mines unrest cuts S. Africa growth forecast to 2.5%. http://au.news.yahoo.com/world/a/-/world/15227799/mine-unrest-cuts-s-africa-growth-forecast-to-2-5/ (accessed October 31, 2012).

African National Congress. (1994) The Reconstruction and Development Programme. A policy framework, Umanyano, Johannesburg.

African National Congress. (1996) Growth, Employment and Redistribution. A macroeconomic strategy. 14 June. http://www.polity.org.za/html/govdocs/policy/gear-02.html

Al-Ali, Zaid & Romdhane, Ben. (2014). "Tunisia's new constitution: progress and challenges to come." OpenDemocracy. http://www.opendemocracy.net/arab-awakening/zaid-ali-donia-ben-romdhane/tunisia... (accessed February 11, 2016).

Amin, Samir. (1989). Eurocentricism. New York: Monthly Review Press.

ANC. (1997) Understanding GEAR. Growth, Employment and Redistribution. The government's new economic strategy. http://www.anc.org.za/ancdocs/pubs/gear.htm

Alexander, Neville. (1993) "Compromise now but struggle will (and must) continue." Democracy in Action, Vol. 7, No.4:12–13.

Ballard, Richard, Habib, Adam, & Valodia, Imraan (eds). (2007) Voices of protest. Social movements in post-apartheid South Africa, University of KwaZulu-Natal Press, Pietermaritzburg.

Bartholomew, Amy & Hunt, Alan. (1990) "What's wrong with rights," Law and Inequality, Vol.9:1–58.

Bearak, Barry. (2009) South Africa's poor renew a tradition of protest. New York Times. http://www.nytimes.com/2009/09/07/world/africa/07protests.html?_r=1&ref=global-h (accessed September 7, 2009).

Bond, Patrick. (2000) Elite transition. From apartheid to neoliberalism in South Africa, Pluto, London.

Bond, Patrick. (2004) Ten years of democracy: From racial to class apartheid. Harold Wolpe Lecture, Howard College. Centre for Civil Society. http://www.nu.ac.za/ccs/

Bond, Patrick, & Khosa, Meshack (eds). (1999) An RDP policy audit, Human Sciences Research Council, Pretoria.

Cox, Anna & Seale, Lebogang. (2008) "Court's eviction ruling a victory for homeless on housing rights," The Star, February 20:7.

Davenport, TRH, & Saunders, Christopher. (2000) South Africa. A modern history, 5th ed., Macmillan, Johannesburg.

Forrest, Drew. (2003) "Social movements: 'ultra-left' or 'global citizens'?," Mail & Guardian, January 31 to February 6:8–10.

Foucault, Michel. (1972) The Archaeology of knowledge, Tavistock, London.

Fukuyama, Francis. (1989) "The End of History?" The National Interest, Summer:3–18.

Gibson, Nigel C. (2008) "Introduction. A new politics of the poor emerges from South Africa's shantytowns," Journal of Asian and African Studies, Vol. 43, No. 1:5–17.

Ginsburg. David. (1996) "The democratisation of South Africa: transition theory tested," Transformation, Vol. 29:74–102.

Gough, Ian. (1979) The political economy of the welfare state, Macmillan, London.

"Government of the Republic of South Africa and Others v Grootboom and Others." (2000) Butterworths Constitutional Law Reports. Vol. 11:1169–1210. Durban.

Greenberg, Stephen. (2004) The Landless People's Movement and the failure of post-apartheid land reform, Centre for Civil Society, University of KwaZulu-Natal.

Habib, Adam. (2003) "State-civil society relations in post-apartheid South Africa," in, State of the nation. South Africa 2003–2004, by John Daniel, Adam Habib, & Roger Southall (eds), HSRC Press: Pretoria.

Henkin, Louis. (1998). The age of rights, Columbia University Press, New York.

Heyns, Christof, & Brand, Danie. (1999) "Introduction to socio-economic rights in the South African constitution," in, A compilation of essential documents on economic, social and cultural rights, by Gina Bekker (ed), Centre for Human Rights, University of Pretoria.

Heywood, Mark. (2010) "Justice and the Treatment Action Campaign," in, In Zuma's own goal: Losing South Africa's war on poverty, by Patrick Bond (ed), Africa World Press.

Hirsch, Alan. (2005) Season of hope. Economic reform under Mandela and Mbeki, University of KwaZulu-Natal Press, Pietermaritzburg.

Hirschl, Ran. (2004). Towards juristocracy. The origins and consequences of the new constitutionalism, Harvard University Press, Cambridge.

Hogan, Gerard. (2001) "Judicial review and socio-economic rights," in, Human rights, the citizen and the state. South African and Irish approaches, by Jeremy Sarkin & William Binchy (eds), Round Hall Sweet & Maxwell, Dublin.

Holloway, John. [s.a] "Change the world without taking power?" http://libcom.org/library/ (accessed September 12, 2012).

Hoogvelt, Ankie M.M. (2001) Globalisation and the postcolonial world. The new political economy of development, 2nd ed, Macmillan, London.

Interactions. (s.a.) "Social, economic and political context in Kenya." http://www.interactions.eldis.org/unpaid-care-work/country-profiles/kenya/social-economic-an... (accessed February 11, 2016).

John, Victoria. (2012) "Still no textbooks: Section 27 takes Angie to court again," Mail & Guardian. http://mg.co.za/article/2012-09-06-section-27-take-angie-to-court-again (accessed October 3, 2012).

Joubert, Pearlie. (2008) "Grootboom dies homeless and penniless," Mail & Guardian, 8–14 August:35.

Kaplinsky, Raphael. (1991). A growth path for a post-apartheid South Africa, Transformation, Vol.16:49–55.

Knoetze, Daneel. (2014). Hangberg: "a view too good for poor people," Mail & Guardian. http://mg.co.za/article/2014-10-08-hangberg-on-a-knife-edge (accessed February 29, 2016).

Kotzé, Dirk. (1996) "The New (Final) South African Constitution," Journal of theoretical politics, Vol. 8, No. 2:133–57.

Landless People's Movement. (2007) "Press release," 27 September. http://www.abahlali.org/taxonomy/term/511

Langeni, Loyiso. (2011) "Foreign direct investment plunges 78%," BusinessDay, 21 January.

Liebenberg, Sandra. 1999. "Foreword," in, A compilation of essential documents on economic, social and cultural rights, by Gina Bekker (ed), Centre for Human Rights, University of Pretoria.

Lodge, Tom. (2002) Politics in South Africa. From Mandela to Mbeki, David Philip, Cape Town.

Makgetla, Neva Seidman. (2004) "The post-apartheid economy," Review of African political economy, Vol.100:263–281.

Mandela, Nelson. (1996) "Opening address by President Nelson Mandela to the Third Session of Parliament," 9 February. http://www.polity.org.za/html/govdocs/speeches/1996/sp0209.html

Mandela, Nelson. (1996a) "Mandela address on the occasion of the budget debate," 20 June. http://www.polity.org.za/html/govdocs/speeches/1996/sp0620.html

Marais, Hein. (1996) "All GEARed up," The African Communist, Third Quarter: 30–42.
Marais, Hein. (2001) South Africa: limits to change. The political economy of transition, 2nd ed, Zed Books, London.
Marshall, T.H., & Bottomore, Tom. (1992) Citizenship and social class, Pluto, London.
Marx, Anthony W. (1997) "Apartheid's end: South Africa's transition from racial domination," Ethnic and racial studies, Vol. 20, No. 3, July: 474–496.
"Mazibuko and Others v City of Johannesburg And Others." (2012) Butterworths Constitutional Law Reports, Vol. 3:239–291.
Moll, Peter G. (1991) The great economic debate. The radical's guide to the South African economy, Skotaville publishers, Johannesburg.
Ndletyana, Mcebisi. (1999) "The civic movement. A toothless watchdog?," IndicatorSA, Vol.16, No.3:34–38.
NEDLAC. (2001) Nedlac Annual Report 2000–2001. Socio-economic report. http://www.nedlac.org.za/docs/reports/annual/2001/socio-economic_ section. html
Ngwane, Trevor. (2003) "The Anti-Privatisation Forum (APF)," South African labour bulletin, Vol.27, No.6:31–32.
O'Connor, James. (1973) The fiscal crisis of the state, St Martin's Press, New York.
Occupiers of Erven 87 & 88 Berea v De Wet and Another ("Kiribilly"), http://seri-sa.prg/index.php/19-litigation/case-entries/293-occupiers-of-erven-87-88-berea... (accessed February 11, 2016).
Odendaal, André. (1984) Vukani Bantu! The beginnings of black protest politics in South Africa to 1912, David Philip, Cape Town.
O'Donnell, Guillermo & Schmitter, Philippe C. (1986) Transitions from authoritarian rule. Tentative conclusions about uncertain democracies, The Johns Hopkins University Press, Baltimore.
Offe, Claus. (1984) Contradictions of the welfare state, The MIT Press, Cambridge.
Purvis, Trevor, & Hunt, Alan. (1993) "Discourse, ideology, discourse ideology, discourse, ideology...," British Journal of Sociology, Vol.44, No.3:473–499.
Republic of South Africa. (1994) Constitution of the Republic of South Africa. Act No. 200 of 1993.

Republic of South Africa. (1996) The Constitution of the Republic of South Africa, 1996. Act No. 108 of 1996.

Republic of South Africa. (1996a) Debates of the National Assembly: Index to interpellations, questions and replies, Hansard, Government Printer, Cape Town.

Republic of South Africa. [s.a] Accelerated and Shared Growth Initiative for South Africa (AsgiSA), http://www.info.gob.za/asgisa

Sachs, Albie. (2003) "The judicial enforcement of socio-economic rights: the Grootboom case," Current Legal Problems, Vol.56:579–601.

Salhin, Amna & Elkhammas, Elmahdi. (2014) "The right to health in Libya: is it a constitutional mandate?" Ibnosina journal of Medicine and biomedical sciences.

Seekings, Jeremy. (2000) The UDF: a history of the United Democratic Front in South Africa, 1983–1991, David Philip, Cape Town.

Sogoni, Slumko. (1990) "Towards a post-apartheid economy," Sechaba, Vol. 24, No.10:13–15.

"Soobramoney v Minister of Health, KwaZulu-Natal" (1997) Butterworths Constitutional Law Reports, Vol. 12:1696–1715.

South African Institute of Race Relations. (1997) South Africa survey 1996/97, Johannesburg.

Statistics SA. (2011) Quarterly Labour Force Survey, Quarter 3, 1 November.

Taha, Rana Muhammad. (2013) "Part 3: New constitution expands social and economic rights, but grey areas remain." Daily News, 4 December. http://www/dailynewsegypt.com/2013/12/04/part-3-new-constitution-expands-social-and-... (accessed February 11, 2016).

Terreblanche, Sampie (Solomon Johannes). (2002) A history of inequality in South Africa, 1652–2002, University of Natal Press, Pietermaritzburg.

United Nations Development Programme. (2003) South Africa human development report 2003. The challenge of sustainable development in South Africa: unlocking people's creativity, Oxford University Press, Oxford.

van Huyssteen. Elsa. (2003) "The Constitutional Court, human rights and democracy in South Africa. A sociological analysis," Unpublished D Phil thesis, University of Witwatersrand.

wa Mutua, Makau. (1996) "The ideology of human rights," Virginia journal of international law, Vol.36.

wa Mutua, Makau. (1997) "Hope and despair for a new South Africa: the limits of a rights discourse," Harvard human rights journal, Vol.10, No. 63:63–114.

wa Mutua, Makau. (2008) "Human rights and powerlessness: pathologies of choice and substance," Buffalo law review, Vol. 56:1027–1034.

wa Mutua, Makau. (2009). "The transformation of Africa: a critique of the Rights Discourse," Buffalo legal studies research paper series.

Wesson, Murray. (2004) "Grootboom and beyond: reassessing the socio-economic jurisprudence of the South African Constitutional Court," South African journal of human rights, Vol. 20, No. 2:284–308.

CONCLUSION

Mariano Féliz and Aaron L. Rosenberg

This book was built on a modest idea: to present several, not necessarily converging studies regarding the production and combat against poverty in the Global South. Such project came about as a result of several days of discussions in CLACSO's conference in the city of Cairo in 2012. The flow of ideas was so powerful those days, in the midst of the "Arab Spring," that we couldn't let them go to waste. From that background, this book attempts to provide a diverse, thorough, and grounded discussion capable of contributing to the struggle against poverty across the Global South.

Poverty is an intrinsically controversial concept and process. Even if in everyday conversation, in the press or in policy discussions, poverty is represented as something self-evident and even crystal clear, it actually feeds into the whole of the world's complexity and contradictions. Situations of poverty result from the myriad processes operating throughout networks of global capitalism; products of the history of colonialism and imperialism. The production of poverty is a deeply political process entrenched within the constitution of contemporary societies, extending to the most profound levels of their very cultural and social fabric.

Poverty is not, however, an agentless process; on the contrary, it is filled with and powered by agency. Concrete actors and institutions work through the social structure in order to produce (their) wealth and attendant positions of power which are often realized together with (other's) misery and marginalization. But this does not mean that population which live in conditions of poverty are passive bystanders. On the contrary, as the chapters in this book show, "the poor" are not passive observers waiting to be helped or rendered helpless in their poverty. They work hard and through concerted channels in order to organize themselves in several ways to confront the processes, relationships, and social actors that have impoverished them. They not only dwell in poverty but struggle against it, against its stigmatizing effects, as well as against its persistence and those who impose it. These articles also demonstrate the manner in which poverty is produced and reproduced by a set of social processes and practices. Poverty as we know it is not just a state, but a social construction, the result of the production and reproduction of value and capital and its attendant systems of thought. Contemporary poverty is without a doubt capitalist poverty, produced and expanded because—not in spite—of the ever-mounting exploitation of labor for its transformation into surplus-value. Féliz's contribution among others shows how the dynamics of capitalist social reproduction in a dependent setting can foreclose an all-out struggle against poverty.

As such, poverty in our days is also the result of the works of capitalist and capitalist-oriented states. In effect, the way in which the creation and persistence of poverty has become tantamount with the dynamics of economic development should force us as both researchers and citizens of the newly glocalized world to open our eyes to an apparently simple fact: namely that neoliberal or developmentalist, developed or dependent, national states and the political forces that run them bear the brunt of the responsibility for the persistence of poverty throughout their limited spheres of immediate influence, and, through their networks of dispersed soft and hard power, across the world. Thomas' reflections on South Africa provide an example of this through their exploration of neoliberal strategies designed to foment "development" in accord with objectives, directives, and models developed in and imposed by American and European financial institutions. Public policies and development strategies cannot be expiated from their role in the promotion of the substantive processes and interests that perpetuate impoverishment of the masses and hinder their agency, as Pérez-Bustillo makes abundantly clear in his contribution.

As the different chapters make explicit, poverty is not a simple, objective fact. The (re)production of poverty is also involved in the continuous construction of the concept of poverty in distinct and often overlapping sociocultural spheres. In a sense, there are a multitude of forms of poverty, and as a relational concept, its definition depends on the side we adopt, or in which we are forced to move, in each and every particular relationship which our individual and collective lives encompass. The chapters in this book abound in a variety of possible ways and means through which we as both observers and participants may identify, understand, and potentially rectify the lived experiences and economic exigencies of poverty throughout the Global South and its diasporas throughout other parts of the world. In particular, these intellectual interventions, based as they are upon the particular circumstances and thoughts of communities in these physical and cultural geographies, show that the "top-down," institutional, academic, definition of the experience of poverty, its causes and consequences do not necessarily (and most likely will not) coincide with the bottom-up interpretation. This is an overarching conclusion we reach upon reading the whole set of chapters, and particularly stressed by Ssempebwa and Nakaiza in their work on several African countries.

Of course, this conclusion cannot simply be taken at face value since the production of poverty through capitalist networks of exchange is at the same time the propagation and strengthening of the ideology of its naturalization, and acceptance on a massive scale. Together with these apparently quantitative definitions of wealth and poverty it must be understood that the rhetoric and study of poverty is embedded within and contributes to the constitution of a particular way of looking at wealth. Development and poverty, wealth and deprivation are not just words, in abstraction of the sociopolitical context of the "society of capital." Putting into question poverty implies at the same time discussing wealth, how it is produced and distributed. Chirisa's chapter shows the ambiguities involved in this debate. Not paradoxically, but probably enlightening to many, this books shows that while an idealized form of capitalism attempts to provide a universal pattern of well-being, the realities of economic scarcity and alienation have led, if not outright forced, people in different parts of the Global South to construct their own, often vastly divergent idea of a good life. Rosenberg's chapter, for example, makes use of popular culture in the form of songs from Kenya and Jamaica in order to formulate and dispute the validity or invalidity of alternate means of generating wealth in economically disadvantaged contexts.

This being said, poverty is not just a subjective feeling or perception. The experience of capitalist impoverishment runs through people's bodies and minds, creating conditions that violently limit their possibilities of happiness and their ability to imagine and to therefore work toward building a future of actual freedom for themselves as well as their families and communities on a variety of levels.

Finally, we would like to close this discussion with the realization that poverty is not and should not be equated with helplessness. Even as capital attempts to build a world or bend it to its own image, those people who are caught up in these complex processes strive to build something else. In many cases these efforts are directed toward the creation of a world based on diverse, even contradictory, values, a world where people's rights come about as the result of the actual struggle for a good living and not the relentless drive of forces which are perceived to be beyond their ken and control. Chiweshe's contribution makes this clear in the context of women's struggles in Zimbabwe. These struggles mold the field for a better future, a future with less poverty and less severe experiences of it. Let us hope that studies of the sort contained here may contribute to this in ways that so many "anti-poverty strategies" from top-notch institutions, be them national or transnational, have not.

ibidem.eu